D1230042

Schooling for Young Riders

Schooling for Young Riders

A HANDBOOK FOR THE HORSEMEN OF TOMORROW

BY JOHN RICHARD YOUNG

Drawings by Randy Steffen

Appendix on judging horsemanship by Carson Whitson

WILLIAM WOODS COLLEGE LIBRARY

NORMAN

University of Oklahoma Press

BY JOHN RICHARD YOUNG

Arabian Cow Horse (Chicago, 1953)
The Schooling of the Western Horse (Norman, 1954)
Champion of the Cross 5 (Philadelphia, 1955)
Arizona Cutting Horse (Philadelphia, 1956)
Olympic Horseman (Philadelphia, 1957)
Angst der Tapferen (Munich, 1969)
Schooling for Young Riders (Norman, 1970)

International Standard Book Number: 0-8061-0890-8

Library of Congress Catalog Card Number: 78-97243

Copyright 1970 by the University of Oklahoma Press, Publishing Division of the University. Manufactured in the United States of America. First edition.

SF
287
Y58
Copy 2

For LINDA'S MOTHER

62001

Contents

Illustrations

Figures

Schooling for Young Riders

Don't give your son money. As far as you can af-
ford it, give him horses. No one ever came to grief—
except honourable grief—through riding horses. No
hour of life is lost that is spent in the saddle. Young
men have often been ruined through owning horses,
or through backing horses, but never through riding
them; unless of course they break their necks, which,
taken at a gallop, is a very good death to die.

—Winston S. Churchill in *My Early Life:*
A Roving Commission

CHAPTER I

Why This Book Was Written

THIS book is, among other things, a true, subjective account of the selection, breaking, and schooling of one particular pony big enough to qualify as a small horse—and, if spirit counts, big enough to rank as one of the biggest little horses that ever ate grass. It is also an unvarnished account of the training of his youthful rider, who started school just as green as he was. This subjective treatment is quite different from the way most books on riding and schooling are written, and it was intended to be. So at the outset perhaps an explanation is in order.

As a rule, most books on riding and schooling limit themselves to telling the reader, in effect: "Now this is how things *should* be done." Often the authors don't even give clear reasons for many of their statements. They blithely ignore the possibility that things might *not* turn out as they *should*. Everything is supposed to work out smoothly from start to finish with never a hitch and certainly no unhappy mention of bumps and bruises and periods of discouragement.

Unfortunately, however, life has a most exasperating way of not always turning out as we think it *should*, and the schooling of a horse is a prime example of this. For, while there are certain basic principles to be followed, every horse or pony is an unique individual with a distinctive personality and his own peculiar reactions. Though they may be aware of this in theory, most novices are a long time in fully grasping this fact. It takes them even longer to be able to analyze and understand the manifold reactions which they find themselves faced with—and which the books they have read do not even mention. This is why we who teach schooling—as distinguished from teaching only riding—so often hear the plaint, "My horse won't do this," or "I just can't make him do that," and "He's so bullheaded!"

This can be confusing and very discouraging to a young rider when he discovers that, as one girl put it, "the horse hasn't read the book." The baffled novice usually has no one to tell him that his predicament is not unique or even unusual. Professional trainers have the same problems multiplied many times over—animals that for one reason or another simply do not react to ordinary methods as the optimistic books say a horse *should*.

The seasoned pro, however, has no time for discouragement; he can't afford the luxury of confusion. If one method doesn't work, he tries something else; if that also fails, he will back off and try a new approach. With unusual problem horses he may even have to invent a "new" method—new in the sense that he has never tried it before and may never have heard of anyone else doing it. (Actually, in horsemastership there is nothing new under the sun. Every trick, gimmick, or gadget you can think of somebody else has tried before, long before you were born.) A horseman's degree of success in overcoming such problems is the most accurate index to his skill as a trainer.

I am reminded here of a girl who came to me with the idea of "learning dressage." An experienced rider of intermediate skill, she had won a fair degree of success in show jumping. Having developed good balance and a firm seat, she should have found it easy to cultivate good hands; yet any horse she rode soon became emotionally upset and developed into a dreadful puller.

I told her that she could not even dream of "learning dressage" until she first learned the difference between a pulling hand and a fixed hand and understood the function and application of each.

"Oh, I know all that junk," she informed me airily. "I gave up that fixed-hand stuff years ago because it just doesn't work."

This is an example of the sort of pitfall I hope to help readers of this book avoid. In theory, this girl "knew all about" the fixed hand, an indispensable aid in educated riding; but when, lacking a good instructor, she found herself unable to get the results her reading had led her to expect, she concluded that the principle of the fixed hand was merely empty theory for bookworms, and she reverted to pulling.

This is what reading "cheerful earful" books often does to young riders. They are misled into thinking that schooling horses should be a mere kindergarten, complete with school bus service to the front door.

But it isn't like that at all. It never was and it never will be.

About sixteen years ago I collected my observations and reflections on horsemanship into a book, *The Schooling of the Western Horse*. It seemed to me that there was a great need for such a book, written in simple, forthright language, expressing a modern point of view, and completely free of any attempt to be "tactful"—a term that may be defined as reluctance to tell the truth for fear of stepping on other people's toes.

At that time, there were only two or three books on the handling of Western horses, and all of them, in my opinion, were years out of date. The writers did not think in terms of schooling a horse; they wrote about "breaking" and "training" —with no clear distinction between the two terms. They seemed to be addressing an audience who only recently had voted for or against General Grant for President. No knowledgeable horseman could have accepted as up to date the viewpoints they expressed. None of the books had the virtues of logic and clarity of expression. All of them left so many loose ends dangling and so many unpleasant facts unsaid that they were of little help to modern readers of limited experience with horses, the very persons most likely to read such books in search of help.

The immediate and continued success of *The Schooling of*

5

the Western Horse far exceeded my expectations. The many letters I have received from grateful readers, I like to believe, have proved my original ideas and my purpose in writing the book sound.

One aspect of reader reaction, however, perplexed me for a while. Though I had tried to express my ideas with utmost clarity, the letters I received made it increasingly obvious that some readers had failed to grasp certain fundamental principles upon which successful schooling depends—and most of those who had this difficulty were older readers, mature men and women. Younger readers—teen-agers and those in their early twenties—showed a much quicker understanding of the ideas I had offered them.

Without the evidence of their letters, I should have assumed the reverse to be true; for is not maturity supposed to develop understanding and judgment? Perhaps, sometimes, it does. But I am convinced that it does not develop increased receptivity to new ideas.

Young people may have much to learn, as their elders often like to impress on them, but they are quite capable of learning —more capable now than they will probably be when they themselves become elders, with a penchant for lecturing the next generation.

That is why, though this book is primarily for young riders who aspire to become real horsemen and horsewomen, I have made no attempt to oversimplify. No one who studies this book or even reads it attentively will be left with the idea that becoming a good horseman is chiefly a matter of assuming a "correct" seat and being able to ride over obstacles without falling off. But I have no doubt that young riders who really want to learn and improve will have little difficulty understanding what I say. If anybody finds parts of the book difficult, it is likely to be the parents. Some may think me too meticulous; others will say that I make riding and schooling seem discouragingly difficult. But, on the contrary, it is precisely this careful attention to seemingly minor details that makes riding easier and schooling a pleasurable task rather than an exasperating experience in frustration.

I mention this matter here because this book is also for the parents of young riders and for teachers of riding who care enough to see that their youngsters get a right start. From beginning to end this book assumes that horsemanship is an art as well as a sport, a recreation which one can enjoy perhaps even more in middle life and old age than in youth; for increased knowledge and experience result in keener appreciation—*if* one has been fortunate enough to get the right start. Many people give up riding when they pass their physical prime simply because they have been imbued with the notion that it is a strenuous form of athletics—and the muscle-flexing way they learned to ride, it is. But one who learns to appreciate horsemanship as an art requiring intelligence and finesse rather than as merely a sport demanding acrobatic agility and muscle might have to be dragged from his saddle to be placed in his grave.

Finally, this is a book for those who enjoy the amusing companionship of ponies and believe that a good pony deserves intelligent schooling quite as much as any horse. Because of their size and their generally superior intelligence ponies often confront their owners with peculiar problems which the average horse owner never has to worry about. I hope that this book will provide some helpful answers.

CHAPTER II

Why Riders Fail As Horsemen

I F ALL the books ever written about horsemanship in all languages were gathered together, I
can hardly make even a wild guess at how large a library they
would fill. Just those written in English would pile up to many
more volumes than I, for one, would care to read, even if I
had the time. For in such a vast body of work there must inevitably be a large number of books which are of little or no
value—books written by articulate theorists who don't know
what they're talking about, others written by practical horsemen who do know their subject but who express their ideas so
fuzzily that often they mislead the reader into thinking that they
mean one thing when in fact they mean something quite different. And then, of course, there are the concoctions of complete muddleheads who know neither what they oraculate on
nor how to write.

Amid this deluge of printed material are hundreds of books
written especially for young riders, the horsemen and horsewomen of tomorrow. A majority of them share certain common characteristics:

Most of them come from Great Britain, where interest in
pony clubs is high.

The authors are usually females with, naturally, a feminine point of view.

Many of the books convey the idea, at least by implication, that success in the show ring is the yardstick by which to measure a rider's skill and a horse's schooling—an idea so completely false that it hardly even merits rebuttal.

Too many of the authors write down, patronizing their youthful readers. They seem to assume that none of their young readers knows anything at all or is capable of learning much. The advice they give, page after page, is elementary to the point of being ridiculous. Some of this, of course, is necessary and proper for equestrian kindergarteners; the trouble is that too often the authors rarely offer more. A smart youngster can skim through dozens of such books without learning anything he doesn't already know.

Practically all the authors are glowingly cheerful. They bend over backward shielding their young audience from the simple facts of life in the saddle. Accidents never happen. Nobody ever falls off. All ponies are miraculously schooled to perfection. Ponies are dear little pals, always eager to please, never willful or contrary. "Taking the bit in his teeth" is merely an expression from folklore. No *nice* pony would think of doing it and all ponies are nice. Just do as the lady says. As in fairy tales, there is always a happy ending.

Most of these cheery works are illustrated, some with photographs, many with drawings. The overwhelming majority of the photographs prove nothing except that the rider's heels are down, the reins are too long (the show-ring influence), and the relative positions of mount and rider are correct; that is, the pony is not on top. Some authors avoid sticking their necks out even this little bit. They eschew photographs, relying on drawings. In effect, they preach, "You should do this; you must do that; here is the correct way"; but, even though the standard of riding they hold out to their readers is hardly beyond the kindergarten level, the authors are careful not to offer any evidence that they can do what they presume to tell others how to do or that any pupils they may have coached can do any of these things. It is so much easier to have an artist take care of fussy details; the author need not even leave her armchair.

As sources of helpful information and instruction, books of this sort, in my opinion, are worse than useless. I condemn most of them as positively detrimental to a budding horseman's progress. For the authors, striving with more enthusiasm than common sense to present the joys of equitation as seen through rose-colored glasses rather than through the clear lens of reality, succeed only in producing a paper-lace Valentine. Intentionally or not, they foist off on their eager but ignorant readers a sentimentalized, anthropomorphic distortion of equine psychology that may for years delay, or even forever prevent, many impressionable youngsters from gaining what they need first and most—a clear understanding of the true nature and mental attributes of horses and ponies, and of what constitutes a sensible working relationship between a rider and his mount.

Perhaps even worse than this fault is another: The authors, by writing down, offering only the lowest of standards on the evident assumption that children are incapable to mastering anything else, leave the youngsters with no worth-while goal to shoot at. When a writer or an instructor is satisfied with standards that could be mastered by a trained monkey on a circus pony, and says, in effect, "This is good horsemanship," can we blame a child for concluding, "I can do that—it's easy. So I must be pretty good"? Then we have in the making one more obnoxious little know-it-all, cockily smug in his own miasmal ignorance, mentally incapable of making any progress for years to come; indeed, he might remain impervious to ideas that go contrary to the little he knows, or thinks he knows, for the rest of his life. It is almost inevitable that in the long run, by his attitude or his example, this misled brat will mislead others. Thus the malign influence of these superficial books on pseudo-horsemanship spreads.

I believe that a worthy book on horsemanship for young riders must offer a goal which even the best of them can attain only by diligent effort. It should direct their eyes to the stars.

To some blasé instructors as well as to those who are in the business only to make a fast buck, this attitude may seem naïve. However, I am well aware of the fact that by the law of averages very few student riders, however enthusiastically they may begin, will ever become stars or even come close to attaining a really high degree of skill. Some lack the physical or the mental requisites; most do not have the driving ambition to become really good, the spur that makes for excellence in any field, particularly one as varied and complex as horsemanship. Often a keen youngster loses his ambition, sometimes so gradually that he is unaware of the loss until one day he realizes that it is long gone. Time, that tireless sneak thief, robs him. Personal circumstances, repeated setbacks, parental indifference, lack of guidance and encouragement, as well as other interests, all combine to dilute enthusiasm to indifference.

As an example, I might mention my own daughter, Sheilagh. When she began to ride, she was quite keen to learn to ride well, but she quickly discovered, as most of us do, that watching someone else do it is much easier than doing it yourself. Difficulties such as we all run into easily discouraged her—she was trying too hard to be good too soon. Acid criticisms from her more experienced younger sister, even when Linda meant her tactless remarks as helpful advice, did nothing to encourage her. Eventually—and, I think, without even realizing it—Sheilagh lowered her sights. Now she is content with an elementary standard of riding that leaves the finer points to those who ride with their brains instead of merely with the seat of their pants.

This has saddened me, and I have often wondered whether the underlying fault was mine, but I don't know what to do about it now. When the weather is fine and she feels the need of exercise, Sheilagh may ride for hours; but when the day is cold or wet or very hot and I have the temerity to suggest that she might profitably forsake television for a while and get out and practice, she is not interested. "There are other things in life," she reminded me on one occasion, "besides horsemanship." Of course, she is right; I know that practically all her friends who ride agree with her. To them, riding is not an absorbing delight and can never approach being an art; it is merely a pleasant outdoor exercise and a social activity, nothing more.

Sheilagh has everything she needs to become an excellent horsewoman except the one basic ingredient that makes all the others jell—a driving ambition to excel. In her, the spark of ambition flickered briefly, then was quickly extinguished. I have seen it happen in other youngsters; I'll see it happen again. Experience enables me to make a safe prediction: One day long before the infirmities of age might make it necessary, Sheilagh will quit riding forever.[1]

I mention this rather personal matter to make it quite plain that I am not unaware of the course many promising young riders follow. For various reasons they never even come close to their potential. Many of them, however, would if they got the right start—and one of the surest ways *not* to get the right start is to be misled by books written by charlatans and equestrian Dale Carnegies who imply that anyone can master horsemanship in a few easy lessons because there is really nothing to it except stop and go and steer with the reins—and, of course, keep your heels down.

[1] Since these words were written, more than a year ago, my prediction has come true, though it is too early to say "forever." Sheilagh has not been on a horse in that length of time. Six months ago her favorite mount, my Morgan stallion, Emerald's Aristocrat, died, and Sheilagh's interest in horses seems to have died with him.

CHAPTER III

How Horsemen Are Not Made

THE great majority of horses and ponies for children are so poorly schooled that it seems almost a miracle that the children who ride them do not quickly lose all enthusiasm for equestrian sports. Some, of course, do. Bouncing over the landscape on a bullnecked pony or an aged crock whose mouth seems to be made of rawhide soon ceases to be their idea of fun. Or perhaps an accident, which proper schooling would have prevented, ruins their nerve. Then what once was fun becomes a nerve-racking ordeal, and the child wants no more of it. Fortunately, however, most children retain their initial keenness in spite of scares and tumbles from mounts they hardly know how to control with any degree of certainty or precision.

The principal reason for this, in my opinion, is that the youngsters are as ignorant as their unlucky mounts. They do not know that their long-suffering pets are poorly schooled. They have never ridden a schooled pony (and wouldn't know how), they have never seen one ridden, nor do they have more than a vague idea of what schooling is.

There are several common causes for this lamentable state of affairs.

Many parents, who themselves ride and want their children to enjoy the sport, don't know how to school.

Neither do a large majority of stable operators who presume to call themselves riding instructors; nor can they teach the theory of what they themselves cannot practice.

Often a parent or an instructor who knows how to school a horse feels lost when confronted with the task of educating a pony. Most ponies are too small to be comfortably ridden by an adult of average size. Even if the animal is sturdy enough to carry weight out of proportion to its size, the average adult rider's legs will dangle hopelessly out of position to be of much use in schooling. Some basic lessons can be given by ground driving or driving to a cart, but eventually mounted work becomes necessary.

Then what?

Then the hapless horseman needs help—either a young rider of much more experience and skill than most children have or an experienced lightweight adult who might have made it as an exercise boy in a racing stable without missing three meals a day. Probably one is as difficult to find as the other.

The usual result of this perplexing predicament is that many parents as well as far too many instructors take refuge in an attitude extremely detrimental to their youngsters' riding education—the attitude that a child's pony is "just a kid's pet." As long as it has four legs and will tolerate a passenger on its back, that is about all one can expect. The comfortable theory is that the child's riding skill, his horsemanship, will develop later.

This theory, however, rarely works out in fact. Sloppy riding habits are easily acquired but not easily changed. A poor juvenile rider usually grows up to be an inferior adult rider.

This is particularly true of youngsters whose families can boast that they "have always owned horses." The young rider who "grew up on a horse" is one of the most difficult pupils to teach—the most difficult of all being his father. This might seem paradoxical, but it is not; it's quite natural and reasonable. The longer most people have owned horses the more smugly cocksure they are that they know all the answers. Frequently they veil their assumed superiority behind a façade of mock humility which takes the form of humorous flippancy intended to cover up their real lack of knowledge, but they betray themselves by their positive antipathy to new ideas. Xenophon himself could not tell them anything which they don't think they know better.

A youngster reared in this sort of family atmosphere seldom goes elsewhere for riding lessons, and when he does they don't do him much good. He has been conditioned to be a smart aleck. He usually has a ready retort to everything, even though politeness may prevent him from always saying, "My father says——" or "That's not the way *We* always do it." He has gotten most of his ideas from his father, who learned from grandfather. It doesn't matter that times change, that new knowledge replaces old ideas, that new discoveries (and the motion-picture camera) have long since disproved many of the old notions that grandfather swore by. No, all that really counts is that father and grandfather grew up with horses, and they have taught Junior all they know, even if half of it isn't true.

Not long ago I had a depressing encounter with one of these horsey-set heiresses to the wisdom of the ages, a twenty-year-old girl who had "grown up on a horse." To hear her proud parents tell it, her next stop was the Olympic team. She had come to try out a schooled horse of mine.

The girl trotted and cantered the horse around the schooling ring, avoiding the corners as if they weren't there. After a while I suggested, "Ride into the corners. Bend him." Bend him? She hadn't the vaguest idea what I was talking about, nor, even after I had explained, could she do it.

A little later I requested, "Do a turn on the forehand."

She looked at me blankly. "What's that?"

I also had to explain in detail how to do a turn on the haunches.

This girl, believe it or not, earned part of her college expenses as the chief riding instructor at a summer camp. She had held the job every summer for four years. It is easy to imagine what the youthful campers learned about horsemanship.

Who is responsible for this sort of farce, this travesty of everything that the term *horsemastership* means? Every deluded parent who ever said of an iron-jawed pony, "He's only a pet," and every instructor who lowers his standards with the excuse, "You can't expect much—after all, they're only children."

This common attitude that young riders are incapable of learning is, I am convinced, the chief reason for the low overall quality of juvenile horsemanship in and out of the show ring and why we tolerate ponies and horses that are little more than green broke. It is not that young riders can't do better; they can. But their parents and instructors, as a rule, do not expect them to. Apparently we have no more confidence in our children's ability than we have in our own. If their standards are low, it is because our own standards are low. Anything beyond an intermediate stage of riding we sanctify, or casually dismiss, as "dressage"—and that's for foreigners, not us red-blooded Americans.

This ridiculous attitude, which seems to be peculiarly American, is hardly consistent with our approach to other sports. Most of our best swimmers are teen-agers, and they work harder than race horses, practicing four or five hours a day seven days a week—and getting up at dawn to do it. They break records almost as fast as the records can be printed, and we feel proud that they are the world's best. Apparently nobody thinks that their coaches are expecting too much of them.

Our young skaters and skiers train just as hard—and will anyone argue that downhill skiing is less demanding than riding a horse?

Does schooling a jumper or a stock horse require any more of a rider than baseball, football, gymnastics—or ballet?

As we grow older, too many of us tend to forget how tough, resilient and adaptable youth is, not only physically but mentally. Again and again in teaching horsemanship I have had this truth brought home to me. Almost always pupils who have the most difficulty grasping and accepting new ideas and putting

Young Love. Most small children have a natural affection for ponies and practically no fear of them. Making sure that they get the right type of pony is the best way to foster these desirable traits, which form the foundation of future horsemastership. Riding, unlike many other sports, can be a lifelong enjoyment, fun from youth to old age. The most important thing is getting the right start, then encouragement and intelligent help. Here Linda's brother Seán, 7, and his sister Kristen, 4, lavish affection on their first pony.

them into practice are older riders—and if a lesson is prolonged, they are usually the first to become tired.

I am not implying that to become a good rider you must start young; that is not at all necessary. But I know from experience that it is much easier to teach an absolutely green twelve-year-old than an adult pupil, and it is very much easier than correcting the faults of an adult rider of some experience. Physically the child is more supple and adaptable, and when trying something he has never done before he isn't thinking, "This is very hard to do," which is the way many adults seem to think. To put it bluntly, older pupils, with a tendency to magnify imaginary or real difficulties, need more coddling than youngsters.

The young riders I am talking about here range in age from twelve to twenty. A few children may be ready to begin learning real horsemanship at ten or eleven, but they are exceptions. Under twelve, the average child cannot hope to be more than a mere passenger in the saddle. Let him be that and enjoy himself, but don't let anyone tell you just because he can kick a pony into a canter that he knows anything about riding.

In expressing this idea I have stepped on more than one set of parental toes, but my opinion is based on experience and it stands. I know all about infant prodigies who "learned to ride before they could walk," wore spurs at six, competed in their first show at seven, and so on. Last summer I saw one of these geniuses, a lad nine years old, win an open jumping class in a large show. Mounted on a 16-hand Appaloosa, he made his adult competitors look silly. But if you think the lad had anything to do with winning, you weren't there—or you've never jumped a horse. He merely pointed the horse at the first jump and hung on. The horse and the lad's guardian angel did the rest.

Later, I made a point of talking with the boy and with his proud parents. What all three of them didn't know about what the child was doing—or wasn't doing—on horseback would have filled all his third-grade school books.

This lad's parents were of a certain type that bears much of the blame for the poor juvenile horsemanship commonly seen in and out of the show ring; yet they would be the last to think that any of the blame was theirs. This is the proud parent—usually a very indifferent horseman himself—who enjoys a vicarious glory in the show-ring successes of his children. His big ambition in life is to have Junior or little Suzy win a tack-room full of trophies and ribbons, regardless of whether the child ever acquires even the rudiments of first-class horsemanship. For this parent, no horse or pony is too expensive if it can win in the ring; that, and that only, is the yardstick of success. Usually the animal is schooled by a professional, who then gives the child lessons on how to handle it in the ring, the way one learns how to ride a bicycle or drive a car. Once the pony begins to collect ribbons, proud Papa, Mama and all their friends take it for granted that their young rider has become an accomplished horseman. The youngster's friends, whose mounts cannot boast of so many ribbons, listen respectfully when the star echoes the pearls of wisdom he has heard from his instructor, and they assiduously copy his style of riding. Thus the baneful influence of the show fanatic spreads like ripples on a pond.

Some children, particularly those with a strong show-off streak, learn to enjoy this; they relish competition. Others are made miserable by the constant pressure of winning to please their parents, who have chosen such an expensive hobby. But whether the kids enjoy it or not, true horsemanship in the sense this book defines the term has almost nothing to do with the process, nor can such mechanically trained show ponies be called well-schooled mounts.

In this book you will find no magic short cuts to success. You *will* find parts of it which you may have to reread many times and carefully ponder before you finally get the message. You will, I believe, find a set of standards worth striving for—and don't be too disappointed if you fall short of attaining some of them. Be patient. Persist. You may taste the exasperating bitterness of failure at times, but you will never fail irrevocably if you are always willing to try again. A good horseman always has a high and ever higher goal to achieve—and the moment you lose this, you are finished. That is why this book, rather than being "easy," is meant to be a challenge. Its purpose is not only to instruct but to prod and provoke and inspire.

The rest is up to you.

CHAPTER IV

Selecting a Suitable Mount

THE term "pony" is rather loosely used. Webster's Unabridged Dictionary defines a pony as "a small horse." According to the American Horse Shows Association, a horse qualifies as a pony if it is not more than 14 hands tall. We still speak of "cow ponies" and "polo ponies" even though the animals we refer to might be registered Thoroughbreds. Some horsemen consider even the Arabian a pony because he is rarely as big as they would like a horse to be.

Perhaps for most practical purposes such vagueness may be sufficient; however, it is of no help whatever to a young person trying to decide whether he should buy a pony or a horse. There is more involved here than merely a question of height. For, no matter what your dictionary or the A.H.S.A. says, a true pony is not a horse, nor can any horse however small be a pony unless he has pony blood and pony characteristics.

It is not uncommon to hear people who own and like horses say, often with a good deal of emphasis, "I don't like ponies." Many pony fanciers, on the other hand, consider most horses downright dull, as stupid as the blundering giants that populate fairy tales. Obviously there must be reasons based on practical experience for such divergent ideas. In this chapter let's consider some of them, then briefly survey the various types of ponies from which to choose a child's riding mount.

I have yet to meet a *good* horseman who did not find ponies interesting and enjoyable or who had any unusual difficulty in handling them. Conversely, I have never known anyone who liked horses but not ponies who, in my opinion, could qualify as a really good horseman. And here, I think, we come to the heart of the matter: horsemen who dislike ponies are disillusioned characters who have been outsmarted by the mischievous little imps once too often. They manage to get along with most horses as long as the horses are not too spirited or too bright, but they simply cannot cope with ponies. Their usual condemnation of the little animals may be summed up in a sentence which Noah probably uttered when he was loading the Ark:

"Ponies are so stubborn!"

Ponies can indeed be stubborn if you let them develop the notion that stubbornness will enable them to have their own way when it is opposed to yours. Of course, the same may be said of horses, but with a difference. The difference is that, as a rule, ponies are "smarter" than horses; they are craftier, they have more cunning, a more determined "will of their own." Having developed more than horses under natural conditions and for a longer period of time, even after a thousand years ponies remain closer to the feral state than their big brothers. During the past centuries—in some cases even in the last few decades—almost all breeds of horses have evolved and considerably changed as a result of man's efforts to breed the kind of animals he wants for a specific purpose; but ponies, with a few exceptions, remain essentially the same as their wild ancestors. Much more so than horses, they represent Nature's inflexible law of the survival of the fittest. This is what we mean when we speak of true pony character and pony characteristics.

And basically this is why more people than will admit it don't like ponies. They find the primitive little animals just too smart for them. Difficulties which they can easily overcome when breaking and schooling an average horse leave them baffled and frustrated when complicated by the willful cunning of a spirited pony. So they condemn ponies as stubborn instead of admitting their own ignorance and lack of skill.

Fortunately, the traits that make a pony different from a horse have advantages as well as drawbacks. Ponies learn very fast; they never forget a lesson—either good or bad. They mature more quickly than horses and are extremely hardy. They can thrive not only on less feed but on feed of poorer quality. Their instinct of self-preservation is very pronounced, a trait that makes them safe and reliable cross-country mounts for children—it also explains why one rarely sees a pony with wire cuts, no matter how dangerous the pasture fences may be to horses. Some horses when frightened or otherwise extremely excited will crash right through a fence, heedless of possible injury. I have never known a pony that would so completely lose his head. On the other hand, if a pony *wants* to escape from his pasture you need a really stout fence to keep him in. (But if the grazing is good, you needn't worry; he'll stay there!)

I hope that I have made obvious the vital importance of choosing a *good* pony or none at all. A poor specimen purchased as a mount or a pet for a child is one of the worst investments on earth.

To give a specific example, I would call the reader's attention to the pictures on page 23. Study the points of this pony as they are revealed in the photographs—they were even more pronounced in the flesh. Notice the coarseness of the animal's head, too large for its body; the short ewe-neck; the poor straight shoulder. Note particularly the pony's dull, "knotheaded" expression, so lacking in good pony character. This pinto, purchased from a dealer, was supposed to be a great bargain at forty dollars. He turned out to be one of the most expensive "bargains" I've ever heard of.

His first owner, a man completely ignorant of ponies but stubbornly determined to get his money's worth, kept the animal for a year and was unable to teach him anything except

The Tragically Unlucky Lucky. If ever a pony was misnamed, Lucky was the one. A forty-dollar "bargain," his life was a testimonial to the greed and shortsightedness of those who owned him. This pony and everyone who misused and abused him would have been luckier if he had never been born. He cost at least thirty times as much as his forty-dollar price. A pony like this one can be the death of a child. At least once Lucky came close to it.

to buck. A professional "horseman" who briefly undertook to educate the pinto met with no greater success. In fact, he made the pony worse by trying to "knock sense into him" with a whip. (Here we have a perfect example of how pony-detesters are made.)

Eventually the pony, inappropriately named "Lucky," changed hands, but this time the buyer had a fair idea what he was getting. Being a born bargain hunter, however, he decided to gamble forty dollars on the chance that he might wind up with a small nag his young children could at least have some fun on. Since none of the kids knew how to ride, this was a most optimistic point of view, the sort of spirit that made a haggard Columbus croak wearily, "Sail on!"

The man asked me to "break" the pony so that his children could at least sit on him without being bucked off. I gave him my frank opinion. I said that any time spent on this little jughead would be wasted, that the best thing would be to get rid of him and write the whole deal off to experience.

I might as well have saved my breath. This fellow also was

determined to get at least his forty dollars back. So I proceeded with the job. Starting from scratch, I went to work on Lucky as if he were a green colt. He really was a lunkhead, but he finally learned what he was supposed to know—not to buck and to respond to simple rein and leg signals, merely that and nothing more. Anything more complicated would have over-taxed his mentality.

My bargain-hunting friend was delighted. He had won his forty-dollar gamble, he thought; his children had a pony to ride. Unfortunately, his elation was a bit premature. In less than a week Lucky proved that in horse- and pony-buying, with very rare exceptions, you get just what you pay for. He ran away with my friend's eleven-year-old son. The lad fell off, made a one-point landing on his elbow, and suffered a most serious compound fracture. The accident crushed the veins in the lad's arm and almost cost him his life. It took a team of surgeons four hours to repair the damage. The doctor and hospital bills added up to almost one thousand dollars.

After that, you probably think, the ill-starred Lucky could have been sold only to a cannery. But, as somebody said—was it Barnum?—"there's a sucker born every minute," and for each one of those there are two bargain hunters born a minute.

Once again the unlucky Lucky changed hands and at the same bargain price, forty dollars.

This time the buyer knew what he was getting, he thought; but he had four rough-and-ready youngsters, and they were all, he said, "good riders." He was confident that they could "take care of" the pinto.

A few months later, however, I happened to ask my friend how the "good riders" were making out with their knotheaded pet. He chuckled with the mock sadness of a man who has proved that he is not the only chump on earth. The new owners could not ride Lucky at all. He had already broken one boy's leg. Now the old man was on the lookout for another bargain hunter to take the expensive little beast off his hands. For at least forty dollars, of course.

I have no doubt that he will find one, but I hope that the next

Brownie: ⅛-Carat Gem. This little Welsh-Shetland gelding is everything that Lucky never could have been. His temperament as a child's mount is almost ideal. He has no "nerves" and no vices; he has never been sick. Sound as a rock, he can go all day, and he'll eat almost anything that isn't chrome-plated. His pure pony characteristics are evident. No picture could mislead even a novice to mistake him for a small horse. Hardy, gentle, alert, and always looking out for Number One, he will do anything for a firm young rider; but a complete novice can't push him faster than a walk. Photographs by Msgr. J. Graham

thrifty sucker will not be found among the readers of this book.

What was wrong with Lucky? To put it briefly, practically everything, but chiefly his mentality. He was not naturally mean; he was not a high-strung nervous animal. He was simply stupid. Observe his head and his expression. It is not a pony head. It is the head of a small underbred horse, too large and coarse for his body. Lucky's head shows no pony characteristics whatever. But the people who tried to make a good thing out of the ill-starred little animal could have studied him all day without ever seeing this. Their ignorance more than matched his stupidity, a hopeless combination. They could teach him nothing because they themselves knew nothing.[1]

Now look at the pony on page 25. He cost considerably more than Lucky, but he has proved himself worth every penny of his price. And he is a pony, not a stunted horse. A crossbred Welsh-Shetland, he is of pure pony blood, with pony traits and characteristics. Though almost a hand shorter, this pony weighs more than the pinto, is about three times as strong, and could run Lucky into the ground either in an all-out sprint or over a long, hard day across country. He can think around ten corners while a jughead like Lucky is bumbling around one. This hardy little bay can be trusted with a five-year-old child.

The three-year-old filly shown in the picture on page 27 is a very good type of riding pony, both in conformation and in temperament. Her light mane and tail, contrasting with her body color, give her a "flashy" appearance that most children —and many adults as well—like. She has good gaits and takes readily to schooling. Her dam was a 15-hand Saddlebred-Arabian; her sire, a small pinto of Hackney and Shetland breeding.

If I have dwelled on the subject of Lucky more than his few merits seem to warrant, I have done so with a purpose. In selecting a pony or a horse for a child, price is one of the least important considerations. I can hardly overemphasize this point. Cheapness is false economy. In the long run, a poor animal will cost you more than a good one. Often the cost is not only in cash but in the pleasure you miss when you use the animal. Then you cannot help realizing that you got just what you paid for, a nag with a leg on each corner and very little in between.

Many riders of all ages are unsuitably mounted not only because they erred in selecting a proper mount but because

[1] By chance I recently learned of Lucky's present whereabouts. He is living the life of Riley on a farm only a few miles from here. For the past five years, turned out in pasture, he has done nothing but eat and sleep—the complete loafer. In all that time no rider has been on his back; he has not done a lick of work. Living on his reputation, Lucky has a good thing. This leads me to wonder: Was that little knothead really so dumb, after all?

Taffy, a Good Type of Child's Pony. This flashy little filly embodies an unusual blend of distinctly different breeds. Sweet-tempered but full of go, she would make a good show pony for an experienced young rider. If I had seen Taffy soon enough I probably would have passed up Tonka, and Taffy would be the "star" of this book. Photograph by Msgr. J. Graham

their pride prevents them from admitting their error. More than a century ago Jorrocks remarked that it was safer to criticize a young man's morals than his horsemanship; today one might apply the observation to girls as well as boys. Countless ponies and horses are ruined for no better reason than that those who own them become stubbornly determined to "master" them and refuse to admit that they really don't know how. They try everything except common sense before they finally give up. It seems that frankly admitting a horse or pony is too much for

one is something to be ashamed of, a reflection on one's courage—or perhaps his skill as a bargain hunter. Nothing, however,
could be more absurd. We are not all horsemen of Olympic
Games caliber and most of us never can be; it is foolish to pretend otherwise. The wise rider must recognize his own limitations or be guided by some adviser who can do it for him.

In selecting a mount for a child, whether horse or pony, the
cardinal rule is: *Fit the animal to the rider*. To expect a youngster with little or no experience to adapt himself to a pony that
requires an experienced rider is to court disaster. If a child is
a harum-scarum roughneck—the sort of brat that our grand-
fathers referred to as "a plucky lad" or a "daring rider"—I think
it is quite all right to mount him on a mettlesome pony that will
put the fear of God into him or at least break a few of his bones
and teach him caution. But this can be overdone; it often is
done unintentionally, the result of ignorance. That is why I
have sketched the brief unlucky history of Lucky.

On the other hand, excessive caution in selecting a pony,
though it may be a lesser mistake, is to be avoided. An athletic
youngster who is really keen on riding and who has potential
ability will not enjoy himself or make much progress in riding
if mounted on a sluggish pony more suitable for his little sister.
Any normal lad—and maybe his sister, too—will soon want a
whip to put some life into such a pony. This reliance on haphazard use of the whip at the very outset of a child's riding
career is distinctly bad. It tends to develop an attitude quite
at variance with the principles of good horsemanship, particularly in fostering the notion that the only purpose of a whip is
to make one's mount go faster. The whip, like the spur, can
be an aid to good riding, but it should be used properly or not
at all. This intelligent discretion in the use of the whip is not
instinctive; it must be taught.

Wise choice of a suitable mount for a child stems from a
combination of common sense and sound horse sense. Two
general rules easy to follow in reaching a decision are these:

In a pony to be used for practical outdoor work—that is, not
exclusively as a show animal—temperament is more important

than conformation. It is easy to buy quality and get more trouble than you can handle. Temperament is of paramount importance.

A pony should be just mettlesome enough to gain and hold its young rider's healthy respect. A child who realizes that his pony has both the spirit and the agility to leave him straddling thin air—and, if badly handled, is very likely to do just that—soon learns to use his head as well as the seat of his pants when in the saddle. This mental alertness is essential to good horsemanship. Without it, we have nothing, nothing at all.

Closely linked with the problem of temperament is the question of sex. Does a stallion make a suitable mount for a child? Are mares better than geldings? Such questions can be answered only in a general way; so much depends on the individual animal and on the individual child—and on the instructor who teaches the child.

A rather common fixed idea among a certain type of horse owners—those who think they know it all but whose real knowledge of animals is only superficial—is that all stallions are difficult to handle, none can ever be trusted, and most are inclined to be "vicious." Never waste time or energy in futile argument with such persons. Your most cogent dialectic will never be able to inspire them with a boldness they naturally lack or with good horse sense.

At the opposite extreme to this point of view, we meet with the optimistic notion that anybody accustomed to mares and geldings can quite as easily handle stallions. I wish that this were true, for personally I prefer stallions; they have more courage than mares or geldings, and I think that as a rule they are more reliable. One who has the knowledge and the skill to appreciate their qualities can never, I believe, be completely satisfied with a mare or a gelding.

I can assure you, however, with a degree of certainty based on much observation and experience that many persons who are quite successful with mares and geldings *cannot* handle stallions and can never learn to. The most convincing proof, I think, is the large numbers of spoiled and ill-mannered stallions to be seen wherever there are ponies and horses. The chief quality that make him what he is is the stallion's nemesis—his natural spirit. It overmatches the puny spirits of those who lack the temperament and the talent to handle him.

In another chapter I shall discuss this subject in more detail. For the present I offer the following general observations; I think that most experienced horsemen will agree.

Stallions show more spirit than the average amateur rider can be trusted to control. Having more dominant personalities than mares or geldings, they can be more "difficult" for a timid or an uncertain rider to train; they usually need a knowledge-able trainer blessed with understanding and a firm hand. Stallions also benefit from more systematic daily exercise than most owners have the time or the inclination to give them. For experienced teen-age riders, who have learned to make a habit of mental alertness, stallions can make excellent mounts. Unfortunately, most children are too careless to handle them properly. For small children, however secure they may be in the saddle, stallions can be ruled completely out.

Mares are less reliable than stallions and more spirited than geldings. They are more prone to fits of temperament and can be a bit troublesome when in heat. However, being as nature meant them to be, they usually show great mettle and courage. They sometimes show an inclination to use their heels too freely, a vice that should be immediately squelched.

Geldings, even the best ones, are merely ghosts of the horses they might have been as stallions. Having had most of their natural fire doused, they make the safest mounts for the major-ity of riders. Usually geldings are more timid than mares, but they seldom have "moods" and can keep their minds on their work.

A question that seems to perplex many novices (while others never even give it a thought) is: What is the "best age" to buy a pony? Is it better to buy a mature animal already trained or a green colt?

On the surface, this appears to be a simple question to answer. Any sensible answer, however, can be given only in general terms; even then it must perforce bristle with *if*'s. For everything depends on the experience and the personal temperament of the child who is to ride the pony and—if a green colt is the choice—on the skill of the person who is to school the colt. It would greatly simplify everything if one could lay down a few exact rules, but experience has convinced me that this is not possible.

Most ponies are so poorly schooled—if you can call the process they go through real schooling—that it is a rare one that reaches maturity without having developed some very annoying faults. Instead of being schooled, the great majority of ponies, it seems to me, are merely taught to carry a rider—and I use the term *rider* in its loosest sense; *passenger* might be a better word.

When you do find a mature pony of good conformation and with good manners, a pony that has been really schooled, this jewel is for sale only at a price that might make you wonder whether his owner really wants to sell him at all, or whether you have picked the wrong hobby.

Such a "made" pony will be worth every penny you pay for him—if he is properly handled and ridden. But to buy a made pony like this for a youngster who is just learning to ride is a sheer waste of money. The child will ruin the pony in a very short time—and in the process he might get himself hurt. Generally speaking, I think, ponies are not as patient under abuse as horses are.

Even if he doesn't spoil the pony or get hurt, the novice who is given such a mount will miss gaining an understanding of what horsemanship really is. True, under a good instructor he may learn to ride the pony fairly well; he may even show it with some success in competition, which the ignorant mistake as the final, unanswerable test of horsemanship. But the child will never acquire even an inkling of what a great deal of time, patience and skill goes into the job of making a finished mount —until he himself tries it. "Those who do not school," stated Colonel M. F. McTaggart, "can never really ride." Such riders are to be seen everywhere; they are, in fact, the great majority.

You can see many of them winning ribbons in shows, confidently mounted on horses or ponies that somebody else has schooled for them. Most of them are completely self-satisfied; displaying their trophies and ribbons inflates their egos. But what they do is not horsemanship, the subject of this book. On a green mount or a spoiled one, this type of rider would be completely lost. They do not know really how to ride.

For this reason I am convinced that young riders who have acquired a firm seat and who are eager to learn should undertake the schooling of a green pony or horse without delay. It is the only way to learn.

Unfortunately, most youngsters are not encouraged to learn schooling; too often they are not even permitted to try. Their solicitous elders assume, without trial, that it is too difficult a task, or they may consider it too risky. But isn't gaining real proficiency in almost anything usually difficult? Few of us are blessed with such natural talents that we can easily master whatever we wish to. Schooling can at times be difficult; you will find nothing in this book intended to make it seem easy. But it is no more difficult than a hundred other things that we all learn to do as a matter of course in growing up, and its rewards are great, a source of lifelong pleasure.

That there is some element of risk in schooling colts no experienced horseman, I feel sure, would deny, but the degree of risk varies from almost none at all to sheer foolhardiness resulting from recklessness and an ignorance of equine psychology. The risk is implicit in a colt's natural friskiness, even skittishness; therefore it depends to a great extent on how systematically and carefully one proceeds with the schooling. It is axiomatic that good horsemanship aims at a procedure so gradual that it avoids upsetting a colt; it is thus that we avoid trouble. There is an element of risk in everything, even getting out of bed in the morning. Life itself is a series of risks. The wise way to live it and to teach one's children to live it is to take the hazards in stride. Parents who worry unduly about such things can be a great handicap to ambitious young riders.

On the other hand, it would be obviously foolish to mount

Partners. The senior partner, burdened by one of his chief cares, is below. After two years of happy-go-lucky trial and error Seán, now nine years old, had become, in his own estimation, a superior horseman. He felt secure in the saddle, on a pad, or bareback; he could boot Brownie into a gallop and usually get him stopped within about fifty yards. With luck, he could even prevent the pony from pausing to nibble grass. But Brownie wasn't fooled; he knew who was really the boss and who would remain boss for about one more year. A young rider's fond parents too often are fooled at this stage of his education. Because he has learned how to stick on, they don't realize that the child knows little more than that. This woeful lack of discernment at the very outset of their riding careers is why so many riders never get beyond an elementary level.

a rank beginner on an undisciplined green colt or on a spoiled pony like Lucky. A novice, who must concentrate merely on staying in the saddle and then learning to control his mount in an elementary way, certainly is not ready to attempt schooling, even if he understood how. Learning position comes first, then elementary control; the finer points must wait. A rider in this kindergarten stage needs a placid mount that has been not so much schooled as made foolproof under all reasonable circumstances. The age of such a beginner's mount does not matter much, for if the rider's education progresses as it should, soon he will want and need a more sensitive mount.

A novice rider, having learned position and fairly good control if he has a competent instructor to guide him, may well proceed to learn schooling without delay. He will, naturally, make mistakes, which it is the instructor's job to explain and correct; but even in spite of the mistakes both the rider and his mount will improve, and the more the rider improves the better job of schooling he can do. Every little step forward begets greater progress.

A rider taught in this way will progress many times faster than if he merely rides while the instructor harps on the mechanics of riding—head up, heels down, elbows in, and so on.

Re-schooling a horse or pony that has been spoiled by bad riding or that has some dangerous habit such as rearing is quite another matter. Correcting or reforming an animal of this sort is no job for a beginner. As a general rule, in fact, reforming badly spoiled horses and ponies is, in my opinion, a rather thankless, tedious task. About the only profit in it is the extra knowledge one may gain from the experience. For this reason, however, and because the number of ponies more or less spoiled by ignorant handling is so great that it is not too difficult to find some potentially good ones, it is sometimes wise to gamble on the price and hope that the purchase turns out to be a bargain.

Sometimes it does; often it does not. But I must repeat with emphasis that animals of this unfortunate background, in need of corrective schooling to make them safe and reliable mounts, are not for novices or timid riders. For anyone but an expert horseman to take them in hand is to risk ending up with another Lucky and with a young rider who has lost his nerve.

Any lingering doubts you may have about this should be dispelled when you read the next chapter.

CHAPTER V

The Gray Stallion

Perhaps after digesting my remarks in the preceding chapters, you wonder how I hope to avoid in this book the faults I criticize in others. I'm not sure I can, but at least I shall try. Let me invite you behind the scenes to look upon an earnest author's travail. Perhaps a brief summary of my troubles in composing this book may encourage you when in your riding and schooling everything seems to go wrong, so completely wrong that you might feel tempted to quit. At least it might convince you that I have not been content to take the easy way.

In the writing of this book everything went wrong, not once or occasionally but a hundred times.

To begin with, once I was committed to the task I realized that a mere cut-and-dried manual explaining in vague, general terms how to do this or that would not be the best way of giving real help. Anyone can merely offer advice and lay down theoretical rules—indeed, the world is full of armchair theorists who know how to do little else. But putting advice into practice and proving that the rules really work is something else. Yet if I could not do this, then certainly I'd have no business setting myself up as an adviser to others.

This decision brought me to grips with a problem that was

to remain constant throughout the book—the shooting of suitable photographs to illustrate major points in the text. I am not a professional photographer; I'm not even a skilled amateur. But my experience with professional photographers has not been too happy. Most of them know little about horses and are almost utterly ignorant of good horsemanship. If a print is sharp and "sparkling" and shows plenty of action, that, they usually think, is enough. It is often difficult to make a good photographer understand why a technically excellent picture may actually serve as a "horrible example" of a horse and a rider doing everything quite wrongly. I realize that somewhere in this world there must be photographers who are also horsemen, but I have not been fortunate enough to meet up with one. Therefore, I decided, it would be simpler to shoot the pictures myself.

Simpler? The job turned out to be a never-ending headache.

Before I learned this the hard way, however, I had a more basic problem—choosing my subjects for most of the pictures to be taken. I wanted a youngster about twelve years old who was completely inexperienced with ponies or horses, a child whose potential as a rider had never even been tested. Then I had to find an absolutely green pony or a small horse—an animal practically untouched by human hands—whose temperament and conformation promised that it would be worth schooling. I wanted just good average specimens, not prodigies.

The first part of this problem was relatively easy. My potential rider was right at home—either one of my daughters, Linda and Sheilagh. Linda was eleven; Sheilagh was thirteen. Their knowledge of horses and ponies was practically nil and entirely theoretical; they knew that horses and ponies had four legs, sometimes kicked, and liked to eat grass. Neither of the girls had ever been on a horse or pony more than a couple of times, and then only for a short while; it could hardly be called riding.

If such ignorance in the daughters of a horseman seems strange, I should explain here that, contrary to common opinion, I do not believe that it is necessary to begin riding very young in order to become a good horseman. I've seen too many self-styled experts of this kind who were the worst horsemen imaginable; conversely, I've known other riders who did not begin until comparatively late in life who developed into excellent horsemen. The average child of about ten is neither mentally nor physically capable of learning really to ride. Certainly, athletic youngsters can learn to "stick" to a saddle; they can have a great deal of fun on horseback, and if they enjoy the sport they should be encouraged. They are, however, actually little more than passengers, able to control a mount only in the most elementary way. Intelligent riding requires headwork even more than good balance and a sturdy pair of jeans.

Thus, I did not push either Linda or Sheilagh into a sport for which they showed no special inclination. If and when they wanted to learn, I knew, there would always be plenty of time.

Before deciding which of the girls to use as a subject for this book, I set about finding a suitable pony. I wanted a pony, or a small horse, with the following qualifications:

> Good temperament
> Physically sound
> Good saddle conformation
> Absolutely green, with no bad habits to unlearn
> Between two and three years of age, old enough
>   to begin schooling under saddle
> Of sufficient size to mature at about 14 hands
> Reasonable in price

Surely, one would think, with so many horses and ponies always for sale, these simple standards are entirely within reason. However, when we set out to find a pony with these qualifications, we found reason to wonder.

Most ponies were smaller than we wanted. Many were just miniature draft horses, with short thick necks and rough choppy gaits, not at all suitable for riding. Those with decent conformation showed the wrong kind of temperament for a child's mount; this was particularly true of registered animals that their owners considered promising "show ponies."

Our fourth and fifth requirements—absolutely green and mature enough to start under saddle—seemed to cancel each other out. A pony colt two years old that is no more than halterbroken, or at least unspoiled by inept handling, is almost as rare as a black pearl. At least, that was my impression when I tried to find one. Every two-year-old we looked at had been "started"; many could be mounted and pulled about by youngsters who knew nothing whatever about riding. Many of the potential "show ponies" had already been subjected to the sort of needless spooking-up treatment gaited horses undergo. As subjects for *re*-schooling most of them would have been excellent.

The small horses we looked at presented an even more discouraging picture: weedy runts that would never be able to hold together under the stress of real work; chunky, bulldog "Quarter Horse types" that belonged in harness; or flighty, stunted "Thoroughbred types" as unsuitable for a child as a hair-trigger pistol. A few good animals of Arab blood were priced too high; none of them qualified as green or unspoiled.

Then one day by pure happenstance we had a stroke of luck; though at the time we did not realize that it was our lucky break, and in fact I almost passed it by.

A friend of mine, Marie Rathman, telephoned to inform me that she had just acquired a pony as a pet for her young son and daughter. The pony was running free in a large hilly pasture on the farm where he had been foaled. I gathered from what Marie said that the animal was practically as wild as a mustang. He had never had a halter on, and no one could lure him into a corral or a barn. Marie, who breeds and shows German shepherds and who is an expert trainer of dogs, admitted that she had no experience whatever with ponies or horses, but it was up to her to catch this pony because everybody else had given up trying. The pony had become so wary that now no one could even get close to him. Would I, she asked, help her catch him?

It was a chill autumn afternoon and Marie lived a good twenty-five miles away; I was fed up with looking at ponies I had no use for, and I had no desire to see this one, probably another scrub refugee from a fox farm. Marie Rathman, however, is one of my favorite people; she had always been most helpful and generous, sharing freely her keen knowledge of dogs. I said I would come; I'd help her round up her children's future pet.

During the drive to the farm where the pony was, Marie filled in a few details. He was a stallion. He had no name. He was not yet two years old. His sire was a registered Welsh pony, his dam a small Arabian. Since birth he had run loose on this hilly farm in the Kettle Moraine, rarely if ever seeing the inside of a barn. The breeder, a friend of Marie's, was retiring from the pony-breeding business. This stallion colt was the last pony she had left, one of her favorites. She had offered him to Marie as a gift in gratitude for Marie's having handled one of her hounds to its championship in the show ring.

I suggested that an unbroken stallion colt might not be the ideal pet for a couple of completely inexperienced youngsters. Marie admitted that she didn't know about that. I predicted that she wouldn't be long in learning.

Fortunately for us, someone had managed to lure the colt into a large corral adjacent to an old barn. He was standing in ankle-deep mud, alertly watching us as we got out of the car. He was dark gray, almost black, about 13 hands tall. His winter coat had started coming in; he looked dirty and shaggy, rather scrawny, and wild. He had excellent legs with plenty of bone, a well-shaped head, and dark, full eyes—watchful eyes that missed nothing. His silver-gray tail touched the muddy ground and his forelock hung more than halfway down his face. He had a distinctly masculine air; even at a distance no one would have mistaken him for a filly or a gelding.

Entering the corral alone, I approached him. The pony wheeled, going away from me at a springy trot. Though his feet were badly in need of trimming, his action was excellent, straight and true. For his age, he looked superbly muscled.

"He's no harness chunk," I told Marie. "He'll make a saddle pony."

Plodding after him with a loop ready, I tried to get within roping distance, but the pony seemed to know exactly what I was up to. He kept moving, always well out of reach. I found it impossible to maneuver him into a corner and close in on him, even with Marie's help. Again and again that gray pony, dodging with catlike agility, eluded us. The treacherous mud did not slow him down at all. He was as sure-footed as a mountain goat. He could explode from a standstill into a dead run in one stride and cut ninety-degree turns.

"Let's shoo him into the barn," I suggested. "Maybe we can corner him in there."

The idea was sound; it just didn't work. The old barn was littered with farm implements and odds and ends of junk, but we could not get that pony into a corner he could not get out of. He outdodged us from one end of the barn to the other. He never bumped into anything, never knocked anything over. He could find "holes" where there didn't seem to be any with the skill of a professional halfback.

I realize that this sounds quite ridiculous—one small shaggy pony making two active adults look like retarded stumblebums —but this pony did just that. His display of open-field running was so fantastic I feared that his luck might run out; I did not want to see him injured. So I opened the barn door, and the pony led us back out into the corral.

By this time the light had begun to fade; dusk had set in. Marie flooded the corral with the headlights of her car. The colt had begun to tire. Marie and I were well ahead of him in that respect. The maneuvering in the mud continued while I cursed my too-short rope—and then suddenly, unexpectedly, the loop was around the pony's neck. Marie had scooped it off the ground and flung it almost blindly. The colt, racing down the fence, had run right into the noose.

I grabbed the trailing rope and took a hip-lock, digging my heels into the mud. The gray colt hit the end and swung around facing me, the noose tight around his neck.

I kept it tight while he pulled and plunged to regain his freedom. When he finally stood still, legs braced and flanks heaving, I eased off a little.

I worked my way down the rope until I could lay a hand on his neck. Though frightened, the colt did not fight. There was no trace of meanness in him and he had sense enough to know when he was licked.

Talking softly to reassure him, I haltered him, then I removed the rope. Marie said that her husband and somebody else would come and get the colt the next day.

"Some kid's pet!" I said as we drove back to her place in the dark. "You'll have your hands full with that lad."

For once, I qualified as a real prophet.

I thought no more of the gray pony for months, except to wonder now and then how the Rathmans were making out with his education. Then one day the following spring Marie telephoned again.

Sunny, she said, was loose. Would I come out and try to catch him?

"Who," I asked, "is Sunny?"

Sunny was the gray stallion colt. He had been roaming the countryside for five days, trailing a twenty-foot rope from his halter. Nobody could get anywhere near him and Marie was hopeful that perhaps I could.

"She must think I'm a magician," I remarked to my wife as we got into the car. "Sunny! At least, they could have called him Smoky or The Galloping Ghost."

Marie met us with a tale of woe. The pony had quickly realized that he was in the hands of innocents and that he had a good thing going. He had practically taken over the Rathman family, the farm and the mortgage. No one knew how to handle him and his natural Prince Valiant arrogance flowered. He developed the nasty habit of nipping and the deadly trick of rearing and striking with his forefeet. After he had almost brained Marie a couple of times, she kept him confined in a corral and forbade her children ever to go near him. The pony went about with a long rope trailing from his halter, and he was watered

41

6 2001

WILLIAM WOODS COLLEGE LIBRARY

and fed through the corral fence. He was a pony with four owners and no master.

This was not the first time he had got loose, Marie told us. Once before he had roamed the countryside for several days, cunningly eluding all pursuers. Finally thirst drove him into a farm yard for water and somebody slammed a gate behind him.

That evening three husky men, armed with ropes, went to the farm to fetch him home. But the gray pony had other ideas. Along the way, he suddenly exploded into action, knocking one of the men into a ditch and nearly rope-burning the hands off the other two as he broke for freedom. That time he was gone a full week.

Now he was loose again, trailing the long rope that almost had become a part of him. Someone had seen him that afternoon in a field bordering the farm. Probably he was still there, Marie said with a marked lack of enthusiasm.

He was there. The gray pony stood quite still watching me saunter toward him across the lush springtime grass. He waited until I was about two hundred yards away; then he trotted off in a wide semicircle, the long rope trailing from his halter. He did not move with his head held to one side to avoid stepping on the rope; he trotted straight and true, but not once did he plant a foot on that rope. Wheeling after him, I watched him vanish into a thicket of scrubby timber clogged with under-brush.

Now, I thought, I'd have him. It seemed hardly possible that any animal could trail a long rope through that dense thicket without snagging it on something. All I had to do was wade in and find him.

I was still blundering about in the thicket when the gray pony emerged into the open, circled around behind me and resumed grazing near the spot where I had first seen him. He watched my second approach, I felt sure, with a rather bored air of must-we-do-this-all-afternoon?

We did not do it all afternoon, for after trying every trick and blandishment I could think of I gave up. Afoot, I had no more chance of getting near that crafty little beast than of reaching the moon by pogo stick.

Three days later we heard from Marie again. A neighbor had caught the thirsty pony in his yard and had tied him to a tree. The little stallion was there now, but nobody would go near him. Would I go out, Marie asked, and lead him back to the barn? Would I, furthermore, try to find someone who might want to buy him? Or perhaps I wanted to buy him? Marie was not particular. She just hoped that I could think of some way to get the wretched beast off her hands.

The Rathmans, like thousands of other people, had had their equestrian fling. Henceforth they would stick to dogs.

I found the little gray stallion tied to a tree where Marie had said he would be.

Judging by the signs, he must have been tethered there for quite a while, perhaps twenty-four hours or more. But as he watched me walk toward him, the little stallion still had his haughty Prince Valiant manner, the proud look-of-eagles.

This was my first close look at him since the previous autumn, and I eyed him now with more than casual interest. Before, I had not given even a thought to the possibility of ever buying him. Now, however, the Rathmans wanted only to be rid of him, and they were finding no takers; nobody who knew anything about this pony wanted any part of him. But I was still searching for a pony to "star" in this book and seemed to be as far from finding the type I wanted as when I'd begun my search. Now the thought suddenly occurred to me: Was this rambunctious little stallion, masterless, unwanted and unloved, the very type of pony best suited to my purpose?

He had grown; I estimated that he would mature at about 14 hands. He was beginning to fill out in the right places. Certainly, he could hardly qualify as unspoiled. In his brief, baby life he had already acquired enough nasty habits and dirty tricks, some of them really dangerous, to give a mature horse a reputation for being "rank." But he was green enough; no one had succeeded in teaching him anything at all.

I found that out as soon as I started to lead him home. He

Tonka as a Two-Year-Old. This picture was taken a few months after I had bought the young stallion. With all the good hay and grain he'd clean up, and excellent pasturage, the colt was beginning to fill out. This photograph illustrates how a healthy, properly fed horse shows a glossy coat without a lot of grooming. Tonka spent almost all his time outside. He seemed to enjoy rainstorms, the more thunder and lightning the better. Gray horses are born black; as they age they fade. If Tonka lives as long as his superb health indicates he probably will, he may end up pure white.

knew no more about leading than when first I'd put a halter on him. Nor did he want to be led. He wanted to lead me. Unable to do that, he wanted to get rid of me. He repeatedly tried to bite me. However, I did not make the mistake of hanging onto him merely by the lead rope, as others had always done. I stayed close to him, with a firm grip on his halter as well as the rope.

When he found that he could neither pull loose nor bite me,

the pony resorted to jibbing and rearing. That had always worked for him, scaring people silly. But it failed to work this time. Our progress was a jerky, erratic zigzag over the grass, but at last I got him back to his stable and shut the door of his box stall behind him. He immediately went to work on the fresh hay awaiting him as if he had not eaten for a week.

"Charming little rascal," I told Marie. "Wonderful child's pet. Sell him to your dearest enemy."

She stared glumly at the gray pony. "Could he be trained?"

"Of course. But the job would cost you more than you could get for him, at least in this area."

For the next few days, off and on, that little gray stallion kept pushing himself back into my mind. I liked him. I liked his looks, his cocky spirit. Secretly, it amused and delighted me that one little raggedy colt had been able to make so many superior intellects look foolish. I was really in a receptive frame of mind when my wife suggested:

"Wouldn't that gray pony be a good subject for the book?"

"Would he?"

"He's green——"

"Green? Spoiled!"

"The right size?"

"He'll be big enough."

"Age?"

"Just right."

"And a stallion. You say you like stallions best."

I was silent.

"A spoiled stallion colt," my wife said triumphantly. "A real object lesson. All you have to do is teach him manners and educate him, then teach Linda or Sheilagh to ride him, take a few pictures, and tell how you did it. And there's your book."

"That's all? Nothing to it, eh?"

"Well, isn't that what the book is supposed to be about?"

"All right. Tell Marie we'll take that gray hellion off her hands."

CHAPTER VI

Diamond in the Very, Very Rough

THE trip from the Rathman farm to his new home was the gray pony's second experience in a trailer. I had very little difficulty getting him in. Suspicious of everything, he seemed to be afraid of nothing. After he had balked at the ramp a few times, I put a tail rope on him; that did the job in a hurry. He went in with a rush.

As a safety precaution I had bought a new halter, made of the finest quality leather. It looked strong enough to hold a horse, and it probably would have. Once the pony was securely tied inside the trailer with some hay to occupy his attention, it seemed like a good idea to let him "soak" there for a while before we started home. Leaving Linda to keep an eye on the pony, we returned to the house to celebrate the transfer of ownership.

We'd been in the house only a few minutes when a yell from Linda brought us charging out into the yard. "He's breaking loose!" Linda told us excitedly. "He had both his front legs out that little door on the side. I pushed 'em back in——"

"How *could* he get his legs through the feed door?" I looked at her incredulously. "It's impossible."

"Well, he did. I pushed 'em back in. He was making the whole trailer rock and shake."

I opened the small door at the front of the trailer and peered in. The little gray stallion gazed down at me with wary interest—and there was not a strap of leather on his head. The fine new halter, strong enough to hold a horse, was lying on the floor. The sturdy brass ring to which the tie rope was attached had been bent egg-shaped, and the crown strap had been cleanly severed at the buckle.

I gazed at the little stallion in awe.

"What shall we call him?" I asked Linda. "Hercules or Paul Bunyan?"

That halter-breaking incident was my first hint of the mighty atom we had acquired. Linda decided to name him Tonka. *Tonka* is the Sioux word for *horse*. Our Tonka was only a pony, but time proved the name appropriate; for the gray stallion turned out to be a "big little horse"—much bigger than most people would care to handle. It was no wonder the Rathmans saw us off with happy smiles!

Several years later, I was told, Marie remarked to a friend, "I was so happy to get rid of that pony I would have *given* him away." I can see her point. For while there was never a trace of real meanness in this colt, Tonka was as brash and cocky as they come. He combined the intelligence of the Arabian with the craft and cunning of a true pony. If you gave him the slightest advantage, he was instantly aware of it—and he took it. As a result, he had developed some nasty habits which had to be corrected before his real education could begin.

His most vexing and certainly his most dangerous habit was trotting up to anyone who entered his corral or pasture, suddenly rearing, and striking at the person's head. He had acquired this habit through Marie Rathman's mistaken notion of how a colt shows affection and playfulness. She had permitted him a few times to place his forelegs on her shoulders, as if he were a playful Irish wolfhound. When he started aiming at her head, however, Marie realized her mistake. But the seed had been planted and she did not know how to uproot it.

His most annoying habit was his penchant for biting. This is quite common in colts, particularly stallions. It is a habit that should be nipped in the bud, immediately and without any compromise. Some ponies and horses can never be trusted not to bite if you turn your back on them because, when they started the nipping habit as colts, their deluded owners thought the youngsters were merely showing playfulness. Later, after the vice had become established, the owners did not know how to break the habit. As a rule, about all the average person can think of in correcting a horse or pony is hitting the animal. This seems to be the universal cure-all. But it isn't. Hitting at the wrong time or for the wrong reason can do more harm than good. I don't think it even comes close to being the best way to correct a biter.

Besides trying to chew your hand off when you were leading him, the gray colt was not properly halterbroken. Dragging frightened people about on the end of a long rope had taught him only that he was stronger than they were. To do anything with him on the end of a lead rope you needed plenty of muscle, as well as enough experience and quickness to keep him off balance. And always you had to watch out for his going up on his hind legs and playfully knocking your head off.

Linda and Tonka. At this time, shortly after we had acquired him, Tonka was still pretty much of a mischievous handful. That was one reason why he was wearing this Mexican horsehair hackamore instead of a halter. Notice how Linda is holding him away and keeping an eye on him. The colt still made a pest of himself at times with his nipping habit. This picture was taken only a short time before he almost brained the loudmouthed bridle-path cowboy who knew all about how to handle stallions.

I wasted no time going to work breaking up all three of these habits. While it is a generally accepted basic rule in training, "Teach one thing at a time," this does not mean that you must waste time concentrating on only one lesson while postponing others. I had no intention of letting Tonka drag me all over the landscape and chew my pants off while I concentrated on teaching him not to rear and strike. He had to learn all three lessons and learn them in a hurry.

Since his striking habit was really dangerous, I forbade the children and my wife ever to approach Tonka in his paddock or pasture except when I was present—and I didn't have to repeat the order. They were not at all eager to have their heads bashed in. Neither was I. Accordingly, I went at the task of reforming him with complete determination.

The young stallion had already formed the habit of coming up to anyone who approached him—he had to get close in order to knock your head off. He'd come at a prancing, swaggering strut, supremely cocky that he was the Champion Stud Hoss of the World. I decided to make use of this habit to begin teaching him to come when he was called, for few animals can be more exasperating than a horse or a pony that is difficult to catch in an open field, one that has to be chased, cornered and captured every time you want to bring him into the stable.

So each time I went out to bring Tonka in I carried a small handout of oats—and several pebbles concealed in one hand. I would call him from a distance. As soon as he started toward me I would halt—the idea was for him to come to me. When he was about five yards from me I'd hold out a handful of oats —but not in my throwing hand, the hand that held the pebbles; that hand was ready for instant action.

At first, of course, the colt tried his Big Stud Hoss act on me. But the moment his forefeet left the ground as he started to rear, I'd let him have it—not the oats but one of the pebbles. I aimed at his belly and his hind legs, and I threw as hard as I could. When a stone hit him it stung, and I meant it to hurt. I took the offensive away from him, the last thing he expected because no one else had ever done it. Yelling, "*No!*" I would jump at him threateningly. Usually I was carrying a lead rope and I'd take a swat at him with it, trying to hit him while his forefeet were in the air. In short, I let him know in every way that the instant he went up on his hind legs he was making trouble for himself and I would not tolerate his Big Stud Hoss antics.

I realize that this sounds pretty rough. It was. Some readers may reasonably wonder why, if this was the way I usually greeted his approach, I did not defeat my own purpose, teaching the colt to run away instead of come when I called. But the answer is quite simple. Tonka met this sort of reception *only* when he made the slightest move to rear; I never made a threatening gesture until his forefeet were *off the ground*. In other words, I carefully timed my correction so that there was a distinct connection between his attempt to rear and my explosive reaction. But if he kept his feet where they belonged, on the ground, and only if he kept them there, then he received a quite different reception—a reward of oats, caresses and sweet words.

In all stages of training, no matter what the lesson may be, the matter of correct timing is of utmost importance. Probably nothing else so greatly influences the ease or difficulty of training. If your timing is wrong, it is practically impossible to make the horse or pony understand what you want him to do. He may be as docile as the proverbial lamb, willing to do anything you desire, but he will never clearly understand what that is— no matter what the lesson may be—if your timing is wrong. There *must* be a distinct, immediate connection between his act and your correction or reward. This is true whether you are merely halterbreaking a foal or working on an advanced exercise in mounted schooling. In fact, the further schooling progresses, the more important this factor of timing becomes.

Whatever his faults, Tonka was never a lunkhead, and the gusto of his appetite matched the keenness of his brain. He much preferred the tasty oats to the stinging stones and he was not long in figuring out how he could get the oats. In a few days he would come trotting up to me, eager for his handout, without any attempt to rear.

A permanent cure, however, was not as simple as that last sentence might mislead you to believe. Most studs have a tendency to go up in front, and Tonka had developed his bad habit unhindered by any real attempts at correction. Though he quickly learned not to rear when I was facing him, the gray colt was by no means trustworthy—as I found out, not at all to my surprise, the first time I cautiously turned my back on him. Then immediately I became fair game again. He probably would have clouted me silly that first time I turned my back on him if I had not anticipated his reaction. He was up on his hind legs taking aim at me when, quickly completing a full turn, I hit him in the belly with the end of the lead rope. Tonka almost fell over backward trying to get away from me. He was the surprised one, not I.

Many persons, I know from experience, would conclude that this little stallion was a naturally treacherous beast, never to be trusted, because he would go for me from behind like this after I had taught him not to do the same thing when I faced him. But this sort of hasty judgment is based on a lack of understanding of equine psychology. It accounts for many errors in training and thousands of spoiled horses and ponies. A fact of equine nature that the average novice handler never grasps without someone to tell him is that horses and ponies must learn everything from both sides. It is not too far from the truth to say that they are not only two-sided; they are four-sided, six-sided, eight-sided.

A simple illustration is the reaction of a pony or a horse that is accustomed to being mounted always from the left side, as most are, when someone first tries to mount him from the opposite side. It is almost a certainty that he will "spook," acting as if he had never been mounted before. Likewise, a pony that will quietly pass a familiar object on one side only, if turned around and required to pass it while going in the opposite direction, is likely to act as if he had never seen that thing before. A horse familiar with the sight and sound of automobiles coming toward him might try to run away the first time a car approaches from behind him.

We might reasonably suppose that anyone who has handled a horse or a pony for even a short time would become aware of this and could draw correct conclusions based on his observation. But we would be wrong. The average horseman, unable to see the obvious right in front of his nose, is inclined to conclude, "He's just stubborn and ornery," and reach for his old standby, the whip.

Thus, Tonka had to learn the hard way that rearing and striking, at all times and under all circumstances, was out, not merely when I was facing him. Teaching him this required constant vigilance for a while. I never turned away from him without watching him out of the corner of my eye and being ready to whirl on him with a yell and a slash of a rope or a flung stone. Realizing that this lesson had to be indelibly impressed on his mind, because if it were not he would remain forever useless as a child's pony, I often went out of my way deliberately to tempt him to take a poke at me so that I would have a chance to correct him.

But Tonka learned fast. He learned that I was as quick as he was and could be quicker and that I was never off guard. On a lead rope or free, he learned to keep a certain distance from me; if he overstepped that invisible boundary, I let him know about it. He learned to freeze in his tracks if I, suspecting he might be plotting mischief, warned him with a sharp, "No!" He soon gave up any lingering notion he might have had of striking at me, but it was several weeks before I trusted him enough to relax my vigilance a bit.

In theory, I suppose, permanently breaking the little stallion of his dangerous habit should have been possible in one tough lesson. In actual practice, however, theory often flies out the window on the wings of fancy. Every pony and horse is an unique individual, having his own peculiar quirks and traits—and any trainer who fails to realize this will never go very far; he will fail with at least as many animals as he succeeds with. The unique individual named Tonka was a very smart, crafty pony that had acquired an excellent working knowledge of human weaknesses. Perhaps an incident during this phase of his training might make it clear why I deemed it wise to keep a wary and careful eye on him long after I might have been justified in accepting him at face value as a thoroughly reformed character.

A neighbor was standing with me near the entrance of the training corral one day just after I had given the gray colt one of his first lessons on the longe line. This bridle-path cowboy professed to know all about how to handle stallions (though he had never owned one) and made no secret of his belief that I was in need of his expert advice. His ideas boiled down to two basic convictions: except for breeding purposes, there should not be any stallions, and the only way to treat a stud was to treat him rough.

We were standing a few yards apart; Tonka, apparently quite relaxed and with the longe line slack, was standing midway between us. Suddenly, without the least warning, he was up on his hind legs and was smashing down at the loudmouthed oracle who knew all about how to handle stallions. By the grace of God, I reacted quickly enough to jerk the pony off balance as his forehoofs flashed downward, but even so Tonka was fast enough to knock the fellow's hat off and almost take a few of his shirt buttons as well.

What suddenly possessed Tonka to make him do this? My explanation to the furious and frightened bridle-path cowboy, "He doesn't like your ideas about stallions," was meant merely to clear the air. (It didn't.) To this day I have not found an answer that satisfies me. I don't know why he did it unless he still thought he might be able to get away with something.

Why he chose our neighbor as his target instead of me, on the other hand, seems obvious. Long after he would not dare to nip me even when I turned my back on him, the colt would still occasionally try to find out if he could get away with nipping my wife and the girls as well as strangers. "With you, he's an angel," Sheilagh remarked one day, rubbing a nipped arm. "With us, he's a little devil."

I cite these incidents to stress an important point: In all training and schooling you do not merely teach a lesson. By frequent repetition over a period of time you must *confirm* it until the animal's reaction becomes a fixed habit.

CHAPTER VII

The Polishing Begins

S HORTLY after starting to work with him, I tried to get some exact information about Tonka's breeding. I went to visit his breeder, the woman who had given him to Marie Rathman. I saw some of the pastures in which he had run and gamboled from the day of his birth until he was almost two years old—hilly, rolling grassland that heaved and dipped and tumbled like a stormy sea. Some of the slopes were about sixty degrees. One look at that wonderful grazing land, so ideally suited for horses, made it clear why the gray colt was so well developed and so sure-footed.

His dam, I learned, was a small gray mare of Arabian and Welsh pony blood, with a fine Arab head. Exactly how much blood of each breed she carried I was unable to learn. My guess is that she was at least half-Arabian, possibly three-quarters or more. I lean toward this belief because of Tonka's size at maturity and his predominantly Arabian characteristics. The gray mare also had a reputation, I was told, for throwing good colts. That was all I could learn about Tonka's mother.

On the other side of the pedigree, our gray stallion's bloodlines were clear, a matter of record. His sire was a registered Welsh pony, Indiana Criban Boy, by Criban Grand Master.

Criban Grand Master was one of the greatest Welsh show ponies in America and a noted sire of the breed.

So it seemed that we had the first requisite for successful training—good material to work with.

Even the best of material needs plenty of work, and I made sure that Tonka got his full share. A child's pony must be fool-proof—because children themselves are not. They are often careless, forgetful, incautious; they woolgather and daydream. You can caution and warn and lecture on safety until you're blue in the face; the youngsters will forget, or they will dare to take a chance. They learn best the hard way—and the hard way usually hurts; it can be a permanent hurt. It is, as a rule, easier to train a horse or pony than the rider. Aware of this, I overlooked no smallest detail in getting Tonka started right.

At the same time I was impressing on him the folly of rearing and striking, I set to work curing him of his penchant for nipping and biting. This is a most annoying habit in any animal; in a stallion it can become as dangerous a vice as in a powerful dog, a source of constant trouble. In the opinion of many experienced horsemen, biting is the worst vice a horse can have. If you are ever safely to turn your back on the animal, the habit must be ruthlessly broken. In dealing with a horse or pony that bites there can be no halfway measures. You can't afford to lose.

There seem to be almost as many "cures" for biting as there are horsemen. Some are rather odd and impractical, such as shoving a piece of hot meat into the animal's mouth. But how often are most of us willing to go about a carrying a chunk of hot meat? Must we wear mittens merely to teach a horse simple good manners? A similar remedy substitutes a sharp-edged stick for the piece of pot roast. But what are we to do when the animal sees—as any smart horse or pony quickly would see—that we are not carrying our stick? The average horseman needs a simpler corrective, one that he can apply any time, any place.

Perhaps, unfortunately, that is why the average horseman—having little more imagination than the animal he would master—is prone to rely on one universal cure-all for every vice, real or fancied—hitting. Hit 'em in the belly, smack 'em on the nose, crack 'em on the rump, whip 'em across the legs. I've even seen men and women hit nervous colts to make them stand still!

I am not a bleeding heart. I have no reluctance to hit a horse as hard as may be necessary if I think it will do some good; but experience has convinced me that hitting is a most inefficient way of attempting to cure a biter. It may, on the contrary, intensify the vice by making the animal "mean"; and if he is struck in the face, it will almost certainly make him head-shy. Whenever possible, it is best to correct a pony or a horse without letting him realize that *you* are doing the correcting. If you can correct him in such a way as to leave him the impression that he, and he alone, is hurting himself, then you have it made.

That was the way I cured Tonka of biting.

To use this method all you need is a straight pin or a sharp nail. I used a horseshoe nail, which is easy to grip firmly. A large safety pin, bent so that it is rather straight, is quite satisfactory. Or you can use a woman's short hatpin, three or four inches long.

Hold the pin or the nail concealed in your hand so that the point protrudes about an eighth of an inch from between your thumb and the second joint of your forefinger. With the other three fingers grasp the leadshank of your horse or pony close to the halter (see page 59). Now start leading him as you ordinarily would, watching him out of a corner of your eye for the first sidewise head movement that precedes a nip at your hand.

The instant he moves his head to nip let him ram his jaw or muzzle against the sharp point. Remember: *Let him do it*. Do not jab at him; make no threatening gesture whatever. Try to keep your hand holding the lead perfectly still and firm. The idea is to let the horse or pony punish himself, leaving him with the impression that you have absolutely nothing to do with hurting him.

You can be certain that only a few such painful "accidents" will be enough to convince even the most persistent nipper that biting doesn't pay and that you are probably part porcupine.

I have never known this simple method to fail, no matter how firmly established the animal's biting habit had become. It worked like magic on Tonka and has been equally effective in curing other horses and ponies without exception.

Anyone can apply the cure. It demands no special skill. All you need is a pin or a nail and the ability to hold your hand quite still when the horse or pony goes for it.

Corrected in this way, a colt will never become head-shy. He does not learn to think of you as an enemy, someone who will hurt him—for you don't hurt him; he hurts himself. He never even knows that you have anything in your hand.

Of course, like all other lessons, this lesson must be confirmed. You cannot expect to cure an inveterate biter in one minute. Always keep in mind that horses and ponies are cheerful optimists; one or two failures to achieve their purpose won't discourage them from trying again. But repeated failures will, especially when it hurts every time. Therefore, in setting out to rid a colt or an old rogue of this nipping habit, keep your nail or pin handy; for a week or two carry it in your pocket so that you'll always have it whenever you need it. Every time you take hold of his leadshank have that secret weapon concealed in your hand. Within a couple of weeks at most, I think, you won't need it any more.

A horse—but almost never a pony—that has been allowed to get away with this nipping habit for a long time without correction will occasionally show signs of reverting to the habit. It will seem as if he has forgotten the lesson of the pin or nail. But you can rest assured that he has *not* forgotten. He is merely feeling you out, trying to see whether he can still pull any of his old tricks again. Get out the nail or pin and let him know at once that he can't.

One day, long after we considered Tonka completely rid of his old habit, he surprised Sheilagh with a sharp nip while she was grooming him. Standing nearby, I saw him do it, and Sheilagh had not been doing anything at the moment that might have hurt him. The nip was pure mischief.

I said, "He needs a refresher." I went to the far end of the

A Cure for Biters. The nail or pin cure for biting is one method that works on all horses no matter how nippy they are. Sheilagh with her beloved Morgan, Corky, illustrates how to hold the lead rope and the pin or nail to teach a horse that biting can hurt him more than it will hurt you. Observe that Sheilagh is holding the lead rope short so that her hand is right next to the horse's jaw; her hand is also out in front of her so that she can see the horse. In this position, a horse cannot swing his head around to bite you without pricking himself on the pin or nail. All you have to do is hold your hand in place and let him punish himself. The nail in this picture protrudes about an inch beyond Sheilagh's thumb and forefinger, but even an eighth of an inch is enough.

barn, which was out of Tonka's sight, and got a horseshoe nail. Returning, I held the nail concealed in my hand. I passed it to Sheilagh behind my back so that the pony could not possibly see it, and Sheilagh concealed the nail in her hand as she resumed grooming him. I say that there was absolutely no way Tonka could have known why I went to the other end of the barn or that I had a nail hidden in my fist when I returned or that I passed the nail to my daughter. The fact remains, however, that *Tonka knew Sheilagh had that nail in her hand.* He knew it instantly. As she resumed grooming him, he stood perfectly still. He might have been a stuffed pony or a statue. Only his eyes moved, warily alert to Sheilagh's every motion.

My daughter tried everything she could think of to lure him into nipping at her again, but Tonka never moved. Then I tried; I all but put my head into his mouth, daring him to bite just once more. But Tonka craftily refused to make a single false move. He stood motionless, a model of impeccable behavior, and I would swear that there was a diabolically angelic glint in his eyes as he warily waited for us to give up.

"It's no use," I said. "He's on to us." And I pocketed the nail.

At that instant the little stallion lifted his head high, curled his upper lip, and cut loose with the most derisive horselaugh any equine ever insulted his owner with.

We laughed so hard we cried.

I offer this incident as an example of how horses and ponies can *sense* our moods. Though we were very careful to conceal the nail, Tonka knew when our mood had changed; he reacted accordingly. When you are scared or angry or coolly determined, your horse or pony will know it. That is why some people always have trouble and others no trouble at all, even when they handle the same animals.

It was not coincidence that when he realized Sheilagh was ready for him with that nail Tonka froze, only his wary eyes moving. This resulted from one phase of his antinipping lessons which supplemented his learning to lead properly. If someone stood close beside Tonka when he was loose in his stall or in a corral, the colt liked to snap his head around and sneak a quick bite at the person's arm, flank or leg.

Some horses and ponies that have been roughly handled acquire this habit as a defense. They learn to dislike being saddled because their saddles are uncomfortable or because they are girthed too tightly. Others, unusually sensitive in the flanks, show irritation and resentment at being touched except very gently. Whatever the reason, these quick bites can hurt. Our first thought, of course, should be to remove the cause: get rid of an uncomfortable saddle, don't girth too tightly, avoid roughness. If, however, the biting is simply the sort of mischievous bullying that Tonka, like many young studs, delighted in, then the habit must be squelched. Instead of removing a source of discomfort, we create one; we make the habit unpleasant to the colt.

Tonka learned this in various ways, all of them sudden and

emphatic. When I was grooming him, perhaps brushing his mane, I would covertly watch him. The moment he swung his head around toward me, he was met by a piston-like jab of my elbow in the side of the jaw. I neither paused in my task of grooming nor did I scold him; I gave no sign whatever that I was even aware of having "bumped" him. But this jarring jolt from my elbow was an "accident" that happened every time the young stallion tried to sneak in a quick nip, thinking that because I was busy grooming him he could catch me off guard.

At first when we handled his front feet, the gray pony could seldom resist the temptation to reach around and grab a mouthful of rump or a piece of kidney. But his will power strengthened amazingly as he learned that an elbow in the ribs, reinforced perhaps by a whack from the hoof rasp in my hand, was an instant consequence of any attempt to turn his head while being groomed or having his feet worked on.

Usually these corrections were accompanied by a sharp reprimand, "No!" Soon the word alone was enough. Eventually Tonka learned that the most comfortable position for him was "eyes front."

Rather surprisingly, Tonka never showed a tendency to kick. In time we were to learn that with other horses in a field he could kick with the best, but he never kicked at any person. As routine precaution, however, I put him through the same antikicking treatment I'd give to any pony or horse which was to be handled by children. This treatment consisted of gently touching him all over with a light pole or stick, with special emphasis on touching his hindquarters, his flanks and his belly. I took care to get him accustomed to having his tail handled and even pulled on. When he had learned to take all this as a matter of course, I filled a small sack with straw and turned him loose in a corral with the thing tied to his tail. The sack rubbed against his hocks, bumping him at every step. When he kicked at it, the sack swung right back against him, bumping his legs. A few repetitions of this and Tonka realized the futility of kicking. In a little while he showed no concern about the bag tied to his tail.

This is an excellent lesson for any horse or pony that seems to be "touchy" behind. No matter how hard he kicks or how long he persists in kicking at the sack, he cannot win.

"Gentling" a Hind Leg. Some horses are "touchy" behind; mares in particular are apt to be spooky about having their hind feet handled. Rough treatment only makes them worse. Tonka never showed any tendency to kick at people, but to be on the safe side I gave him the usual treatment I'd give any green colt, as described in the text. Here Linda and Sheilagh demonstrate another effective way to take the kick out of a spooky horse and teach him to yield his leg when you want to pick up his foot. Sheilagh holds one end of a soft cotton rope looped around the colt's lower leg. As Linda slides her hand down the leg to pick up the foot, Sheilagh exerts a slow, steady pull on the rope, lifting the foot straight out behind. Should the colt try to kick or pull away, Linda holds a riding crop in her right hand, ready to smack him on the leg. In this lesson timing is of prime importance: the whip must be used at the exact moment *the colt kicks or tries to pull away. A hit a moment too soon or a moment too late teaches him nothing. A hard or rough rope that might burn the leg should never be used.*

That first time we had put him into a trailer, Tonka had made a discovery that it is never good for a horse or a pony to learn—that he is strong enough to break his halter or tie-rope if he chooses to exert his full strength. That left me with the problem of convincing him not to try it again. Halter-pulling is a nuisance habit, and it can be dangerous. A loose horse can get into all kinds of trouble, and a loose stallion can cause double trouble. So Tonka had to learn to stand tied without attempting to pull under all ordinary and most extraordinary circumstances. This is an essential phase of the halterbreaking process. Even with those rare, unusually phlegmatic colts that never make a first attempt to pull back when tied, the lesson should never be neglected. It is better to be sure that there will never be a first attempt than to wait for it to happen.

I made sure that Tonka would break no more halters by tying him every day for short periods with, at first, a tail rope and, later, with a body rope. Occasionally I combined the two. The photographs on pages 64 and 65 show the body-rope method. There are two important points to remember: The rope should be tied to a point somewhat higher than the horse's head, and there should be only a little slack in the rope. The high position makes it almost impossible for an excited horse or pony to get a foreleg over the rope and become tangled, and any pull he exerts has to be in a downward direction. This lessens the degree of purchase on the ground he can get with his forefeet: the harder he pulls back, the more he lifts his entire forehand off the ground. The small amount of slack in the rope gives him little room to maneuver.

Of course, the rope should be tied with a knot that can be jerked loose instantly if the pony or horse should lose his footing.

Once I had him securely tied in this way, I actively urged the little stallion to pull back. Rattling a newspaper in front of him, I "spooked" him. The instant he pulled back, Tonka felt the sudden bite of the rope under his dock. Startled, he instinctively jumped forward, causing the pressure of the rope to slack off. I showed my approval by speaking to him and stroking his neck. Then suddenly I rattled the paper again, and the young stallion instinctively reacted as before. But the third time, though wary and suspicious, he did not pull back; the tie rope remained slack. I gently "sacked him out" with the newspaper, and Tonka stood still.

I left him tied like that for about half an hour, watching him from a distance. A couple of times he cautiously tested the rope as if to see whether it would still "bite" him under the tail. Convinced, he stayed put, keeping the rope slack.

Untying him but not removing the tail rope, I led him about

No More Broken Halters. A spooky horse is a dangerous horse. A horse that suddenly throws a tantrum or panics when you are working on his feet can put you in the hospital. He can also injure himself. I have handled too many "perfectly gentle" horses that were dangerous nuisances to be the least bit lenient in halterbreaking a colt. I am as strict in teaching this critical lesson as I would be in reforming a kicker or a biter.

Unfortunately, many backyard horse owners think that their pet is halter-broken if they can lead him without dislocating an arm and if, under ordinary circumstances, the horse will stand tied, usually in a stall. To my mind, however, a properly halterbroken horse is one that leads at all gaits on a slack line and can be depended on under almost any circumstances never to pull back. These two photographs illustrate what I mean. They show what might be termed one of the final exams for a properly halterbroken horse and the use of a body rope as explained in the text.

In both pictures at the moment the shutter snapped I was firing a gun almost under Tonka's nose. The first time (left) he was obviously startled

—*but you will notice that his tie rope was not taut. In the other picture (right), taken a few shots and less than a minute later, he stood firmly to the gunfire, and the rope remained slack.*

Confirmed halter-pullers are certain proof that the trainer does not know his business. Use of a chain around the muzzle or through the horse's mouth indicates that the trainer has no imagination.

"But," you may be thinking, "I'll never fire a gun on horseback. I don't even have a gun." You don't need one. The point of the lesson is not to train a horse for hunting trips but to make him steady to unexpected sounds and sights; for example, the backfire of a car. Bang a pair of garbage can lids together in front of a horse. Rattle a newspaper or a sackful of tin cans under his nose. Suddenly open an umbrella in front of him. Tempt him to spook until he gives up doing it. Build up his confidence. Teach him that strange sights and sounds will never hurt him but pulling back on his halter rope will. By proper use of a body rope or a tail rope and with a little patience, even the most skittish horse can be taught never to pull back. Photographs by Msgr. J. Graham.

for a few minutes. Using oral commands that I would later use in mounted work, "Whoa" and "Walk," I made him stop and start repeatedly. If he showed even the slightest sign of lagging, I gave the lead rope a little jerk to remind him.

I concluded this first lesson with a feed of oats; then I turned him out.

Every day for the next couple of weeks I tied the colt in this way or I used a body rope. The body rope has the same effect, though it works differently. If a horse pulls back, the rope tightens around his middle; the harder he pulls the more tightly it squeezes him. The instant he steps forward to escape the pressure, the rope slacks off.

Some colts, it seems, respond better to one or the other of these two forms of tying; it depends on the individual. In one way, I think, the body rope, though slightly milder, may be the better of the two: it conditions the pony to respond to the pressure of the rider's legs even before he is ever ridden.

It is important to bear in mind that while a body rope can be of small diameter and rather "hard," like sashcord, a tail rope should be of soft-woven cotton or nylon at least half an inch thick. A tail rope that is too small and too hard can abrade the dock, leaving it skinned and sore. This is to be avoided, for then correction becomes punishment.

In less than a week Tonka could not be forced to pull on a tie rope, no matter how we tried to spook him. He might shift his feet a little, but he would not pull back (see pages 64 and 65).

Meanwhile, the little gray stallion was learning other basic lessons.

He began to get used to carrying a bit in his mouth. I started him with the bridoon of a double bridle because it is smaller than an ordinary snaffle. Removing the bit from the bridle, I tied a cord to one of the rings, gently slipped the bit into Tonka's mouth, and holding it in place, ran the cord up behind his ears and down to the opposite ring, where I tied it. Then I threaded another cord through both rings so that it passed over the colt's lower face like a noseband. About six inches from the rings I knotted both ends together and drew them snugly up his face to the cord that passed behind his ears, and there I tied them.

Then immediately while the colt was champing this strange thing in his mouth, I gave him a full feed of oats. That took his mind off the bit. After he had cleaned up his grain, I let him wear the bit for about half an hour; by that time he seemed hardly aware of it.

The purpose of the cord that crossed over his face was, of course, to prevent the snaffle from sliding sidewise in his mouth, but it also held the bit high in his mouth so that from the outset he would never get his tongue over it or try to ball his tongue under it. Tonka learned to accept the bit without any fuss.

For about a week I put it on him each time he was fed his grain. He learned to eat hay with the bit in his mouth, too. Then I substituted a larger snaffle, the same bit he was to wear when I'd drive him in long reins and, later, ride him.

In this introduction of a colt to the bit gentleness is of critical importance. Horses and ponies that are "mean to bridle" are made so by rough handling. Never forcibly jam a bit into a horse's mouth. Avoid letting the metal bump against the animal's teeth. Once the bit is in, take care not to hurt the colt's ears as you slip the crown of the bridle into place. If necessary at first, unbuckle the bridle. The little extra time this requires won't be wasted; it will pay big dividends in the long run. A tall horse difficult to bridle can be most exasperating, but only patience and gentleness will improve him. Always remember that somebody made him that way.

While Tonka was absorbing these basic lessons, he was also absorbing an abundance of good feed. I grained him twice a day, and he grew plump and sleek. I know that it is commonly held that ponies should be fed very little grain or none at all. When applied to a small child's pony I agree with this idea. When a pony is to be worked hard, however, I see no reason why he should not be fed as well as you would feed a horse under similar circumstances. I wanted Tonka to be in good, hard flesh and feeling good, for he was in for a lot of work.

Perhaps if I had been able to foresee how he was going to work—and how he'd work me—I'd have skipped the oats.

CHAPTER VIII

Longeing--Theory

Horses and ponies are pragmatists. They care nothing about theories that fail to work. In fact, they care nothing about theories at all. This is what makes the theory of longeing so interesting. Eventually you'll have to put aside your book and get out there in the ring with your four-footed nontheorist, who will always have a few ideas of his own.

Until about a generation ago, the majority of American horsemen were almost as nontheoretical as their horses. Some, indeed, were positively antitheoretical. Faced with any idea that seemed new, they were prone to reject it as so much high-falutin' nonsense without even giving it a trial.

One such idea was the practice of working a colt or a green horse on the longe line as a basic step in the animal's education. Outside of the army, longeing was regarded as a panty-waist English or European practice; most American horsemen knew little or nothing about it.

Today, however, one has only to look about and talk with professional trainers, including those who specialize in developing stock horses, to realize that most of them recognize the value of longeing and make use of it in their training systems.

Unfortunately, even today most amateur horse owners never

know how much they could discipline a big spooky colt or aid the physical development of a puny one, because they know nothing about the technique of longeing. The professionals, who do know, are rarely inclined to shed any light on the subject. Why should they, with families to support? But if more amateur horsemen understood the technique and the benefits of longeing, the number of colts that have to be started—or reformed—by professionals would drop sharply.

Longeing properly done is much more than merely a way of exercising a horse or pony by shooing him around on the end of a line—in spite of a popular book on riding which misinforms its readers that longeing is nothing more than "shooing" in circles. Longe work is an important step in an intelligent system of training utilized at a time when many colts begin to wrong.

On the longe line a trainer can nip potential faults in a colt before they have a chance to take root, as well as correct faults in a mature horse. Longeing can develop a colt's muscles and his gaits even before he is mature enough to be ridden. It makes teaching prompt obedience to oral commands easy, thereby giving the trainer more control. It enables us to correct faults and rapidly improve a youngster's manners, carriage, headset and gaits. On the ground, we can see results instead of having to rely on horseman's "feel," which takes time to develop.

Probably the first mistake of a novice undertaking longe work without experienced help is to assume that a green horse can be properly longed in a halter. His second mistake commonly is to use too short a line—because his next error is to use too short a whip; he thinks anything he can brandish at the horse or pony will do—or in a pinch he can throw a rock. These three initial errors do much to explain why so many novices quickly get the idea that longeing is pretty much a waste of time, merely a way to give a stabled horse or pony needed exercise.

However, with most horses, especially big, lively colts—and this applies to ponies as well—a halter is no good for longeing. It fits too loosely, permitting only a minimum of control.

Worse, it teaches a colt to pull; it undoes everything you have taught the colt in halterbreaking. The harder he pulls the more uncomfortable he becomes. Eventually he will begin to resent the work; then instead of getting better he will get worse. And there is always danger, as the halter shifts position, that the buckle will injure his eye.

A Halter Is Not for Longeing. We frequently see in magazines with a Western slant pictures of trainers "longeing" a horse by means of a rope attached to the halter—even a rope halter. Usually the horse is galloping close to the wall of a round pen with the rope sagging, while the "trainer" holds the other end of the rope in one hand (usually the wrong hand) about waist-high, or even lower, and looks nonchalant. But this is longeing in name only. What the man is actually doing is just letting the horse gallop around and around, usually to work off excess energy before the trainer mounts him. If the trainer took the slack out of the rope and attempted really to control the horse, the halter would be pulled crooked and dangerously close to the animal's eye. In this picture the halter has a ring in the reinforced noseband, making it more similar to a cavesson, but even so the loose fit is evident. You need not be an expert to realize the very small degree of precise control it permits. As a rule, being longed in a halter upsets a horse and only encourages him to develop bad habits.

The best headgear for longeing is a cavesson. The cavesson was designed for longeing, and if you are going to do the job right it pays to get one. Given the ordinary good care any leather gear deserves, a cavesson will last a horse's lifetime.

In this country there are two types of cavessons commonly available—the English style, a very strong, heavyweight cavesson with metal plates concealed inside the leather noseband, and the lighter, milder United States Army cavesson with a more flexible noseband padded with felt.

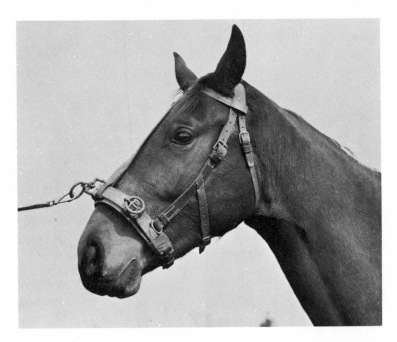

The Cavesson, English Style. Heavy duty cavessons of this type cost about as much as a good double bridle—and they're worth it. Properly cared for, they will last for many years. The heavy noseband is reinforced with leather-covered metal plates. A rambunctious horse can really feel a hard jerk on the line; he'll learn to pay attention fast. The longe line is snapped to the swivel ring at the front of the noseband; if side reins are used, they are attached to the side rings. Notice that the cavesson is secured not only by a throatlatch but by a strap under the jaw as well. A cavesson should fit snugly without being uncomfortably tight so that a horse cannot pull out of it or break it, and no matter how hard he may pull on a circle there is no danger of the cheek-strap buckle poking him in the eye. On colts with fine heads and necks, such as Arabians, this type of cavesson is unnecessarily heavy: the trainer must have equestrian tact to avoid undue severity.

Another type, which seems to be a compromise between these two, is a lightweight German cavesson with a chamois-covered noseband reinforced by hinged steel plates.

I wouldn't say that any of these three is "best." Much depends on the horse or pony—and on the handler. Probably for a strong, rambunctious colt inclined to be hard-headed or for a horse with habits that make him a bit difficult to handle, the English cavesson might bring him into line more quickly.

Any type of cavesson properly adjusted should fit snugly. Never adjust it loosely, as you would a halter. It should stay put no matter how hard you or the colt may pull on the longe line.

Should you have no cavesson immediately available but *do* have a snorty colt you are eager to start right, you can get quite effective results with a good hackamore—assuming that you understand how a hackamore works and know how to use one (a subject we'll pick up later). In fact, in some ways a hackamore can be more effective in correcting certain faults than a

The Cavesson, United States Army Style. This is the type of cavesson commonly used at Fort Riley when it was the Cavalry School. Though much lighter in weight and considerably milder than the English cavesson, in all other respects it is basically the same. It is milder because the noseband is padded with felt instead of being reinforced by metal plates. Hence, a hard jerk on the line is not so severe. It is, therefore, probably the best type of cavesson for a novice to use on the average horse. It is the only type we have ever used on Tonka. The fit should be snug without being tight. A good general rule of adjustment is: If you can slip four fingers inside the throatlatch and two fingers inside the jaw strap and the noseband, the fit is right. The noseband should be set low rather than high; between an inch and two inches above the corners of the lips is about right. The higher the noseband is set the less control you have.

73

cavesson. It can be very helpful in the first stage of developing a desirable headset, and a colt accustomed to blithely ignoring the command, "Whoa!" will have his blithe outlook suddenly sobered by a few pulls on the hackamore accompanying the order.

Perhaps the chief drawback of the hackamore is that it can so easily be overused. One hard pull too many on the hackamore can make a colt dread longe work. This, of course, should be avoided. Throughout all schooling we want to make every lesson as pleasant as possible.

Novices who first undertake to longe a colt commonly assume that the animal should fear the whip—otherwise, how do you "make him go"? But this assumption is one of the first links in a chain of errors. A colt should never be taught to fear the whip. The whip is not an instrument of punishment; it is merely an extension of the trainer's arm, a baton with which he gives cues. The colt must learn to respect the whip, just as later he will learn to respect and obey the bit and the rider's legs or spurs; but he should work unhampered by fear, for a frightened, worried horse or pony cannot learn.

Strangely enough, hand in hand with this notion that a horse should fear the whip we find the practice of using a type of whip which the horse need not fear at all as long as he stays out at the full length of the line, as he should. This is the common buggy whip only about four feet long, much too short to reach the horse or pony unless the trainer unduly shortens the line—or unless he has instilled the animal with fear of the whip, and then the "reaching" is psychological.

An efficient longeing whip has a shaft from six to eight feet long, with a lash of about the same length or a bit longer. With the horse moving on a circle of about thirty feet, the trainer can then reach him. Ponies can be worked in smaller circles commensurate with their size. Once the animal has learned what the whip signifies, it is rarely necessary even to touch him with the lash.

One of the most important functions of longeing is the development of smooth, free, relaxed gaits. No matter what a horse or pony may later specialize in, his degree of success will depend on his ability to cover ground efficiently—smoothly, at times rapidly, always with a minimum of effort.

Too often, however, this beneficial effect of longe work is completely lost by the amateur trainer working a horse or pony in too tight a circle. Using a short whip, the handler finds that he has almost no control over the animal. He tries to rectify this by shortening the line, bringing the colt within reach. This tight circling demands more agility, "handiness," than an awkward colt or a green horse is capable of without strain. A colt can benefit from work on very small circles only after his muscles have been developed and suppled and he has acquired balance and agility.

Therefore, your longe line should be at least twenty feet long. Even if you stand on one spot—as, at first, you shouldn't —this will enable you to work in a circle of more than forty feet after the colt has settled down. A circle of this size is plenty tight enough for a big colt during the first few weeks of longeing.

If you are lucky enough to have a circular pen or a small corral to work in, starting even the spookiest colt is easy. In a large corral it is best to start near a corner; then you have two sides of the fence to help you. If you must work in an open field—unhappy thought!—shorten your line as much as necessary and start walking concentric with the colt in a position near his hindquarters.

Hold the whip so that the butt is near your thumb, the shaft coming out past your little finger and slanted down toward the ground. If you have to urge the colt to keep him moving, you can flick him with the lash by simply rotating your forearm. Always try to touch him with the lash below the hocks. A touch on the lower hind legs will more effectively make him move than if you used the lash on his rump.

Generally, an easy trot is the best working gait, but the main thing at first is for the colt to learn to go round and round, staying out as far as the line permits. If he stops, turns and faces you, don't move in to his head; step around toward his

Longeing in a Halter. These pictures illustrate some of the hazards and headaches that usually result from trying to make a halter do the work of a cavesson. They were taken when Tonka was four years old, after he had been gelded. Feeling frisky, he was giving Linda more trouble than if he had still been a stud—and was being worked in a cavesson or a hackamore.

In the first photograph (left) the colt was just plain goofing off. Circling to the right, he was watching a couple of other horses off to the left. His mind wasn't on his work; he was paying no attention to Linda at all. Notice how the halter was pulled askew and high up under his jaw, allowing Linda little real control.

In the second picture (middle) Tonka, without command, had

hindquarters, flicking the whip with a twist of your wrist. Let him take any gait until he settles down. Watch the line for sagging. If the colt shows a tendency to veer in toward the center, move him out by pointing the whip at his shoulder.

Frisky colts, having a tendency to go too fast, often pull quite hard on the line at first. They should be slowed down, not only as a matter of discipline but because, being physically soft, they can quickly work themselves into a lather. They must be taught at once to obey the command, "Whoa!" On such overeager hotbloods a hackamore often has quicker effect than a cavesson. Pull them (at either trot or gallop) when the inside foreleg is off the ground. Few horses or ponies need to be

speeded up to a canter. The angle at which he was leaning shows that he was going too fast; the taut line as well as the slight outward set of his head proves that he was pulling hard, a cardinal sin in longe work.

The third picture (right) shows what happened when Linda tried to slow him down and make him behave. He kept right on going at his own pace. To slow and halt him Linda had to shorten the line, reducing the size of the circle; but, as her posture and her expression make quite clear, she was having a real tug-of-war.

At this age Tonka knew better, but he was feeling good and knew that he could get away with this kind of performance in a halter. Any smart, frisky colt quickly learns this.

pulled more than a few times in a hackamore before they will halt on command only.

If a colt proves really difficult to stop when being worked in a cavesson, the trainer can guide him head-on into the fence, preferably at a corner. If working in the open without the aid of fences, shorten the line until he is moving in so tight a circle he has to stop.

Whatever the difficulty, be quiet; never shout commands. A horse on the longe line can feel any nervousness or uncertainty by the handler as clearly as he can with a rider.

Once he has settled down you can proceed to teach oral commands; these will be a great help when you are ready to ride him. I use *Walk, Trot, Hup!* (for the lope), *Whoa*, and *Change. Hup!* is uttered rather loudly, sharply; I give all other commands in a normal tone. Later, when the colt has learned what the business is all about, I make use of one more order, *Trot Out*. This is a demand for more speed at the trot.

"Change!" These photographs show how I get what the professors call "a change of hand"—in plain English, changing directions. When teaching this to a colt first halt him with the command, "Whoa." When stopped, he should continue to face in the direction he was moving. Changing the line and the whip to opposite hands, I take a long step or two to the left, order, "Change," and turn the colt's head in toward the center. Then I give the command to walk or trot, reinforcing the order if necessary with a touch or a mere flourish of the whip. Once the horse understands what "Change," accompanied by a light pull on the line, means, the halt can be eliminated. Without pausing, the horse simply wheels around.

Change means reverse directions. Here is an example, in detailed steps, of how it is done:

With the colt moving on a circle to the left, I prepare for the change by shifting the longe line from my left hand to my right, at the same time transferring the whip from right to left. Then I say, "Whoa."

As the horse halts, I command, "Change," and pull on the line, turning his head in toward the center. At the same moment I take a long step or two to the left, using the whip (often merely as a gesture) to encourage him to complete the turn about. The instant he is headed in the right direction, I command him to take whatever gait I want him to take. After he has completed one or two circles, I halt him to pat and praise him for a few moments; then I immediately get him moving again.

Of course, after he has learned to respond to "Change," the halting and caressing are omitted; we merely continue working.

To change from right to left I simply reverse my movements.

With a green horse or pony it may be necessary at first to shorten the line considerably and give him several pulls before he gets the idea. You may even have to walk up close to him to get him turned around. Be patient. Do not hurry him—and never, never let him come in to you. Once you let him get this habit, he'll soon be walking all over your toes. "Whoa!" should mean stop right there, now, and stand there.

When a colt has begun to work well, taking any gait on command and moving freely and calmly, you can concentrate on improving his gaits and developing a good headset. After several days of work in the cavesson you might find it wise to switch to the hackamore, or vice versa. Later you may want to use side reins or draw reins, perhaps attached to a snaffle under the cavesson. We shall revert to these various details later.

Always the trainer must guard against monotony. It is very easy for a colt to become bored with the same old routine, eventually becoming soured on the whole business. If this ever happens to your colt, you're really in trouble, for the animal is likely to remain so, and there is almost nothing you can do about it except take the blame. The fault is entirely yours; you goofed. Therefore, try to vary each lesson as much as possible. Demand frequent changes of gait, pace and direction. Halt the colt often and make him stand; let him relax. Vary the size of the circle by gradually taking in and letting out the line while the colt is moving—this helps to develop his balance. When using side reins or draw reins, give him brief periods of complete relaxation; let him stretch his neck.

A colt that has had six months' or a year's work on the longe will make much more rapid progress when it is time to begin mounted schooling than one that has never been worked but was allowed to "grow up naturally." Physically and mentally he will be so much further advanced that after only a few saddles you can begin putting the finish on him.

So much for the theory of longeing. . . .

Those loud horselaughs you hear in the distance are coming from Tonka. He is eagerly waiting to show you how these fine theories work and what you may expect when you put this book down and step into the ring with your own colt.

Enter Tonka, the nontheorist.

CHAPTER IX

Longeing--The Nontheorist

WHEN beginning work on the longe, Tonka was, I believe, in better physical condition than most colts his age usually are, except, perhaps, pampered young Thoroughbreds ready for training. Well fed, he was equally well exercised. With the door of his box stall always open, he was free to run and graze in a ten-acre pasture luxuriantly grassed. Except for the brief periods when I brought him in for daily lessons, he spent practically all his time outdoors.

I mention this to dispel any notion that he might have been overfed and underexercised from being cooped up in a stall most of the time. He had plenty of opportunity to work off his excess energy.

Nonetheless, of all the animals I've ever handled none ever gave me half as much trouble in the beginning as this gray pony colt. For troublesome trickiness and all-round contrariness I put Tonka in a class by himself. He instinctively knew every trick in the book, and he used them all; then he proceeded to write his own supplement to the book, inventing new dodges *ad lib*. I have taken husky Thoroughbreds, colts that had been raced, and have had them longeing fairly well within ten minutes; but for about two weeks Tonka made me look, and feel, like a novice with two left feet and ten thumbs. At least twice he had me flat on my face in the dirt, dragging me like a stoneboat while I clung desperately to the line. Maybe my bruised ego won't let me recall a few other times.

Some colts, the first time they are put on the longe, are a bit difficult to start; you have to lead them, gradually paying out the line, then urge them to keep moving. But getting Tonka moving was the easiest thing in the world. He rocketed around like mad. The difficulty was in hanging on to him and getting him stopped—except when he wanted to stop. If I'd had a snubbing post I would have used it. Holding him was like holding a roped bronc. He paid no attention to oral commands. The only way I could stop him at first was to haul in on the line hand over hand until he was almost trampling my toes. For a colt his size and age—not yet two years old—he was amazingly strong. That, indeed, was the most deceptive thing about him. I had thought he would be easy for me to handle no matter what he did, but I have handled mature horses that could not match that small stallion's explosive strength. Tonka made me appreciate how much horse Justin Morgan must have been.

The colt interspersed these race-horse antics with sudden stops—not when I wanted him to stop but when he took a notion to stop. He'd swing around facing me, ears up, nostrils flaring. I'd say, "Walk," and give the line a little shake. Tonka wouldn't move. I'd repeat the order—and suddenly he would take off as if jet-propelled, perhaps in the opposite direction or, worse, straight away from me. His movements were incredibly quick and without any warning preliminaries.

It was my misfortune at the time that I had no small corral or pen to work him in. Our corral was quite large, so that the best I could do was to try to keep him in a corner. The way he pulled, however, we usually wound up wandering all over the place, with me resisting every step. The more line I gave him, the faster he would go. When I hauled him in close to slow him down, he'd stop suddenly—and come walking in to me. I would point the whip at him and tell him, "Whoa," or "Stand." Whether he'd obey or take off at a gallop was always a question.

I tried to end each session—I hesitate to say lesson—on a successful note, which in this instance is certainly a relative term. If the colt promptly obeyed even one command or did anything right near the end of a workout, that was when we quit for the day.

Gradually, of course, Tonka did begin to do things right, but not before there were times when I felt like using a club on him, times when I thought I must have been crazy to think that he would ever make a suitable child's pony. I thought I'd never get him straightened out. Sometimes we would end a session with me convinced that at last he was beginning to learn something—and the next day he'd be as wild as ever, or worse.

Then one day, about two weeks after we'd started this longe work, Tonka gave me one of his typical horselaughs. With no warning whatever, the four-legged brat proceeded to show me that he could do everything I'd sweated to drill into him if he wanted to. Moving with the snap and precision of a circus pony, he astonished me with a perfect demonstration of how a horse should work on the longe. Promptly obeying every command, he walked, trotted and cantered without any pulling; then he halted, remained standing and changed directions. He put on so faultless an exhibition that I could not escape the feeling that all along he had deliberately been cutting me down to size, showing me who was boss—or at least who *wasn't* boss.

I was elated. We'd turned the corner. I had it made.

My elation was short-lived. For the next day the little monster was his old self again, putting on his wild mustang act.

Right then I realized my big mistake, an error you may already have suspected. I'd been too softhearted with this young smart aleck; I had made the mistake of not being consistent. When breaking him of his biting and striking habits, I'd been absolutely strict and more than slightly tough, but on the longe line he'd looked so small that, unconsciously, I had thought of him as a mere pony, and only a colt at that. It had seemed unfair to put a hackamore on him and give him what he was asking for —and so on. This sort of soft-headed thinking is quite common among persons who really like animals as distinct from those

83

who merely like to use them; it accounts for a great number of spoiled horses and ponies, as well as poorly trained dogs, especially small, bratty dogs named Pierre or Fifi or Darling. I would not have made the same mistake with a horse. And I never made the same mistake again with Tonka.

I knew several things now I had not been sure of before:

Tonka understood all my commands. He knew what to do.

Mentally and physically he was capable of doing all I expected of him.

He was not only a tremendously strong colt but he had great stamina as well. Some of our strenuous workouts had lasted an hour or more, but the stallion had never shown signs of being tired.

From now on, I resolved, there would be no more nonsense. I was through being soft.

It is often at this point, I believe, that many good colts are spoiled. The handler realizes that he made certain mistakes, and suddenly he loses patience—with himself as well as with the colt. He tries to make up for lost time, forgetting that the hasty way is the slowest way. He becomes rough and harsh, instead of merely firm and determined.

Recently at a show I saw a bridle-path cowboy, a lout who must have weighed at least two hundred pounds, leading a lovely little weanling filly. He had the chain of the lead shank looped around her delicate muzzle, as if he had hold of a rank stud. Some noise or movement suddenly made the filly start and shy, as colts will do. The big fellow, instead of pausing for a moment to soothe her, grabbed the lead with both hands and yanked it a couple of times as hard as he could. Under such brutal abuse the little filly almost jumped out of her skin.

Yet, I have no doubt, that fellow—having the imagination of a toad—thought he was doing the right thing; he was "taking the nonsense out of her" almost before she was old enough to learn. Actually, however, such extremism does anything but speed up a colt's training. In the long run, it does infinitely more harm than being a little too easy. If it doesn't sour a colt and make him mean, it usually dulls or kills his spirit. He loses all spontaneity; he does what he has to do with the listlessness of a machine. And he will never like or trust people.

Of course, for some persons merely this and nothing more is enough. They don't care a hoot whether their horses like and trust them or hate them. All they look for is mechanically good performance. Their horses are merely means to an end, usually either financial gain or personal ego inflation.

I am quite well aware of the fact that there are some horses and ponies that—like people—turn out to be anything but lovable. I know from experience that a professional horseman can hardly lose his heart to every animal that passes through his hands. Nevertheless, I am firmly convinced that indifference to

"Horsing Around." Probably parts of this book might give you the idea that the only way to school a horse or pony is to work him and drill him without letup day after day. But all work and no play is a good way to sour a horse. There's such a thing as just going for a pleasant ride to enjoy the air and the scenery. Any intelligently planned training regime should include off days, play days, horsing-around days. Here are Tonka and Linda in some of their lighter moments—which have been many. The colt always enjoyed frolicking in deep snow after a storm—he has never had a blanket on and the barn doors are always open. A good word to remember in schooling is camaraderie. *If your horse or pony does not look on you as a friend, no matter what else you achieve, you have failed as a trainer.*

85

the mental attitude of a pony or a horse we would train makes truly *excellent* horsemanship impossible, and it makes no difference how close to perfection the animal may learn to perform. If the happy, spontaneous spirit is lacking, the trainer has failed.

Tonka certainly still had his spontaneous spirit intact, while my spirit was a bit bruised after his perfect performance, which was immediately followed by one of his worst. So the next day when we entered the big corral, the stallion was wearing a hackamore with a rawhide bosal to which the longe line was attached at the heel knot underneath his chin, and from that moment Tonka's harum-scarum, wild mustang days were over.

Among most riders today, and practically all young riders, there seems to be widespread ignorance of the technique of working a horse in a hackamore. Very few young riders understand how a hackamore functions; some are even confused about what a hackamore is. Patented gadgets advertised as hackamore bits, or as "new" and "improved" training hackamores, are merely strangling devices designed to "control" a horse by shutting off his wind when the rider hauls in on the reins. Such contraptions have almost no relationship to the true Spanish *jaquima*, of which "hackamore" is an Anglicized corruption.

When a person unfamiliar with the hackamore first sees a horse wearing one, he is apt to jump to the conclusion that it is very mild. Because no part of it enters the horse's mouth, it appears to be merely a kind of fancy halter. This idea is so common even among persons who have been around horses long enough to know better that some hackamore misusers have been known to brag, "My horse has never had a bit in his mouth"—as if that were something to boast of. In fact, it merely reveals the speaker's ignorance, for the hackamore was intended and designed as a means of preparing a horse for the bit. If that ultimate end is avoided, then the hackamore loses its chief purpose.

In the wrong hands, the hackamore can be a very severe instrument and can easily ruin a colt. Within its own limitations

The Hackamore. A hackamore can be as mild or as severe as the rider using it wants to make it. It may be made of rawhide, horse hair or even soft cotton rope. The bosal (noseband) may be heavy or light, thick or thin, stiff or soft. Whatever the materials, a hackamore should be carefully adjusted to fit the individual horse—and to suit his temperament. A hackamore wrongly used can spoil a colt more quickly than a snaffle. As a rule, I'm convinced, inexperienced riders do better if they forget about using a hackamore and begin with a mild snaffle. A young rider ambitious to learn the technique of hackamore training should first learn from an expert—if he can find one. Photograph by J. D. Harper.

it is effective, but its limitations are narrow; you cannot stretch them without creating trouble.

The critical part of a hackamore is the bosal, including the heel knot. This is the tapered noseband that fits loosely around the muzzle. The bosal may be of smoothly braided rawhide or of braided horsehair; it may vary in weight and diameter from a heavy one about an inch thick to a light one of about three-eighths of an inch. It may be so braided as to be very stiff or rather "soft," pliant. The exact way a bosal is made depends on its purpose, how it is to be used. For example, a heavy bosal would be used on a bronc or a green horse to teach him what he was up against and to "soften him up"; a lightweight one would be suitable for a colt that had graduated to carrying a bit in its mouth.

Whatever the bosal's size or degree of stiffness, the heel knot must be of proportionate weight. The knot must be heavy enough so that when the hackamore is properly adjusted on the colt's head with the reins slack, the knot hangs free underneath the lower jaw. There should be no pressure against the underside of the jaw except when the rider uses the reins.

Obviously, making a good hackamore is a highly skilled craft. Expertly using one on a colt is a fine art.

Proper adjustment of the hackamore depends on how high over the nose the bosal is placed and how snugly it fits under the jaw (see page 87). The more loosely it fits, the milder is the effect. If the bosal is too loose, the effect of a pull on the reins is practically nil; if too tight, it will make a horse sore and fretful, and eventually callous. He will become heavy and learn to "go through" the hackamore, ignoring the reins.

The hackamore operates on the principle of pulling—this is one of its chief limitations; for in advanced schooling the bridle reins should rarely be pulled. When the rider pulls a rein—straight back for a halt or to either side for a turn—the horse or pony must learn to give to the pull: he stops or he turns. The quickest way he learns this, a way that impresses on him the power of the hackamore, is for him to be pulled hard the first time or two he is worked in a hackamore. Once a colt learns that he can be doubled, and that the harder he resists the more being pulled is going to hurt him, he usually becomes very willing not to argue the point—unless he is pulled too hard too often. At this point the trainer's discretion, his understanding of the particular colt he is handling, becomes all-important. This discretion and understanding are summed up in the handy phrase "equestrian tact."

When I was a boy one of my heroes was a professional horseman with the unlikely name of Willy Wacker. Willy was wizened, weather-beaten, rawhide-tough, and he had a great gift with horses. He not only could start a green colt as well as anyone I ever saw, but he could also finish the job, turning out a reined horse the average rider could hardly stick on without grabbing the saddle horn.

The thing that struck me most forcibly about Willy's work, however, was the uniformly good manners of all the horses that passed through his hands. As a professional, he took them as they came, and he handled all breeds; but, whether fiery or sluggish, hot-blooded or cold, a horse that Willy finished kept its natural good disposition intact. When he got a spoiled horse that someone else had messed up, that horse soon quit acting spoiled.

Eager to learn the secret of this magic consistency, one day I asked him, "Willy, what do you think is the most important thing in handling horses? I mean, the one thing a good trainer must have above everything else?"

"It's knowing when to go easy," Willy answered, "and when to get tough. Everything else comes after that."

It seems to me that this is the best capsule expression of the essence of intelligent training that anyone ever uttered. The modern tailor-made phrase "equestrian tact" can be misleading, and too often it is. It is likely to give novice horsemen the idea that avoiding trouble in training is the main thing. Certainly it is important, up to a certain point; but beyond that point, any experienced horseman can tell you, there are bound to be times in the training of some horses and ponies when trouble simply cannot be avoided. Then the trainer is a fool who substitutes "tact" for determined firmness. He will be storing up more trouble for himself—and for the animal—than he hopes to avoid.

On the other hand, old Willy Wacker's way of defining tact is absolutely clear. There is no mistaking what he meant—that there *are* times when the trainer must "get tough," when he must convince the horse once and for all who is boss and who is always going to be boss. If he fails to do this when it should be done, someone else will have to do it later. Then, too often, it can be really rough on the horse; for by that time the animal will be considered "old enough to know better."

This was the lesson that I was determined to teach Tonka the day I led him into the schooling corral with a hackamore on his head for the first time.

Instead of starting him circling at once, I lined him up alongside the fence; then I suddenly spooked him with the gallop command, "Hup!" and a whack on the rump. Startled, the stallion took off at a dead run down the fence. This time I was using a forty-foot line; I let him race almost the full length before I took a hip-lock on the line and hollered, "Whoa!" Tonka hit the end of the line running all out, but this time he wasn't wearing a lightweight cavesson with a comfortably padded noseband. That heavy rawhide bosal packed real authority. Following his nose, the stallion spun around in a 180-degree turn and came to the quickest stop he'd ever made.

I could have laughed aloud at his startled expression as I strolled up to him, gathering the slack line in folds. Tonka just stood there looking baffled while I patted him on the neck and spoke to him as if he had done something wonderful.

Allowing him only a few moments to puzzle over this rude shock, I positioned him parallel to the fence, facing back the way he had just come. Again I spooked him into a run. This time I pulled him to the other side. When the line snapped taut as I commanded, "Whoa!" the sharp check, spinning him about, took a lot of starch out of his neck.

That pony, snorting and blowing, moved real gingerly and carefully to keep the line slack as I led him to the center of the big corral and started him circling with the order, "Trot." I made no attempt now to keep him in a corner or even close to the fence. Tonka had approximately forty by thirty yards of elbow room in which to stage the wildest wild mustang act he cared to put on.

But that little rogue seemed to know that I was just waiting for him to begin his usual antics. I am sure that he sensed that I wanted him to act up. For he would not. Suddenly he was a model of sedate decorum, trotting round and round with never the slightest pull on the line.

Tonka had learned the power of the hackamore.

To confirm the lesson I worked him at a gallop as well as a trot, halted him repeatedly and made him change directions. The first couple of times when he did not halt instantly on command, I pulled him and pulled hard. Before the lesson ended, he was doing quick, sliding stops on command with the line slack.

Perhaps at this point there is a question in your mind: Was it fair for me to spook the young stallion into a run, then spin him to an abrupt halt? It was not only fair; it was necessary. I had to impress on him that when all chips were down I was indisputably the boss, that no matter what he did I could effectively counter his every move. To learn this, he *had* to make mistakes. If necessary, he had to be *made* to make mistakes, at least in this first lesson in the hackamore. If he should have put on a faultless performance, so that I should have had no excuse to pull him, he would have learned nothing. Always in schooling, a colt should be allowed to make his own mistakes or even be tempted to make them. Otherwise the trainer will have no opportunity to impress on the animal what it should do and what it should not do.

I realize that there is a mystic distinction here which, to a logical, matter-of-fact mind, may be confusing. For instance, when schooling a horse to jump it seems hardly sensible deliberately to make him fall in order to teach him to jump carefully and to clear all obstacles with plenty of margin to spare. Quite the contrary, falls are precisely what we want to avoid. But we should make a point of teaching him to jump big and to concentrate on every obstacle by such means as passive poling, placing a broad jump immediately after an in-and-out or vice versa, differently spacing various jumps, and so on. By such legitimate means we permit or even induce the horse to make mistakes until by experience he develops into a good jumper. If we do not do these things, the horse will never become a good jumper—the mere fact that he will jump means almost nothing.

Perhaps the method of training that most clearly exemplifies the idea I am emphasizing here is the way a good trail horse is made. The trainer, if he knows what he is doing, deliberately exposes the horse to every kind of obstacle, sight, sound and scent that he might ever meet in the show ring or across country. In short, he offers the horse every excuse to spook and then patiently corrects him.

A colt that never makes mistakes in training, or is never

Ground Driving Must Be Done Right. Driving in long reins is a logical sequence to longeing and a proper preliminary to driving in harness. Even if you don't intend to drive in harness, it's a good way to teach a colt elementary rein cues. Some trainers, however, usually stock horse specialists, don't like ground driving at all. They believe that they can teach a horse better from the saddle— and undoubtedly some of them can. For if you don't have some experience in driving, if you forget how easy it is to hang on the reins while standing as the horse circles around you or when walking behind him, it is very easy to spoil a colt's mouth, teaching him to hang on the hands and eventually to pull.

For this reason I do not recommend ground driving in a bit unless the trainer is an expert driver. I always begin driving in a cavesson with the reins attached to the side rings. If the colt has learned his lessons on the longe, the cavesson gives you plenty of control. You need not worry about hanging on his mouth, yet if he plays up or if something spooks him, you can hang onto him without damaging his mouth.

These pictures show how Linda and Tonka learned ground driving together. (In one picture, left, only her legs are visible behind Tonka's right foreleg.) An important point to note is that the inner rein leads directly from the cavesson to Linda's hand. It is not run through the stirrup leather, as is the outer rein that crosses

behind Tonka's quarters. This method of adjusting the lines teaches —in fact, almost compels—a green horse or pony to bend naturally on the arc of the circle so that he looks the way he is going, a lesson that must be confirmed in mounted schooling. If Tonka were circling to the left, the positions of the reins would, of course, be reversed.

Some high-strung colts, when that outer line first touches their hind legs, spook a little and may want to run. The handler can easily control this just as he did on the longe: decrease the size of the circle by shortening the reins.

Most colts, however, quickly settle down and ignore the line touching their legs—after all, this driving in a circle is merely a refinement of work on the longe. The next logical step is for the trainer gradually to move to a position directly behind the horse and drive him straight ahead. Now it is very important, even when using a cavesson, not to hang on the lines; with even the mildest snaffle in the colt's mouth, it is doubly important. The horse— moving at a walk, of course—must be allowed complete freedom of his head and neck. Only after he moves forward willingly, do you begin teaching him to turn and halt in response to light pulls on the lines. Don't forget that he knows the command, "Whoa!" Use it. For turns left and right make up your own commands.

Tonka's No-Nonsense Rig. Tonka's goofing off on the longe with Linda was mere frisky naughtiness compared to his wild horse antics when I started working with him. The rig shown in this picture had a lot to do with settling him down. Here he is wearing a rawhide hackamore with a standing martingale. Both the martingale and the reins tied to the saddle horn have enough slack in them to allow him complete freedom of movement—as long as he moved the way he should. But the instant he tried any such evasive tricks as throwing his head up to run or—as he occasionally did at first— bogging it down to buck, he got hurt. He hurt himself, while I on the other end of the line looked innocent and apparently had nothing to do with it. The moment he quit his tricks he was comfortable again. Tonka got the message fast. In this rig even the most unruly colt can quickly be brought to order.

This Is Finished Longeing. There is little to be said about this picture. It speaks for itself. Tonka is calm but alert. His trot is regular, cadenced. There is no pull on the line. Observe how Linda is holding the whip, as described in the text. All this picture doesn't reveal is the amount of work that made it possible. Photograph by Msgr. J. Graham.

permitted and even induced to make them, will sooner or later prove his lack of experience—and often at the most inopportune moments. Thoroughly understanding this principle is one of the great secrets of successful schooling.

For the next two weeks Tonka worked only in the hackamore. He had the power of the hackamore thoroughly impressed on him. I do not mean to imply that every day for the next two weeks every time he made the slightest mistake I tried to pull his head off. On the contrary, after that first lesson I pulled him hardly at all, and then only as lightly as possible—little pulls that served to remind him that I could get tough again if he made it necessary.

In addition to longeing him, I also commenced ground driving him in the hackamore. I drove him in long reins, walking

95

behind him, and taught him to stop, turn and back a few steps in response to light pulls on the lines. After the second or third day he learned to yield to my fixed hands; I could halt, turn and back him without pulling at all.

I got him used to carrying a saddle, and sometimes I turned him loose in the big corral with the hackamore reins tied to the saddle horn just short enough to induce him to flex slightly. The colt learned that by tucking in his nose he could avoid pressure from the bosal.

At first, I turned him loose with the hackamore and saddle on for only five or ten minutes at a time. I gradually increased the periods up to an hour; that was the maximum time I permitted. For this flexing, however mild it may seem, requires muscular effort of the neck to which a green horse is not accustomed. If it is prolonged to the point of fatigue, the colt will begin to lug on the hackamore, like a horse wearing a bit that hangs on the hands. This will soon make him sore, then callous, and eventually completely soured.

This is why I repeat for the sake of emphasis what I said before: The hackamore has very strict limitations; it can very easily be overused to spoil a colt. Its effectiveness depends 99 per cent on the skill and the discretion of the trainer.

In a later chapter you will see proof of this—why Tonka, though he could be ridden easily in a hackamore, never developed into a real "hackamore horse."

CHAPTER X

Making Time

I ONCE took on the training of a very frisky three-year-old stallion with this suggestion from the colt's owner:

"You might longe and ground drive him for about a year before you begin riding him."

Reflecting on this, I realize that I muffed a chance to make some very easy money; I could have dragged out the colt's basic schooling for at least a couple of years, and the owner would have been satisfied. I did not, however, act on the suggestion, nor would I do so today. Squandering that much time on just basic ground work with a colt big and strong enough to carry a rider outraged my sense of professional efficiency.

Instead, about a week after having started him I was riding the colt. This does not mean that his training on the longe and in the long reins was cut short or in any way neglected. Ground work and mounted work went along together hand in hand. But I saw no reason for wasting time drilling the colt on the same old thing—and only the same old thing, over and over and over—before introducing something new. While being careful not to rush him, I taught the colt as much as I believed he could absorb as fast as he was ready to absorb it. And I follow the same system today.

The point I wish to make here is that, while slipshod hastiness is never excusable, it is quite possible to be quick and efficient without being hasty. I can see no sensible reason for doddering along a week short of forever with simple fundamentals the way the English like to do it. In England, every step in the breaking process of a colt is treated not only with great care—which is right—but as a prolonged major operation, which is ridiculous. (Perhaps this is why so many English horses, though very quiet to handle, rarely have good mouths.) Obviously, all steps in a colt's education are important, but some are more important than others. Not to realize this shows a lack of discernment between what is really critical in a finished horse or pony and those things which may be taken in stride.

It seems to me that it also usually indicates a misunderstanding of the axiom of intelligent training, that we should teach only one thing at a time. Of course we must teach only one thing at a time, but with eight to twelve working hours in a full day, there is plenty of time for several different lessons, including time between lessons when the colt is free to relax and rest—an important part of any training schedule.

I anticipate objections here. You do not have eight or twelve hours a day, you say, to devote to horse activities, or even five or six hours. You have to go to school; in the evening you have homework. Or perhaps you have a job, either a full-time job or a part-time job after school and on weekends. So? Obviously, the less "spare" time you have to work with your horse or pony, the more slowly his education—as well as yours—will progress.

If you really don't have any spare time at all, then there is something wrong with your schedule; you are trying to cram too many activities into each day—or you are frittering away many more hours than you realize. If you really don't have any spare time, how are you managing to read this book?

Everybody has exactly the same amount of time—twenty-four hours a day. We all have various tasks and obligations that eat up that time—but the time is there. What we don't all have is the same drive, the same amount of ambition. The busiest persons are those who accomplish most. By budgeting time and channeling their energy, they always find a little "extra" time to accomplish more. They make full use of time, while the great majority of us goof off.

As an illustration of how we can double up lessons while following the basic principle of teaching only one thing at a time, a particular time, let's assume that you have just acquired a two-year-old colt as green as grass, that you have your own barn, or that you keep the colt some place near home where you can get to him every day within a reasonable time. Let's also assume that it is Saturday or Sunday, or that school is out for the summer; at any rate, you have practically a full day ahead of you. Now I ask you to consider the following schedule for the day:

Time A.M.	WHAT YOU DO	WHAT YOUR COLT LEARNS
6:00	Water, feed colt with snaffle on	To carry a bit in his mouth without fuss
7:00	Remove snaffle; turn colt into corral or paddock while you muck out the stall	
8:00	Bring colt in; tie him up, groom him, pick out his feet (*Since we are assuming that the colt is really green, each step of this job is done thoroughly, without the least hurry. The grooming is less important than the over-all handling. Whether it takes one hour or two hours does not matter. But it must be unhurried and thorough.*)	To stand tied To be handled all over To have his feet picked up

9:30	Put on cavesson. Lead colt to training or schooling ring. If necessary, use body rope or tail rope.	To lead willingly, with line slack
	Longe colt	Obedience on longe line Oral commands
	Lead colt back to barn	To lead quietly
10:30	Groom colt If he is cool, water him	To stand tied To be handled all over To have his feet picked up
11:30	Turn out to pasture, or return to stall and feed with snaffle on	To carry the bit
12:00	Remove snaffle, even if colt has not finished eating. Allow complete rest in pasture or in stall	

P.M.

2:00	Bring colt in, or lead him out of stall; tie him up	To lead quietly To stand tied
	Handle him all over	To be handled
	Gently introduce him to the saddle; let him see it, smell it; put it on him several times; then girth it just snugly enough to stay in place. Lead him about with saddle on	To wear a saddle To lead quietly
3:00	Put hackamore on; turn colt loose in corral with reins tied to saddle horn for about five minutes	To yield to the hackamore
	Longe briefly with hackamore and saddle on; perhaps conclude with a brief introduction to ground driving	Oral commands To carry the saddle To yield to the hackamore To respond to long reins and get used to lines touching hind quarters

| 4:00 | Lead colt back to barn; groom; turn him out or put him away | To lead quietly
To be handled |
| 6:00 | If colt is kept in overnight, water and feed with snaffle on; pick out stall; remove snaffle | To carry bit
To be handled a little, perhaps caressed |

I am confident that anyone who follows a schedule such as this for about one week should—unless he is hopelessly all thumbs—be able to ride his two-year-old in an enclosure at the beginning of the second week.

If you will take the trouble to analyze this schedule, you will see that it enables you to give your colt ten *different* lessons in twenty brief separate training sessions in a single day. None of the lessons demands more of the colt than he is capable of learning. The routine is not strenuous; in fact, much of the time the colt has only to stand still. He is well exercised and he has adequate rest. You teach only one thing at a time, but you don't waste time.

This schedule is approximately the one I followed with the frisky three-year-old. It varies considerably from the one I have followed with Tonka. The two colts were very different. So were my own circumstances; I had to budget my time differently. This hypothetical schedule is simply to illustrate how much can be accomplished without undue delay if you make efficient use of your time and clearly understand what teaching one thing at a time really means.

In the foregoing timetable we have assumed that for at least one day of the week you are free of other obligations and can put in a full day's work with your colt, besides catching up on stable chores. We all know, however, that most days are quite far from this ideal. Even when school is out for the summer, you will usually have other things to do—maybe even a full-time job. If you live in the North, there will be days in winter when only an Eskimo would want to ride (as I write this the temperature outside is thirty degrees below zero); in summer the fly season can be a miserable time for riding. Therefore, whatever kind of schedule you make up, keep it elastic. Never follow a rigid routine. A schedule that may prove excellent with one horse or pony might need some changing for best results with another animal. And while we have assumed that you have only one colt, your own, to school, it may be that you have the job of looking after several horses or ponies as well. Obviously, this would cut into the time you'd like to spend with your own colt; his progress necessarily will be somewhat slower. But that is not important. What is important is that you learn to make full use of whatever time you do have.

That is a lesson most of us never learn.

CHAPTER XI

I Goof

I HOPE that I have not given the impression that in urging efficient use of time I am advocating hurry-up methods. I am unalterably opposed to hurry-up methods—unless they get better *final* results than slower methods. This automatically removes them from the category of rushing or gimmickry. There are some things you cannot hurry —notably developing a good mouth—and I would be the last to suggest that you should try.

However, some steps in schooling can be taken almost in stride, but there is no good reason to attempt them immediately; it doesn't save time. For example, if your colt is a weanling you *can* longe him briefly and easily, but there isn't much point in doing so unless circumstances make it necessary to keep him cooped up in a stall day and night. Then, of course, the youngster needs some exercise. But if he is out at grass most of the time, as at that age he should be, he will get all the exercise he needs. About the only lessons you can teach him are the simplest—to be handled all over and to lead well, fundamentals that build up his confidence in you and in the world in general.

When this colt becomes a yearling there are still only a limited number of things you can do with him. You can longe him for short periods every day and lead him about, or "pony" him, to show him the sights so that soon almost nothing will look strange or spooky to him. But what else can you do with him at this tender age? Get him used to a bit in his immature mouth and a saddle on his back? Why bother? These are simple lessons that take very little time. But suppose you do this; what have you accomplished? You will still have to let him mature for a year or more before you can ride him. In waiting for a colt to grow up you are not wasting time; in rushing his education you will be wasting not only time but the colt, too. I have known of a few ignorant parents who "broke" weanling colts to saddle and bridle, and then let their young children ride the wretched little animals. Some of these proud parents were so proud of their own idiocy that they even submitted pictures of their kids mounted on the colts for publication in magazines—and ignorant editors printed the photographs.

I have yet to see a horse or pony whose education as a colt was rushed that turned out to be any good.

As a general rule, I think that even a well-developed horse colt should be at least two years old before being burdened with the weight of a rider, unless the rider is a very experienced child or a small adult who weighs no more than one hundred pounds. I like to stick to this rule because until a colt is about three years old his bones and tendons are still developing— and the more heavily topped he is from what often amounts to forced feeding, the greater the strain on those young legs. If feasible, I even prefer to stay off a colt's back until he turns three years old—a statement that almost any unctuous "improver" of running horses will say qualifies me for a padded cell.

The larger a colt is the clumsier he is likely to be and therefore the more liable to possible injury.

Ponies, smaller and more rugged, are usually more durable, perhaps because they mature earlier. I estimate that a two-year-old pony is as mature as a three-year-old horse colt; a three-year-old pony is as physically developed as a five-year-old horse.

I started Tonka very slowly. I went about it as if I had "all the time there is." Even after I found out, on the longe line, how extraordinarily strong and agile he was, I still did not intend to ride the colt until he was a full two years old, or more. However, experienced horsemen whose opinions I respected were so impressed by his sturdy physique and his action that I began to wonder whether perhaps I was being too conservative. After all, there are exceptions to all rules.

One thing that did much to convince me that Tonka might well be an exception was the very evident fact that he needed about twice as much exercise to keep him happy as the average colt needs. Even when I cut his grain ration to almost nothing, he was still full of bounce. Unless I channeled this superabundant energy in the right directions by rigorous schooling, I realized, it was almost inevitable that it would spill over in some very undesirable directions.

Still, I hesitated. Even the experienced advice of so wise a horseman as my friend Colonel R. S. Timmis, a former captain of the Canadian Army International Jumping Team and commandant of the Royal Canadian Cavalry School, to start riding the young stallion did not immediately sway me.

Then one day a chance incident quickly put an end to my indecision and made me realize that Timmy, as usual, was right.

I have mentioned that, except when I brought him in for workouts, Tonka was always free to come into the barn or go out to graze, and that regardless of the weather he spent almost all his time outdoors. But one day I happened to notice that he seemed to be spending more and more time in the barn—but not in his stall. His droppings indicated that he had formed the habit of standing just inside the stable doorway, in a position from which he could look out over his private pasture.

The first time I noticed this I thought nothing of it. The second time I began to wonder. The third time I saw the droppings in the same place I became really curious. The pony's stall was thickly bedded with straw; the manger was always full of hay. Why, if he wanted to stay inside, should he prefer this one particular spot close by the doorway? And why, I wondered, when I was about had I never seen him standing there?

Tonka's First Fan and Linda's Friend. Colonel Reginald S. Timmis, a former Chief Instructor to the Royal Canadian Cavalry School and a member of the Canadian International Jumping Team, was enthusiastic about the. little gray stallion from the beginning. The colonel's great experience both as a judge and as a rider here and abroad enabled him to see Tonka's potential, and his occasional advice and suggestions were invaluable.

The thought never occurred to me that when he stood there just inside the doorway he was a dark gray ghost in the shadows, practically invisible to anyone outside even a short distance from the barn.

I decided to find out what the colt was up to, but an observant hired man saved me the trouble.

"That stud of yours," he informed me, "hides in the barn waiting for somebody to try a short cut through his pasture. He lets 'em get to near the middle of the field, then he comes busting out of the barn. He almost runs 'em plumb through the fence. I've seen some guys dive under on the fly, with Tonka one jump behind 'em."

I decided right then that Tonka needed a lot more work than he'd been getting on the longe.

At this time the gray colt was about three months short of being two years old. However, there was no trace of coltish awkwardness in the way he handled himself. He was already accustomed to a saddle from his work in the hackamore. I introduced him to the feel of weight on his back by giving Linda a leg up on him in the stall. Linda, who weighed about eighty-five pounds then, sat on him while Tonka ate his oats. Tonka was too greedy to pay much attention. Afterward, I had her get on and off several times. The pony made no fuss about it.

The following day I had Sheilagh, who weighed one hundred pounds, do the same thing. Tonka accepted the whole business quite casually. After I led him out into the yard, Sheilagh remounted, and I led the pony about the yard. This was to give him a chance to adjust his balance with unaccustomed weight on his back.

The lesson would have ended as smoothly as it began if Sheilagh had been an experienced rider—which, it pains me to admit, is another way of saying if I had first reminded myself how inexperienced she was. Unfortunately, I goofed; I should have mounted him in the yard myself. For in her effort strictly to follow my instruction, "Sit perfectly still," Sheilagh gripped the pony with her legs, accidentally digging her heels into him. Suddenly Tonka exploded. He shot skyward in a tremendous end-swapping buck. Sheilagh shot even higher and hit the ground about five yards away.

Fortunately, the ground was soft and she was not hurt, but her nerve was shaken, her confidence badly damaged. Hoping to undo or at least partially rectify the harm I had caused, I urged her to remount at once, and Sheilagh had the courage to do so. We went on with the lesson, and I was extra careful to allow Tonka no chance to repeat that first buck; but I felt like kicking myself a country mile. It was a bad start. I

Sheilagh and Tonka, After the Fall. The gray colt was about two-and-a-half years old here. He had learned manners, but Sheilagh was still wary when mounted on him. In fact, even now, years later, she still lacks confidence on him—and Tonka knows it. Thanks to his strict training, he won't try to do anything about it; he will go as well for Sheilagh as for any other competent rider. Yet, with her in the saddle, there is always a hint in his manner implying, "I'm doing this because I'm so good-natured. You aren't making me do it. I can dump you any time I want to, and don't you forget it." All this is the result of just one "little" mistake in the beginning, and the blame is all mine.

could only glumly guess what later effects it would have. But I had only myself to blame.

By putting a green rider up on a green mount, I had violated one of the most elementary rules of schooling—and an even more elementary rule of starting a novice rider. The fact that I'd only been leading the colt and had intended to do nothing more was a poor excuse. "The road to hell is paved with good intentions." Tonka, quite justified in bucking, had caught me napping. And if I knew that pony's quickness in learning a lesson, particularly anything to his own advantage, he was going to give me reason to regret this "little" mistake.

I set down these embarrassing facts without any glossing over for definite reasons:

First, to show how easy it is to find yourself in a sudden storm because, perhaps for only a few moments, you acted thoughtlessly or were overconfident that whatever might happen you could handle the trouble.

Second, to stress the importance of your strict attention to even minor details in your own riding and schooling.

Third, to show the far-reaching effects a "little" mistake of this kind can have on a colt, as well as on a beginning rider whose nerve has been shaken.

I kept Sheilagh on the pony for only a few minutes while I led him about, but that was long enough for me to realize miserably that the harm had been done: Sheilagh's nerve was shot. When I told her to dismount, she did so with frank relief —and she was not to get on Tonka again for more than six months. That one unlucky fall set her riding education back at least a full year.

Feeling like the most stupid fool on earth, I glumly led Tonka over to the big corral, swung the gate shut, and mounted him myself.

CHAPTER XII

Willy Wacker's Way

FROM the moment I stepped up on Tonka and he started to move, I realized that I need never have worried about his ability to carry weight. Though I may have looked too big for him, he carried me easily. There was no feeling of uncertainty or hesitancy in the way he moved. The first few times I urged him to trot, he loped, easily and smoothly. He did not feel like a pony at all. He moved like an Arabian, and better than some Arabs I've ridden.

I kept him moving mostly at a smart trot to loosen him up—this is the best working gait. When he tried to go too fast or broke into a lope I turned him into the fence. The ground work we had done began to pay off now; so did his knowledge of oral commands. He yielded readily to the hackamore so that I did not have to pull him hard. About every three minutes I'd slow him to a walk for a while. I turned and halted him frequently and made him stand while I got on and off—from both sides.

As a general rule, a ten- or fifteen-minute lesson is long enough the first time a colt is ridden, but I worked the gray stallion about twenty minutes, and he was cool when I dismounted.

For the next six months I rode him almost every day, gradually increasing the length of the lessons as his back hardened. Acutely aware of my initial error with Sheilagh, I was very careful never to give the pony the slightest excuse to buck again. Always before mounting, I warmed him up thoroughly on the longe. These warm-ups lasted from about five minutes to as long as half an hour; it depended entirely on how frisky the colt seemed to be. There need be no set rule about this. You must rely on your own observation and judgment, your knowledge of the individual animal. However, this preliminary warm-up before mounting a colt or a green horse or pony, particularly one that is kept in a stall most of the time and comes out fresh with pent-up energy, is important. For it can prevent a great deal of trouble you might otherwise encounter if you were to mount before the youngster has had a chance to "unkink."

Quite frequently, when pressed for time, I hastened this limbering-up process by first longeing for a few minutes, then tying the free end of the line to the hackamore and ground driving the colt, with frequent turns, halts and a few reinbacks. (When employing this method, the reins of the hackamore should be tied to the saddle horn with sufficient slack to allow the colt to turn freely. If you are using an English-type saddle, tie the reins to, or loop them under, the stirrup leathers.)

I wouldn't say that either method was "better" than the other, but certainly the ground driving limbered him up faster. The frequent turns and halts also served to get his attention more quickly.

No matter how brief or prolonged this warm-up might be, when I mounted Tonka was ready to work.

Some horsemen, particularly those who specialize in training stock horses, concentrate from the very first mounted lesson on "reining." They work a colt mostly in circles and do a great deal of turning, stopping, even reining back. Almost everything they do is directed toward the one end of getting a colt to "handle" and to stop always on his hocks. Often the colt is shod behind while his forefeet are rasped almost down to the quick to make him tender and to impress on him that the brakes are in the rear. The final result usually is to produce a horse or pony that moves as if he were walking on eggs.

There was a time when I would have started a colt like this, too; because I did not really think about it, I merely accepted and followed a standard procedure. In time, however, I gave up the method, convinced that it is as artificial as the methods employed in making gaited horses and Tennessee Walking Horses. Experience in schooling hunters and jumpers killed my taste for a mount that moves as if he were treading on eggs. I learned to prefer a horse that moves as Nature intended him to move—boldly, with long, free, straight strides that cover ground with maximum efficiency and minimum effort.

I still believe in schooling a horse or pony to stop on his hind feet, in balance; but a truly balanced stop results from collection, which depends on impulsion—free, energetic forward movement, with every stride marked by drive and spring. This, I believe, is the first thing to work on when schooling a colt. Develop impulsion first. Strive to get the colt to move at all gaits as naturally as he would go without a rider. In due course, collection will come easily—and it will be true collection, not a false imitation induced by sore feet.

Trainers who like the shoe-behind-and-rasp-in-front type of methods prefer them because such methods give them what they want in the shortest length of time—and what they usually want (because their paying customers want it) is a show horse, an animal that can win ribbons and trophies for a couple of years, making its owner proud and the trainer look good, before it is retired for breeding or sold at a handsome profit—and all this long before the animal has even reached its physical prime at seven or eight years.

I realize that the harsh economic facts of life might make such practices necessary, but personally I cannot accept them. Ribbons and trophies leave me unimpressed. I do not believe that simply because a horse or a pony wins in shows it is worthy of admiration or is a good performer under saddle or in harness or is even a good specimen of its breed. I've seen many winners that were none of these things; I have seen too many ignorant and biased judges; and I know too much about the sly tricks that get by under the unholy name of "showmanship."

To me, there is only one true test of the merits of a riding horse or pony, and it can be only guessed at in a show ring. That test is how easily, safely and pleasurably he can carry his rider over a country. Whether he works stock or doesn't know a gopher from a cow, whether he can jump big fences or will merely hop over fallen tree trunks in his path, makes no difference; such specialities can be learned. But work out-of-doors is a horse's *raison d'être*. If he isn't a good cross-country mount, as far as I am concerned he is nothing. Anything over and beyond this that a horse or a pony can do is, of course, commendable. *But this comes first.*

Accordingly, during those first six months I rode him, Tonka spent much more time becoming familiar with the countryside than working in the corral; and when I say "becoming familiar" I mean just that. For the gray colt had spent practically all his brief life in the tranquil quietness of isolated pastures; there were a thousand things he had yet to encounter but which he would have to get used to.

For example, he must have waded through wet spots in pastures innumerable times; yet the first time I faced him at a little puddle on a blacktop road, he seemed to think that I was asking him to leap into a crater of molten lava. He regarded telephone poles as towering giants waiting in ambush for us. I don't know how many he abruptly stopped to snort at and then cautiously passed at a mincing side-step before he finally accepted them as a part of the landscape. An approaching car loomed as a monster from outer space; a truck or a tractor, even if it was only standing in a driveway or in a field, seemed to be a sure sign that the world was coming to an end.

I found this particular phase of the colt's training a source of constant interest and amusement, for of all the horses and ponies I've handled none was ever more alert to everything that went on about him than Tonka. His senses were incredibly sharp; he had the wary alertness of a wild mustang. He showed the Arab's trait of slightly turning his head from side to side as he walked, and his ears were never still. The rustle of a squirrel in a tree, the flight of a distant bird, a flickering shadow—he missed nothing; and it was often minutes after he'd become aware of something before I understood what it was. He was always a furlong or five minutes ahead of me. Riding him across country or along a quiet country road was a constant wonder and delight.

Above all else, Tonka had the stallion's way of going. It is difficult to describe this exactly, perhaps because it is a blend of various things; but I think anyone who has ridden a good stallion will understand what I have in mind. Let me put it this way: You could have mounted that gray colt blindfolded and without ever having seen him, but within fifty yards you would know that you had a stallion between your legs, not a gelding or a mare.

His every movement gave you a feeling of reserve power that had nothing to do with mere size, and his bold manner matched that. With slashing forefeet, he nearly killed a couple of surly dogs that ran at him barking and snapping. At times I had the feeling that I was riding not a pony but a war horse. Tonka would have been in his glory carrying a conquistador into battle.

Riding him in a hackamore, I let him go on a loose rein. My chief concern on these leisurely cross-country jaunts was to teach him obedience to the legs. This is the keystone of all schooling—that the horse should promptly and willingly go forward at the call of the rider's legs.

To teach this all-important lesson the rider should carry a short stiff whip or a crop (a quirt is too flexible). An instant *after* you have applied your legs, tap the colt on the shoulder with the whip or on the barrel just behind the calf of your leg. He will quickly learn to respond to the legs without the whip. Once the colt has learned to obey promptly the rider should make a point of gradually decreasing the amount of leg pressure, so that the colt responds to the lightest cue.

In teaching this lesson, never wear spurs. Superficially, it might seem quite logical that spurs would be helpful in this lesson, that they could do the work of the whip; but it almost never works out that way. Instead, spurs are almost certain to make even a sluggish colt fretful and nervous. Even the most expert riders, able to apply the spurs with precision and delicacy, are slow to use them.

For ordinary purposes, I am convinced, the average rider has no real need of spurs at all. He may think that spurs help him to look more like a true cavalier, but he should be more concerned with what his horse thinks of him.

Before Tonka was confirmed in obedience to the legs I found myself with a couple of difficulties to be solved. Since these problems sooner or later occur in the training of almost all horses and ponies, it might be helpful for me to explain how I overcame them with Tonka.

The first difficulty was his stubborn refusal to walk through water, even a small puddle he could have stepped over without wetting a hoof. Practically all horses and ponies have to overcome this apparently absurd fear of water, even those that have run outdoors since foalhood and have crossed water many times in pastures. It seems that the weight of a rider unsettles them at first and leaves them unsure of their footing or of their ability to escape if bogged down.

Never underestimate this fear of getting bogged down; even the boldest horses and ponies have it. Unlike predatory animals, which are natural fighters, the horse's first instinctive reaction to danger is flight; he relies on his fleetness to escape enemies. Hence, it is only natural for him to dread anything that threatens his mobility. This is why a horse, fearful of a little water, will calmly walk on slick ice, which is really dangerous while a puddle of water is not. The ice looks and feels firm, therefore the animal steps on it with confidence.

After making a couple of mild and futile efforts to get the stallion across puddles, I decided not to make an issue of it. Tonka had the muscle and the determination to make a big battle over this triviality. It was up to me to avoid a useless battle and win the war by using my brain—a thing so many horsemen are reluctant to try. No matter what the strong-armed buckaroos tell you about "mastering" a horse, there are times when you get best results by being easy. Old Willy Wacker had said it all in one sentence.

In breaking Tonka of biting and striking I'd been tough, strict. I had not given him an inch or let up on him, for these were intolerably dangerous habits to be eradicated swiftly and ruthlessly. However, there was nothing so critical or urgent about overcoming his natural reluctance to get his feet wet. Therefore I did not immediately bear down on the colt just to prove my "mastery." Instead, while Tonka probably thought he was getting away with something, I waited for a rainy day.

That was not long in coming and it was made to order for my purpose—a twenty-four-hour downpour that left Tonka's corral looking like a small lagoon. There were a few high spots, but two-thirds of the ground was fetlock-deep under water.

The morning after the deluge I turned the gray pony loose in that corral without any breakfast. Tonka very obviously didn't like it. He stood on the high spots, keeping his feet dry, looked suspiciously at the shimmering water and snorted.

Wearing rubber boots, I stepped into the corral with an armful of hay. I let the hungry colt grab just one mouthful before I heaved the hay out near the center of the lagoon. Then I leaned against the gate, curious to see how long it would take the young stallion to decide whether to get his feet wet or go without breakfast.

It didn't take him long. For perhaps two minutes he paced back and forth along the edge of the water, looking curiously like an angry tiger. He'd sniff at the water, snort, switch his long tail and stamp a foot. But that pony loves to eat, and his greediness finally impelled him, step by step, into the water toward that islet of hay. In another minute he was feeding, as relaxed and calm as if he always ate breakfast this way.

Later he cleaned up his grain from a rubber feed tub I set down in the water, weighted with a rock in it to keep it from floating about. That day and for as long as the wet lasted I rode him in the corral, splashing back and forth through the

Wet Feet vs. a Healthy Appetite. Many horses show what seems to us an unreasonable fear of crossing water. Knowing that the water is shallow and the bottom is firm, we are apt to lose patience with their timidity. This is a mistake. Remember that the horse doesn't know how deep the water may be. He has a natural dread of bogging down. Colts that have free access to open water in a pasture soon get over this, but others can be a real problem. This young Arabian was an example. Aravic had a much greater initial fear of water than Tonka showed—in fact, I think Tonka's fear was 50 per cent bluff; he was just putting on one of his acts to try me out. But both colts got the same simple treatment. They were given the choice of getting their feet wet or going hungry. It didn't take either colt long to decide that he'd rather wade in and eat. No whipping, no spurring, no pulling on the halter rope, no waste of time: it was as simple as that.

big puddles. And that was the end of Tonka's fear of water underfoot. In a few brief lessons, without any fight, fuss, or wasted time, I'd led the colt to overcome a natural fear which leaves some horses stymied for months or even years.

This is only one example of how training and schooling can be simplified and made easy by the use of a little horse sense.

Whenever we can achieve our ends without provoking a

fight, then we are showing true mastery. Strong-arm tactics are very rarely necessary. Usually they reflect only a bully's meanness and sadism and prove that one who must constantly resort to them lacks the first essential of a good trainer: he isn't at least as smart as the horse.

We like to speak of horses' intelligence and brag about our smart ones, but it is ignoring facts to pretend that even the smartest horse has more than a very limited mentality. He learns best by constant repetition of lessons adapted to his mental level. Yet how often in our handling of him do we search for the simplest, clearest methods of reaching his understanding? Instead, it often seems, most of us go out of our way to make training as complicated and illogical as we can.

Then we blame the horse for being "crazy-headed" or stubborn, and we reach for the bat.

The second problem Tonka presented me with on these cross-country rides was somewhat similar to his refusal to cross water. He balked at ditches, even ones so narrow and so shallow that they hardly merited the name. I found out about this the first time I tried to ride him out of a field into a road. He seemed to think the ditch was the Grand Canyon. He flatly refused to get within a yard of the edge, sidling back and forth along the brink with the brisk suppleness of a high school horse.

Obviously, this required a different solution from the water problem. To get him through water I could wait for a rainfall; if necessary, I could have flooded the corral with a garden hose. But we do not live in earthquake country, and I certainly was not going to strain my back digging a ditch in the corral just so that Tonka would learn to hop over it. The colt had to learn to take ditches as and where he found them. It was my task to get this lesson over to him without provoking a fight.

One of the quickest ways to start a fight—and to end up with a spoiled mount—is to force a colt up to something he's afraid of and set to whipping or spurring him to get him past or over it. Open jumping classes in shows are filled with wild-eyed, iron-jawed horses that have been spoiled in this way. The problem called for a bit of subtlety.

The First Step Toward Leg Obedience. Even a small colt too young to be mounted can quickly learn this lesson. Here Linda is pushing with her fist against Tonka's ribs while drawing his head toward her and commanding, "Move." Tonka responds by moving his hindquarters away, pivoting on his forehand in a circle. When mounted, this makes it easy for him to understand pressure from his rider's leg. He soon learned to obey just the oral command, "Move." Linda should have placed her fist about six inches lower. This lesson should be taught from both sides. Each time the horse takes a step, no matter how small, the pressure should be relaxed; then push again for another step.

For a week I kept him away from ditches and stayed off roads. Riding across country, I concentrated on teaching the colt prompt obedience to my legs. For the first time, I actually let him run a little. I encouraged him to take off at a gallop in response to a light squeeze of my legs and the command,

"Hup!"—an order he had learned on the longe line. Tonka took to this work with zest. He loved to run.

These sprints were short, never more than one hundred yards, and they almost always ended in a diminishing spiral or a large circle while I slowed him down gradually, never abruptly. When he had halted I showed my approval with words, pats on the neck, sometimes even a handful of oats or a piece of an apple. After a minute or so we would proceed on our way at a relaxed walk; for the next quarter of an hour or more I wouldn't ask him even to trot. Then I might lightly squeeze him into a canter, slow to a walk, and canter again. Perhaps before we returned to the stable I'd ask him for one more brief sprint.

In a couple of days Tonka had the idea quite clearly: the slightest pressure of my legs meant, always, *forward*; sudden strong pressure was a demand to blast off and go all out until I used the reins.

This lesson is essential for any saddle horse or pony ever to be called well schooled, but a trainer must use a good deal of tact in teaching it properly. Otherwise, he is likely to produce a nervous, flighty mount that soon becomes run-crazy and is difficult to stop, such as can be seen in barrel-racing events.

A naturally hot colt, eager to run, can very easily be taught to jump into a gallop. With such a colt, the trainer's critical problem is maintaining calmness; he must concentrate more on the slowdown and halt than on the quick getaway. He must be careful never to let the colt get the notion that galloping can degenerate into running away. And he must be able to do this without hanging on the colt's mouth. With a colt of this type you may find that perhaps only one lesson a week is sufficient; more than that will get him too excited.

On the other hand, there are sluggish coldbloods that need a touch of the whip before they learn to respond promptly to the rider's legs, and they may need a refresher lesson almost every day; two or three fast starts within an hour's time won't even ruffle their composure. With animals of this type I consider a wide, flat strap better than a whip or a crop. The strap does not cut or sting them as a quirt or a whip would, but it makes a noise when it smacks; this usually wakes them up fast. Yet, not being really hurt by the strap, they don't build up a resentment of the lesson.

The rider should apply the strap, or tap with his whip, a split second *after* he has used his legs.

When the colt obeys the legs, the rider should be certain to give him an absolutely free rein, letting him gallop at least fifty yards or more before making any attempt to check him, and he should never be checked abruptly. This is the only way the colt can understand that he has done the right thing. A sudden pull on his mouth will only confuse him; it contradicts the signal you gave with your legs.

After a week of this leg obedience work Tonka's response had become practically automatic. He had learned to react faster than he could think. He was ready to face one of those dreaded ditches again, I hoped.

I carefully avoided making a big deal of this; I tried to play it low key and cool. But one thing I made sure of: the first time we faced the ditch, we were headed for home. This little detail often is the deciding factor whether a horse does something or refuses to do it. It is also a good thing to keep in mind when first galloping a colt. If he is headed toward his stable, once he gets going he may not want to stop until he gets there.

I was riding the stallion at a walk along a road bordered by one of the fearsome ditches when I reined him in a ninety-degree turn and suddenly clapped my legs to him, hard. Tonka reacted before he was even aware of facing the ditch. Bounding forward, he was at the brink before he knew it; his own momentum practically forced him to jump. He cleared the ditch with feet to spare, and the moment he landed I began telling him how wonderful he was.

I think he believed me. He acted real proud of himself. We hopped back and forth over that ditch half a dozen times, and the pony seemed to think it was fun. He had overcome another bogey, and his manner left the impression that he had done it all himself.

CHAPTER XIII

In the Ring

THIS period of quiet hacking benefited the young stallion in several ways. Physically, it legged him up, hardened his back, and blunted the edge of his vast energy. On the mental side, it did much to steady him as he grew accustomed to more new sights and sounds. Without losing his keen alertness, he gradually quit demonstrating the truth of the old saying that there are only two things a horse will spook at—things that move and things that don't move.

These rambles over the countryside, however, were more than mere leg-stretching and sight-seeing excursions. I always managed to sneak in a little basic schooling along the way.

For example, when at the walk I never let the colt just slop along any old way. I made him *march*. Riding with loose reins, I encouraged him with repeated squeezing of my legs to extend himself and to lengthen his stride. It was never long enough to satisfy me; I always demanded a little more.

This work at the walk is important in the schooling of all horses, though much too often it is neglected, but it is doubly important in the schooling of ponies. "Pony gaits" is a common descriptive term; when applied to a horse, it is used in a derogatory sense. It refers to short, choppy strides, a "trappy" way of going. This is characteristic of ponies; no amount of schooling can completely eradicate it. But schooling can considerably lengthen the strides at all gaits, and the more this trappy way of going is eliminated, the better a cross-country mount your pony will be. We must never forget that the ultimate practical aim is to cover ground—and to enjoy the ride. So we want a smooth, elastic stride, with a minimum of "bumps."

Like most green mounts, at first Tonka, instead of moving ahead in a straight line, would wander from side to side. If left to his own devices, he would have zigzagged and serpentined all over the landscape, eventually turning back home. Surely, nothing seems simpler than moving straight ahead, yet this tendency to drift aimlessly is quite common in colts. It indicates lack of impulsion or "drive." The remedy is to ride the horse vigorously forward, if necessary even changing gaits and increasing the pace. Once he is moving straight ahead, the original gait and pace can be resumed. But this fault requires constant vigilance and it is where so many riders fail as horsemen. They can ride for a lifetime, but they ride "with their legs hanging down." They never learn how to use their legs to make a horse march and go up into his bridle.

However, even this most beneficial of exercises, like anything else, can be overdone. You should remember that a fast extended walk is as strenuous an effort for a horse or pony as it is for a man. A colt needs frequent breaks; fatigue can turn him sour, the one thing above all we want to avoid. Hence, I never kept Tonka at the fast walk for more than a few minutes at a time. Then I'd let him relax, letting him set his own pace for about a minute, or I'd halt him and make him stand—a thing he made it plain at first he didn't like to do; he always wanted to go. A practical saddle mount, however, must learn to stand quietly whenever and wherever his rider requires it. I reinforced this lesson often by dismounting and remounting several times from either side while the stallion stood with the reins slack (see pages 124 and 125).

On these rides I also began very lightly to rein him in simple turns and in large figure 8's, using my weight and legs as well as the reins to cue him. After longeing and ground driving,

An Essential Lesson: Stand To Be Mounted. The generally accepted "correct" way to mount a horse is for the rider to start from a position near the point of the horse's left shoulder and facing directly or diagonally toward the rear. This is a safe way of mounting an unruly horse or a strange one that you can't trust, one of these spoiled darlings that might cow-kick you in the pants. But otherwise, in my opinion, this method has little to recommend it. If you must mount your own horse or pony in this way, it is positive proof that you have not taught a most elementary lesson—to  *stand still while being mounted and remain standing until cued to move off.*

Horses acquire the habits of jittering around when mounted and starting off before the rider is ready for two main reasons: Ignorant riders permit them to do it without any attempt to correct the fault, and clumsy riders actually provoke them into doing it by snugging the reins tight to "control" them (the worst fault), digging a boot toe into their ribs, pulling the saddle crooked, then sitting down with a spine-crushing thump. Such stupid treatment makes even phlegmatic horses cranky.

Tonka—anything but phlegmatic—learned to stand still and to remain standing after the rider was seated. In the accompanying series of pictures Linda demonstrates how and why.

In the first photograph (left) observe Linda's position. She is standing beside the saddle, not up near the point of Tonka's shoulder. She is facing to the front, and her foot in the stirrup is pointed to the front; her toe can't possibly dig him in the ribs. She has the reins in her right hand, which grips the pommel; her forearm is resting on the seat. Her left hand is free to make any correction necessary—and the reins are slack.

(Tonka was so indifferent to the proceedings that he was looking at passing riders in the field beyond. As I snapped the shutter, Linda was using the left rein to turn his head toward the camera. Otherwise she would have placed her left hand on his crest.)

In the second photograph (middle) Linda has sprung up. She stands balanced in the stirrup with her foot still pointed ahead and her weight partly supported by her hands—and the reins are still slack. Tonka stands as calmly as an old plug; he couldn't care less.

In the third photograph (right) Linda, firmly supported by her hands, is swinging her leg over to sit down. Tonka hasn't moved a foot—and the reins are still slack.

I emphasize the slack reins, for they are the secret of teaching this lesson. Even with the greenest colt, no matter how high-strung, the rider always begins with the reins slack. He keeps them slack as long as the horse stands still. But the moment the animal moves, whether forward, sidewise or backward, the rider steps down and away from him and sharply corrects with a jerk on the reins accompanied by the command, "Whoa!" or "Stand!" He never tries to take his seat with the horse in motion.

To most good horsemen jerk is a dirty word; it has a connotation of abuse or cruelty. It is amusing to watch for the euphemisms many writers resort to in their efforts to avoid the word, even when jerk is precisely what they mean—and what they themselves, when necessary, do. However, an occasional jerk on the reins, whether corrective or accidental, never spoiled any horse's mouth; it certainly won't spoil a mouth that isn't even made. It's constant hanging on the reins that spoils a mouth.

These corrective jerks on the reins need not be severe; indeed, after the first few corrections a mere twitch of the reins is usually enough. After each correction soothe the horse with a few pats and soft words. Then, with the reins slack, begin again. Don't hurry, don't fuss, don't struggle. Repeat and repeat until the horse stands. If the horse starts off of its own volition once the rider is in the saddle, he checks with the reins and an oral command.

The average colt will learn this lesson in only a few minutes. Spoiled horses take a little longer. Thereafter the lesson needs only to be confirmed.

Still Standing. Here in the photograph on the left are Linda and Tonka three years later, doing the same thing. This time Tonka isn't looking at passing neighbors, so Linda's left hand is where it belongs. Both are older, wiser, more co-ordinated, a closeknit team. Tonka is grayer; Linda is bigger. Otherwise things are pretty much the same—hand on pommel, forearm on seat, eyes and toes front—and the reins are still slack and always will be.

With all this concern about mounting, we might as well show how to dismount. A quick way, but not too easy, is just to fall off. A more comfortable way is shown in the photograph on the right: swing your right leg over, lean on your hands, slip your other foot from the stirrup and drop down. And lay off your horse's mouth; keep those reins slack! Train your horse to be mounted and dismounted from both sides.

this simple reining came easily to him. I had only to take the slack out of a rein with my little finger to stop or turn him.

Longeing and ground driving, I might as well admit here, are two chores that do not exactly enthrall me. I can easily understand the attitude of trainers who prefer to skip these basic lessons. Yet, though I sometimes find the work a bit dull, I never skip it. For I know from experience that when mounted schooling begins, this dull groundwork will pay off and prove its worth. Then you find out how much further advanced your colt is than he would have been if you had given in to the temptation to skip this phase of training and, as they say, "just go to riding him."

At all times I used the reins as lightly as possible. To put it another way, the resistance of my hand was *weaker* than his resistance; but it never let up until he ceased to resist. The instant he yielded, I also yielded. In this way Tonka gradually became very light in the hackamore.

I minimized rein cues even further by preceding them with weight cues. For example, to turn right I first shifted my weight slightly to the right stirrup—a shift so slight that people who watched me do it could not see it. Then immediately I'd take the slack out of the right rein and move my hand out to the side the way I wanted him to turn—a leading rein, not a pulling rein. If the young stallion did not promptly start to turn, I waited for a few moments; then I slightly increased the tension on the rein, still holding my hand out to the side and keeping it fixed in place with no more pulling than a slight flexing of my fingers.

It wasn't long before Tonka was turning in response only to my weight cues. I needed to rein him only for a very sharp turn.

The importance of this fixed hand in schooling rather than a pulling hand can hardly be overemphasized. It provides the only way that we can begin to develop a really good mouth. For the secret of success is to yield the moment the horse yields, not two or three seconds later. But if you are pulling on the reins, you cannot instantly feel when the horse yields and at once relax your hand to reward him. But this *immediate* reward is our only means of conveying to the horse that he has done right. A time lapse of only a few seconds leaves the horse without any connection between his action (obedience) and our reaction (reward).

Throughout all training this one fundamental principle never varies: When the horse resists, we oppose him; when he obeys, we instantly yield.

Some readers, who have seen too many cowboy movies, may wonder here why I do not talk about neckreining. At this elementary stage of schooling, neckreining is something you don't even think about. When you are ready to think about it, your horse should be past the hackamore stage.

When you see "hackamore horses" in shows that appear to neckrein with lightness and precision, don't be fooled. They are not really hackamore horses, except according to the A.H.S.A. rule that defines a hackamore horse as one no more than five years old that has never been *shown* in a bit. But that doesn't mean that, at home, these horses haven't been schooled in a snaffle or a curb bit. They have. About the only time they wear a hackamore is at shows.

Tonka was fit and hard when I cut down on the cross-country work and began to concentrate on schooling in the ring.

We began with work over the cavalletti.

Cavalletti are an Italian invention. They consist of heavy wood rails, about four inches in diameter and about sixteen feet long, affixed to triangular supports at both ends and elevated twelve inches above the ground measured from the top. Six or more poles are placed parallel in a line one behind another at regular distances—usually three or six feet apart—so that they form a grid or an obstacle course over which the horse is ridden on loose reins at a walk and at a trot.

Cavalletti were first used at the Italian Cavalry School as an aid in schooling horses in the forward system of riding (not merely the forward seat) formulated by Captain Frederico Caprilli (1868–1907). Today the basic principles laid down by Caprilli are universally accepted by the world's foremost international riders, but the intelligent use of cavalletti in schooling is still little understood in this country.

In the accompanying pictures you will notice that the cavalletti I use vary from those of the Italian design, which are centered in equilateral triangular standards so that, however you may turn the standards, the poles are always the same distance above the ground. My cavalletti can be used in three positions: with the poles flat on the ground; raised about four inches off the ground; and ten inches off the ground. I believe that this makes them more versatile and useful in schooling horses and ponies that differ in size and in stride. It seems illogical to have the bars set at the same height and placed the

1

Left hand passive and held low, yielding as horse turns head. If necessary, hand resists overbending.

Left leg passive, or acts behind girth to sharpen turn.

Right hand moves out to side with no rearward tension on rein.

Right leg maintains pace.

2

Left hand is passive or yielding.

Left leg is passive at girth or moves back to hold croup from swinging out.

Right hand exerts slight rein tension to rear.

Right leg, behind girth, maintains pace.

3

Left hand is passive, or acts to hurry turn.

Right hand moves to left rear across neck.

Legs act to control turn either on center or haunches.

4

Left hand is passive.

Left leg is passive.

Right hand moves to left rear but not across neck.

Right leg pushes croup to left.

5

Left hand is passive or may apply leading rein.

Legs maintain pace.

Raised right hand, with no tension to rear, presses rein against neck.

The Five Standard Rein Effects.

same distance apart for both a 13-hand pony and a 17-hand hunter.

The original purpose of cavalletti was to help to develop the balance and agility of jumpers, as well as to correct certain faults such as rushing. The horse is ridden over the poles at a trot on loose reins. The rider, as passive as possible and well forward in the saddle with most of his weight in the stirrups, does absolutely nothing to "help" the horse. The horse has complete freedom to find and adjust its own balance as necessary. "As necessary" depends, among other things, on how far apart the poles are spaced. This distance can and should vary according to the individual animal's needs and its degree of training, as well as the length of its stride.

This last requirement, the length of the stride, demands that the poles be spaced with some care, not just haphazardly. We don't want the horse to hit the poles, breaking stride and getting all fouled up as he stumbles over them. We want him to step lively over those poles at a smooth, cadenced trot, taking them in stride and without any feeling of apprehension. So the correct spacing for any individual horse or pony depends on the trainer's judgment; he must find it by trial and error—and he can't afford to make too many errors before he gets it right.

I might add here that the use of cavalletti for the purpose of developing a colt's balance and agility has nothing whatever to do with the use of poles scattered haphazardly on the ground as an obstacle in trail horse classes. In a show, the poles, scattered any old way, are used merely to test the horses' willingness and carefulness in walking through the "obstacle."

This is the way I got Tonka used to cavalletti, and the way I usually start most colts:

In the schooling ring I laid one pole on the ground close to and at a right angle to the fence. Leading the colt, I walked back and forth over it several times. Each time I'd halt and pat him a few times before turning around to repeat.

Moving to the center of the ring, I let out the longe line and started Tonka circling at a trot. He had plenty of room to pass the pole near the fence without having to go over it. After he had circled a few times, I shifted position toward the fence so that as he came around again he was moving close to the fence and heading directly at the pole on the ground. The fence prevented him from running out on that side while I, controlling him with line and whip, was ready to check a runout toward the center.

So Tonka, of course, never one to do the expected, slid to an abrupt stop, as suspicious of the pole as if he had never seen it before.

I walked up to him, led him over it, and started him circling again. This time as he came down the fence, ears cocked forward and eyes on the pole ahead, I flicked the whip at his hocks and said, "Hup!"

The colt went over the pole. More precisely, he jumped almost four feet high, landing about fifteen feet from where he had taken off. Then he exploded into a gallop. I just hung on and let him go.

He made six or seven circuits like this, each time going at that insignificant pole on the ground as if it were a triple-bar jump. Bit by bit his leaps flattened out, and then he was jumping in stride. I moved toward the center of the ring, drawing him off the pole, and slowed him to a trot, a walk, then a halt. Slipping him a handful of oats, I praised him extravagantly.

It is not to be supposed that most colts, or even many of them, are likely to react in Tonka's explosive way to the simple matter of stepping over a pole on the ground. The vast majority of colts, when handled sensibly, make very little fuss about it, just as some will cross their first ditch quite casually. I relate here how Tonka took his introduction to cavalletti merely to warn readers what they should *be prepared* to expect. It all depends on the individual horse or pony. The gray stallion's reaction, I believe, was simply an indication of something we were to learn later—that he is a natural jumper; he has not only ability but desire to jump, seeming to enjoy it.

Again starting him, I longed him at a walk for a few minutes, then put him into a trot; step by step I moved back toward the

Cavalletti. In each of these pictures, you will notice, the bars are set at different heights, with a consequent difference in the horse's action. These cavalletti can also be used with the bars flat on the ground. In doing this exercise the rider should assume a jumping position with his seat clear of the saddle and his weight well forward. The horse should be given the utmost freedom to handle himself without any help from the rider. Only if the horse fails to

pole near the fence. This time I anticipated his hesitation, said, "Hup!" and flicked the whiplash. He jumped at a canter but slowed immediately when I commanded, "Walk." Finally, about the fifth or sixth time, he crossed the pole at a trot. I put him over about a dozen times, then halted him, had him change directions, and made him do it a dozen times the opposite way.

Then we quit for the day, returned to the barn, and he got a good feed of oats.

The following day we repeated this; then I added a couple of poles. I spaced the three poles about fifteen feet apart, allowing Tonka to take two full strides between each pair. I longed him over these several times, moving parallel to the fence, and the colt made no attempt to break out of an easy trot. He had learned to accept the poles.

This, and merely this, was one of my two purposes in intro-

move straight forward should the rider interfere, as Linda has straightened Tonka with the left rein over the lower bars. In both photographs Linda shows her pet fault—looking down and to one side instead of straight ahead. No matter how often she is corrected, she sooner or later repeats the error. "Nobody," she excuses herself, "is perfect—not even Tonka."

ducing him to the cavalletti on the longe line; the other was to let him try it a few times without weight on his back. Since Tonka was such a strong colt and blessed with excellent natural balance, I constantly had to remind myself that he was still only a two-year-old pony and that my weight plus that of a saddle was a fair burden for a mature horse. However, real work over the cavalletti is done with the horse carrying a rider, not only because of the extra effort required but because it is only in this way that he can develop the balance we seek—balance under saddle.

For this work now we need at least six bars on the ground; a dozen bars would be better. The bars can be placed down the middle of the ring rather than near a fence. For the first few days I prefer to space them so as to allow the colt two or three full strides between pairs.

After a thorough warm-up—including some small circles in

the corners to limber him up—trot the colt straight down the middle of the ring and ride him over the poles. Don't let him slow down and walk over. Trot! The first couple of times you may have to sit down in the saddle and use your legs strongly, holding him straight with the reins. But as soon as the colt goes straight and freely at a trot the rider should be as passive as possible. Riding with loose reins, allow the horse complete freedom. Keep off his loins by getting forward in the saddle with most of your weight in the stirrups. Should the colt hit one of the poles or stumble, don't let him stop or turn out to one side. Push him ahead until he has gone over all of them.

Continue down to the end of the ring keeping him at a steady trot, turn along the fence, trot back to the starting point, and do it again. Do it a dozen times or until he trots over the poles freely and smoothly. Then let him relax, walking around the ring on loose reins. After a few minutes repeat the same procedure, this time starting from the opposite end of the line of poles. Put him over a dozen times. Then quit. Take him out for a relaxing walk across country or put him away for the day—anything to let him know that he has done well.

I like to repeat this exercise for two or three days before making any changes. With an awkward colt I might do it daily for a week. Then I either move the poles closer together, decreasing the number of strides between from three to two or from two to one, or I leave the poles where they are but turn them over, elevating them off the ground. I don't think that it makes any difference which you choose to do first. You might even do both at the same time: leave some of the poles flat on the ground, turn every alternate one up, and vary the distances between poles. It all depends on the individual colt. Your ultimate end remains the same—to trot him over all the poles elevated off the ground without any extra stride between pairs.

The first time you do this, I think, you will find it a pleasant surprise—and perhaps quite an eye opener about the firmness of your seat and your balance. Trotting over poles about ten inches above the ground without an extra stride between poles is an excellent gymnastic exercise for any horse, developing the

Agility Plus! Tonka has always been full of funny surprises. To me, one of his most astonishing stunts is to gallop *over closely spaced cavalletti, jumping the bars singly as a series of in-and-outs. The first time he performed this amazing feat of agility, in an exuberant mood and of his own volition, I doubted what I saw. He moved so fast, bouncing up and down like a rocking horse, that I could not quite believe that he was really galloping. Linda was up on him and I told her, "Make him do that again." She retorted, "I'm not making him. He's doing it." Turning around, she let him canter at the grid again, and Tonka repeated his display of Fancy Dan footwork, never touching a bar. Here—with Linda in a full-moon jumping position—is a picture of him doing it.*

muscles, spring and free play of the joints. The movements are quite similar to those of the high school passage, and when you experience them, you may understand why some horsemen turn to dressage riding almost exclusively and why the passage has been called the most beautiful of high school airs.

In this work over the cavalletti it is important to remember always that we are doing school exercises; the work is not an end in itself. No matter how frequently the horse may hit a pole (if we have them properly spaced to fit his stride), we should not think that he is failing the exercises. He cannot fail; he can only improve. All horses misjudge and hit poles, no matter how long they have done the work. Therefore, never show impatience and never punish for a mistake.

CHAPTER XIV

Saddles and Seats

Saddles make seats. If you habitually used a Mongol saddle or a Gaucho or Cossack or Mexican or Arab saddle, the saddle's inherent design would shape your seat. Eventually you would ride like a Mongol, a Gaucho, a Cossack, a *charro*, or an Arab, whether you wanted to or not. Obviously, this makes your choice of a good saddle for the kind of riding you want to do a matter or prime importance. If the saddle is designed wrong, your seat will be wrong. If it isn't comfortable for both you and your mount, a long ride will be an unpleasant, perhaps a painful, ordeal. Almost all experienced riders have tried a good number of saddles before finding one that fills all their requirements. The wise novice will not be in any rush to squander money on a saddle simply because the manufacturer spends a lot of money advertising it. The dubious fact that a certain model is the favorite of Red Nottholer, the famous rodeo star, does not mean it will be ideal for you.

In this country there are two general types of saddles—the "English" or "flat saddle" and the Western or stock saddle. (A separate type, no longer manufactured but still occasionally to be found, is the McClelland saddle formerly used by the army.) The labels "English saddle" and "flat saddle" are merely convenient terms to designate hornless non-Western saddles. Actually, some so-called "flat saddles" have seats as deep as some stock saddles, and rather than being exclusively English, they may be of German, French, Italian, American, Argentine, or Japanese manufacture—the last two being excellent examples of "economy" craftsmanship to avoid.

Even aside from the country of origin, the terms "English saddle" and "flat saddle" are too vague and inaccurate to tell us anything more than that a saddle lacks a horn. For these so-called "flat saddles" come in a variety of designs, each usually intended for a specific and even a specialized purpose. In a general way they may be divided into five distinct designs:

1. Extremely lightweight "postage stamp" saddles used in flat racing and steeplechasing: stripped of all nonessentials, these are made to aid the horse's running efficiency, with no regard for the rider's comfort or stability.

2. Forward seat saddles: these are intended primarily for jumping and cross-country galloping; some models, usually of Italian design, are more extremely "forward" than others, such as the German jumping saddles which often have quite deep seats (see page 139).

3. Dressage saddles: these, usually of German or French design, have a fairly deep seat and a narrow throat. With or without knee rolls, they enable the rider to sit deep and have a better "feel" of his mount.

4. Cutback saddles: these saddles are used on Saddlebred and Tennessee Walking Horses in shows; many Arabian and Morgan exhibitors also use them, aping the Saddle Horse fanciers. The name refers to the design of the saddle; the front is "cut back" to expose more of the horse's forehand, an attempted illusion that fools nobody. The rider sits erect or even with torso slightly to the rear with his seat against the cantle (see page 140).

5. Park, polo and hunting saddles: these are the original "English saddles," with a basic design older than the American label. Sometimes called "general purpose" saddles, they might

more accurately be referred to as backward seat saddles. Many polo players and fox hunters have abandoned this style of saddle in favor of forward seats, which today may be seen even in appointment classes. Riding forward in this kind of saddle can be difficult and uncomfortable.

Even if we ignore the racing saddles, which for ordinary purposes are impractical, this leaves us quite a selection of saddles to choose from—a wider variety, in fact, than our list indicates, for each type includes different models to suit different tastes.

Obviously then before buying a saddle we should know in at least a general way what kind of riding we plan to do so that we may have a clearer idea of what we shall need than just the hazy notion of an "English saddle."

Unfortunately, the average rider knows so little about saddlery that he cannot even distinguish between good and poor workmanship, much less good and poor design. He knows when he finds one saddle more comfortable and secure than another, but he can seldom put a finger on the important differences and say exactly why.

Western riders are no more knowledgeable than their flat saddle contemporaries. They are, in fact, the biggest suckers in the world for slick advertising. They'll buy almost anything if they can be persuaded that a famous rodeo star or some fast-talking "clinic" professor designed it or uses it or recommends it. They seem to judge the worth of a saddle by its sheer weight and bulk—the bigger the better. They will pay extra for fancy details that have absolutely nothing to do with the saddle's worth as an aid to better riding. This would be a harmless vanity if it were always secondary to those practical qualities which add up to a superior saddle, but the average Western rider hardly knows what practical horsemanship is, he has been so thoroughly brainwashed. However, he is firmly convinced that he knows and is inclined to look down with superior tolerance on any way of riding different from his own. This explains as well as anything else why he usually knows so little about what he thinks he knows so much.

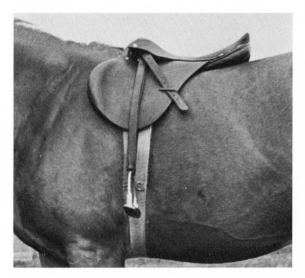 

A Forward Seat Saddle. Saddles of this type (left) are designed primarily for fast galloping and jumping. The stirrups are hung close to the front of the tree and the skirts are cut forward for the rider's knees. Beneath the front edge of each skirt is a concealed knee roll for greater security. Most of the time when galloping and jumping the rider has his seat completely off the rear of the saddle with his weight in the irons. He rides over the horse's center of gravity, leaving the hindquarters free. Notice that the tread of the stirrup slopes downward to the rear; it also slopes downward toward the horse (See right photograph). Such offset stirrups are designed to aid the rider in depressing his heels and "breaking" his feet outward at the ankles for a secure leg grip. Photograph by C. Whitson

Photograph on right: The off-center location of the stirrup leather loop in the iron, when the rider puts weight on the stirrup, depresses the inner side of the iron even more than the picture shows. Some riders find these offset stirrups helpful; others do not like them at all. Linda detests them. I prefer them. Perhaps most riders who dislike offset irons, I'm inclined to think, are those with very flexible ankles; they just don't need any extra help in keeping their heels down.

The Cutback. A glance is enough to tell anyone that saddles like this are not made for forward riding or jumping. The rider sits back with long leathers and his feet ahead of him. An excellent rider on a fine horse can look quite the elegant cavalier in a cutback saddle, but such riders are rare. The average show rider, pounding along hopelessly behind the horse, is a ridiculous caricature of a horseman. With a saddle like this, he could hardly sit otherwise, even if he knew how.

The average Western horseman today is strictly a pleasure rider. He competes in shows but not in rodeos. He almost never has an occasion to work livestock on horseback. There isn't a day of his life when he *has* to build a loop and throw a lariat—and if there were, he couldn't rope a mounted moose head more than three feet away. The severest strain he ever puts on his saddle horn and rigging is when he mounts and dismounts or, on exuberant days, when he teams up with a buddy in the shovel race.

Yet he likes to jog about in a saddle built to the specifications of a professional steer roper, complete with breast collar and flank cinch. The idea never occurs to him that his ordinary pleasure horse needs thirty-five or forty pounds of wood and leather on its back about as much as it needs five-pound shoes—or racing plates. Least of all does our bridle-path cowboy ever stop to think that having all this excess gear between himself and his mount hardly makes for the togetherness that is so necessary for good horsemanship.

But try to tell him this and see how far you'll get before he interrupts or turns away.

Besides the twin faults of excessive weight and general stiffness as a result of using heavy leather, the majority of stock saddles are poorly designed for riding that demands real finesse. Most of them, even the most expensive custom-made jobs, have seats designed to keep the rider *out of balance* with his mount. This elementary fault in riding is perpetuated by the insidious built-up seat that forces the rider back against the cantle, thus keeping him behind the horse's center of gravity.

It is a fundamental of good horsemanship that the rider should sit in the lowest part of the seat. In fact, gravity makes it impossible for him to sit any place else unless he makes a deliberate, contorting effort to avoid doing so. But since almost all stock saddles have seats that slope up to the fork from a low point near the cantle, the rider is forced behind his mount's center of gravity even at a walk, and much farther behind at a trot and gallop.

This "plowboy seat" is further accentuated by the forward position in which the stirrups are usually hung, close to the fork of the saddle tree. Manufacturers even advertise their "free-swing" stirrups intended to make it easier for a rider to shove his feet forward as he lolls back against the cantle.

In a jumping saddle this forward position of the stirrups is correct; for fast galloping and jumping it is an asset to both horse and rider. For then the rider's seat is mostly off the saddle with his weight supported by, or balanced over, his feet in the irons, his knees and his lower thighs, and even to some extent at times by his hands on the horse's neck. The horse's center of gravity is far forward and the rider leans forward accordingly.

However, when you have to ride like this in a stock saddle in order to stay in balance with your horse, you aren't going to lean very far forward before you feel the saddle horn in your belly. Even aside from that, you won't be riding what any judge would recognize as a stock saddle seat, at least if he knows his A.H.S.A. rule book.

As if the built-up seat and forward-hung stirrups were not enough to hinder his riding, the typical Western horseman uses a saddle several inches longer in the seat than, as a general rule, he needs. What ever started this fad of the long seat I don't

A Typical Stock Saddle. Notice the steeply sloping seat, low near the cantle, high near the fork. (Because of the high camera angle, the slope actually is even steeper than the picture shows.) A seat like this, with the stirrups located well ahead of the lowest part, is ideally suited for forcing a rider in most ordinary circumstances behind his mount's center of gravity. Carrying even a lightweight rider almost on his loins tires a horse unnecessarily and hinders the all-important action of his hindquarters. This saddle weighs about forty-five pounds, with four layers of heavy leather between the rider's legs and the horse. All the fancy stamping and carving in the leather cannot make up for the basically poor design. *Photograph by D. Strassman*

A Good Saddle: The Neil Mc-Grady. Here is a plain, workman-like saddle of excellent design. From a horseman's viewpoint— and the horse's—it is worth ten times more than the fancily stamped saddle. The deep seat is not unduly built up from cantle to fork and the stirrups are hung close to the lowest part of the seat. These features place a rider in balance the instant he sits down. A saddle like this is a boon to a hard-working stock horse. A lightweight version makes a fine pleasure and show saddle. Courtesy Glendive Saddlery

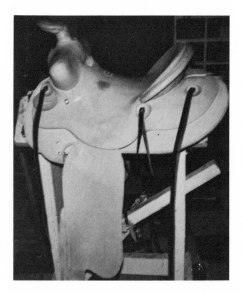

know, but it is as firmly established as the cult of the loose, sloppy rein. Many riders apparently want their seats big enough for them to lounge in the saddle rather than ride in it. The overlong seat is one of the principal reasons why we see so many sloppy seats among Western riders.

An acquaintance of mine once attended a horsemanship "clinic," and after watching the proceedings for a while he asked the professional who was running the show, "How do you figure the correct length of the seat?"

"For anybody," blared the professor, "from six to sixty, sixteen inches!"

My friend didn't waste time asking any more questions.

This reply makes as much sense as saying that everybody should wear a size seven hat or a size nine boot. But the professional "professor" who laid down this absurd dictum has many amateurs convinced of the correctness of his thinking.

If these riders had a broader knowledge and more experience, however, they would simply laugh at such sweeping generalizations. If they weren't semihypnotized by skillful showmanship, they could see the error instantly, as my friend did.

Finished horsemen the world over use saddles with short rather than long seat: riders of the Spanish Riding School, whose equipment is the same today as it was two hundred years ago; officers of the famous Cadre Noir at Saumur; Portuguese *rajonadores* who fight on horseback against cat-quick Spanish bulls; and the expert horsemen of all nations who compete in dressage in the Olympic Games. In some European military academies for training army officers new cadets were taught the fundamentals of a good seat—even those who had experience in riding—in special training saddles so designed as practically to force the rider to sit in a correct position—and stay there without having to make any special effort to do so. These saddles had short, deep seats; they allowed the rider no extra room in which to slide back and forth between the pommel and the cantle—which is what so many Western riders seem to want to do. The stirrups of these saddles, like those on good dressage saddles, were located close to the middle of the seat so that the

A Charro Saddle. This fancy Mexican rig shows the short seat so typical of well-made saddles favored by skilled horsemen the world over. A good saddle should place you in the right position and make it easy for you to stay there. Rodeo Cowboys Association rules make it mandatory for bronc riders to use saddles of a certain minimum length in order to make the rider's job more difficult. Old-time bronc riders, before the R.C.A., sensibly favored shorter trees than are now allowed. Photograph by M. Whitcomb

rider's feet were positioned almost directly under him; he could transfer all his weight to the stirrups without even leaning forward to readjust his balance. A commonly known tree of this general design is the old army McClelland saddle. Stripped of all frills and nonessentials, the McClelland put United States Cavalry troopers, many of whom had never been on a horse in civilian life, right where they were supposed to be on horseback.

It is a fallacy to think that simply because a man is six feet

The Phillips Saddle. Shortly before the army abolished horse cavalry, this saddle was designed as an all-purpose saddle for officers. Similar to saddles used at Saumur, the French Cavalry School, the Phillips is suitable for any type of riding from schooling to jumping. Materials and workmanship are of the best. With the demise of the cavalry, the army auctioned off many of these fine saddles at a fraction of their actual cost. If you are lucky, you might still come upon a used Phillips for sale. If you do, buy it before the owner has a chance to think twice.

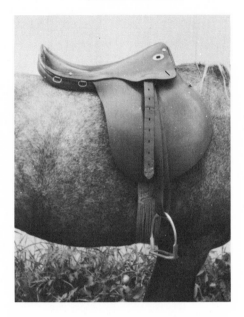

tall he needs a sixteen-inch saddle seat. That depends entirely on his build. If he is slim-hipped he will probably find a thirteen-inch seat a much better fit, while his five-by-five wife, whose pear-shaped figure strains the seams of her Levis, may be the one who needs a bigger seat.

I am six feet tall, and the only stock saddle I have ever used on Tonka is the same one Linda uses, a lightweight JRY Special Schooling Saddle with a twelve-inch tree.[1] Even in heavy winter clothing I don't find that it cramps me. Persons who have used this saddle have been unanimous in their agreement on its merits. They include riders who had never straddled a stock saddle before. They did not have to adjust their seat or "learn to ride the saddle." The saddle put them in correct balance, and they could concentrate on riding their horse.

A lot of breath and ink have been wasted on superficial explanations of the differences between "English riding" and "Western riding" and "the stock saddle seat" contrasted with

[1] The JRY saddle may be obtained from the Glendive Saddlery, Glendive, Montana.

The JRY Special Schooling Saddle. When Linda was still only a baby, I designed this saddle for her oldest sister Dawn. It is the only stock saddle we have ever used on Tonka. It has withstood years of hard usage, yet it weighs only about twenty pounds. To one accustomed to saddles built like elephant howdahs it looks deceptively small, but I have used it on horses of all sizes and shapes. I especially like it for starting colts—no excess weight. Notice how low it "sets" on the horse's back and that the seat has no build-up at all. The stirrups are hung close to the middle of the seat; you don't have to lean forward to get your feet under you. This saddle makes riding with the horse easy and natural: you just sit down right where you belong, and you have no trouble staying there.

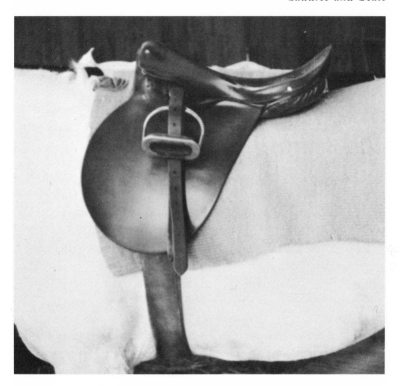

The McTaggart Saddle. This forty-year-old saddle, the only one of its kind in America, was a forerunner of present-day, all-round saddles designed for both dressage and jumping. The seat is several inches shorter than those of most English-type saddles so that when the rider is seated in balance he does not have any excess cantle jutting out behind him. In some of the action pictures in this book Linda was using this saddle. Almost every rider who has tried this saddle liked it; the few who didn't were accustomed to knee rolls. A confirmed stock saddle rider used this saddle on trail rides in the Rockies and found it to be "the only flat saddle" she could ride all day, uphill and downhill, without feeling stiff and sore at day's end.

"the flat saddle seat." Many Western riders sincerely believe and frankly admit that they know nothing about "English riding." Some hard-boot horsemen are just as humble about their ignorance of Western riding. In my opinion, both are wrong. They have never really *thought* about horsemanship, and very often the reason they haven't used their own brains is that they have meekly accepted as truths the half-baked notions of ignorant elders and professional pundits who don't know what they're talking about, either. There are no *fundamental* differences between the two styles of riding. Skilled horsemanship is basically the same wherever you find it. A rider who really is a horseman can ride any way the peculiarities of his mount and individual circumstances call for.

In Europe there is a big annual competition to determine the world's champion show rider over jumps. It is a test of riders rather than of horses and one of the most coveted prizes. The best horsemen from all over Europe, the British Isles, and our own Olympic team riders vie for it. Each rider competes on two of his own mounts, but he has to ride each of the other horses of every one of his competitors as well. Thus, if there are a dozen riders in the competition, each contestant must ride twenty-four horses, including his own pair. The rider who finishes with the least total of faults wins the championship.

While it is true that all the horses are show jumpers, each is an individual with its own peculiar ways. Furthermore, they have all been schooled by more or less different methods, according to various "systems," and by different horsemen, and each, of course, is accustomed to its own rider's personal style. These differences are often quite as marked as the difference between a horse "trained English" and one "trained Western." For example, a German Hanoverian horse might have been schooled to take a very firm hold of the bit, demanding a degree of support from the rider that verges on pulling, while another, perhaps an Anglo-Arab from France, might have a very light mouth. The horses differ in size, length of stride, temperament, the way they like to be handled, the way each jumps best. Accordingly, to have any chance of winning this supreme test

148

of horsemanship, a contestant must be able to subordinate or adjust his own style of riding to suit each horse he rides—and he has only a couple of minutes to get used to each mount before riding in the ring. In other words, a successful rider must be both versatile and adaptable, able to emulate the style of each of his competitors.

This is the quintessence of skilled horsemastership.

Now consider: What are the differences between the English style of riding and the Western style?

In the former you hold a rein or, with a double bridle, a pair of reins in each hand. The Western style calls for the reins to be held in one hand.

In flat saddle riding you *usually*—not always—keep the reins stretched so as to have at least a light contact with the horse's mouth. But there are many times when you let the horse relax on a loose rein.

In Western riding you *usually*—not always—leave a little slack in the reins. But there are many times, particularly in schooling, when you don't. In "Western" classes for Arabians the rule book specifies riding on light contact.

In English riding you sometimes turn on a direct rein—though if you know your business you will use whatever rein effect or combination of effects circumstances may require.

In Western riding you turn by neckreining—but in starting a green colt you "plowline" him, holding a rein in each hand, and you spend a good deal of the time schooling that way, too.

Now, considering these superficial details, what is the basic difference between the two styles of riding? Is there even one critical thing in either method of handling a horse that any competent horseman cannot do? If there is, I can't pick it out. The only possible difficulty I can see is that a rider accustomed to riding most of the time on contact might have a tendency to hang on a Western horse's mouth, but anyone who does this on *any* horse can hardly be called a competent horseman. Thousands of Western riders do it so constantly that they don't even know they are doing it, nor do they realize that they halt their miserable horses by *jerking* on the reins.

The different lengths of stirrup leathers is often cited as a big difference in the two styles of riding, but this idea hardly bears scrutiny. A flat saddle rider schooling a horse, or just out hacking, may use as long a leather as any stock horse rider. Most riders who specialize in dressage do a lot of riding without any stirrups at all. Some jump riders do the same to develop "glue in their pants" against a time when they may lose a stirrup when jumping. Most professional ropers ride with leathers short enough to be quite suitable for jumping. A proper length of stirrup leather is governed by what kind of riding you do as well as by the length of your horse's stride; the longer the stride the shorter the leather. The only really important thing is for the rider to be in balance with his horse—not merely in balance *on* the horse but *with* the horse.

CHAPTER XV

Linda Up

Six months is a long time for an eleven-year-old to wait to get on her own pony; the time seems to stretch out forever. But Linda was patient, content to groom, feed, muck out, watch, and listen, and sometimes sit on Tonka as he munched hay in his stall. More than once I thought of not making her wait any longer, but memory of Sheilagh's initial experience made me resist the temptation. At last, however, the day came when I told Linda, "Now it's your turn."

We saddled the colt, put the hackamore on and led him into the corral. For about ten minutes I warmed him up on the longe; then I gave Linda a leg up and started Tonka, still on the line, moving at a walk.

Since it is practically impossible for a beginner to concentrate on acquiring a firm seat if he also has to think of controlling his mount, I tried to keep this first lesson as simple as possible. I controlled Tonka on the longe; Linda had no reins to worry about. All she had to do was sit still, get used to the feel of her mount and develop confidence.

In fact, for the first three or four days I even refrained from telling Linda how to sit. I let her sit naturally, telling her only to relax and to keep her lower legs slightly away from the pony's sides. I think this is the best way to start any beginner,

 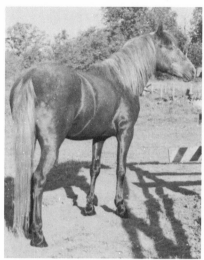

Tonka As a Three-Year-Old. Always a very masculine colt, at this time Tonka already showed to a very marked degree all the characteristics of a mature stallion. He seemed to strut and swagger rather than merely walk. His manner gave the impression that he thought himself as good as the best, if not better. Here is one of his first pictures after he had become accustomed to a snaffle. The other photograph shows him patrolling his private pasture where he "laid for" unwary trespassers. Note how a year of work on the longe and under saddle has muscled him up. With a country-boy haircut at both ends, he might have passed for a small Quarter Horse.

for I have found that most children, if not beset by too much advice at first, naturally adopt a fairly well-balanced seat. After all, there aren't too many ways of straddling a horse, and the fine points can come later.

Tonka behaved admirably and Linda, a natural athlete with good co-ordination and balance, was enjoying herself. In a couple of days she could comfortably sit a trot, but I waited a couple of days more before I began to shape her seat. Here essentially is what I told her, taking one thing at a time:

Sit on the lowest part of the seat.

Sit tall and supple, but sit *down*. Don't brace on the stirrups so that you push your rump back against the cantle.

Look ahead, over the horse's ears. Tilting your head forward to look down causes you to round your back, upset your balance and no longer sit tall.

Let your arms hang naturally, shoulder muscles relaxed. Rest your hands on the horn or fork of the saddle without hanging onto it, or on your thighs, palms down.

Let your lower legs hang close to the horse, but don't get into the habit of holding them snugly against him. If you do, he will soon become insensitive to light leg pressure—the very opposite of what you want.

Place your feet in the stirrups so that the treads are under the widest part of your boot soles. The inner edge of the sole should be against the inner side of the stirrup, the side closer to the horse (see the picture below).

Relax your ankles so that your heels are lower than your toes.

Let your feet turn out naturally. Don't try to ride pigeon-toed.

When you sit in this way, your stirrup leathers, viewed from the side, will be vertical. As a general rule for most persons, if, without leaning forward or tilting your head, you can see your toes, your feet are probably too far ahead and the stirrup leathers are not vertical.

Either in a stock saddle or a "flat" saddle this seat is basically

Foot Position. Most novice riders get into trouble because they lose their stirrups. They lose their stirrups because too often they are taught to rely chiefly on grip to maintain their seat. But grip is only for emergencies; then it is an instinctive reaction. Most of the time a rider's balance is from the feet in the stirrups. Therefore, we should pay some attention to how we place our feet in the irons. The tread should be directly (not diagonally) across the widest part of the boot sole with the heels pushed down and the inner side of the foot against that side of the arch closer to the horse.

a schooling seat, a balanced seat suitable for all usual purposes. With a few slight modifications, notably shortening the stirrup leathers, it can be used equally well for speed riding, jumping, roping or anything else you may want to do. You may change the details, but the principles remain the same: you stay in balance with your mount.

It seems appropriate at this point to list and refute a few moth-eaten notions that should have gone out with plate armor, though we find them still being expounded by befuddled ancients who try to teach beginners by first confusing them:

The rider's shinbone should be vertical.

If it is, the stirrup leather cannot be; it will be ahead of the vertical. Hence, pressure on the stirrup will push the rider's weight off balance to the rear, causing him to pound more or less on his mount's loins.

Press the knees tightly against the saddle; avoid "the fatal triangle" of light.

This error goes with the vertical shinbone or the shin ahead of the vertical. We see it in many old photographs of soldiers, cowboys, polo players and fox hunters when they were trying to look their best for the camera. However, at a halt or when riding at a relaxed walk there is nothing wrong with letting the knees move away from the saddle; to do so is quite natural. As leg pressure increases at the faster gaits, or when we urge our mount to speed up the walk or move collectedly, the "fatal" triangle disappears. The important area of contact is the rider's legs below the knees.

Keep your elbows in.

If you make an effort to do this, you will inevitably ride stiffly, with eventually disastrous effect on your horse's mouth. Instead, let your upper arms hang naturally, quite relaxed. Think of your arms, including the hands, as rubber bands that elastically give and take to every movement of the horse's mouth.

In general, my first instructions to Linda boiled down to one rule: "Sit tall and supple, and be relaxed." For a beginner, I believe, relaxation and *going with* the horse should be stressed

The Whip. All riders should practice enough to become adept at carrying a whip. Even if they rarely use it, they should know how. Some riders, mostly women, do not want to learn. They are sentimental about their horses even when the beasts are spoiled brats (that's why they are spoiled), and they think of the whip only as a symbol of punishment. This attitude is foolish. The whip, properly used, is an aid, an extension of the rider's legs. In schooling it is almost indispensable. Learn to carry it in either hand. Carried as shown, a mere twist of the forearm, a flick of the wrist, brings it into play behind the girth.

first, even at the sacrifice of correct position. Suppleness and balance are the keystone and the essence of good riding—add tact and sympathy for the horse and you have the secret of skilled horsemanship. It is easy to correct the seat of an inexperienced rider who is relaxed even to the point of sloppiness in the saddle, but it takes considerably more time and attention to relax a novice whose first lessons were chiefly drills in keeping his heels down and his elbows in.

One of the most common questions young riders ask is, "How do you post?" My usual reply is, "First let me see you ride a trot without posting." For experience has convinced me that a rider who has not learned to sit a trot with at least a fair degree of comfort and security can rarely learn to post properly. He will merely use his stirrups to bounce up and down, often showing about six inches of daylight between his seat and the saddle and in general looking as ungainly as Ichabod Crane.

At the canter and the gallop, I believe, relaxation should be stressed quite as much as at the trot, even when the pupil's ultimate aim is to learn the forward jumping seat. Until you can sit down snugly and comfortably on a moving horse, you are not ready to perform any acrobatics on him—and posting is a mild form of acrobatics while the jumping seat is perhaps the ultimate.

So I didn't even mention posting to Linda, and she didn't know enough about riding to ask. Linda learned to sit flat and ride in balance with the young stallion, supple and relaxed. Then, still ignoring the reins, I set about teaching her to use her legs.

People have a penchant for speaking with a knowing air of "good hands" and "bad hands" in riding, and usually they don't know what they're talking about. But I have rarely known anyone to discuss good legs and poor legs in riding. I suspect that this is because the average rider never realizes the importance of legs and cannot distinguish good leg action from poor. Thumping his mount in the ribs with the heels or roughly prodding with the spurs is about as much as the average rider ever learns.

Yet I would say that proper use of the legs is about 75 per cent of good riding. Hands certainly are important; until we develop them—and develop them we must, for they are not a natural gift—we can never become finished horsemen. But if the legs don't create impulsion in the horse, the hands have nothing to work on. The most sensitive hands cannot make a horse supple and light except when co-ordinated with the action of the legs.

Let me give you a specific example:

One day I was giving a lesson to a middle-aged pupil, an intermediate rider of fair skill. This man has light though uneducated hands, but he had known almost nothing about how to use his legs before coming to me. He had had a few lessons from Saddle Horse "experts," but only a few; that was all he needed to realize that he wasn't learning anything he didn't already know—chiefly, how to stop and turn a horse with the reins only.

For this particular lesson I had mounted him on my Morgan stallion Emerald's Aristocrat, commonly called "Corky." He

Bareback Riding. I think it is very questionable whether riding bareback or riding without stirrups "strengthens" a young rider's seat, as so many teachers profess to believe. (Except for a few dressage specialists, I don't see many of them practicing it, and I wonder how many of them are merely accepting what they were taught without bothering really to ponder the matter.) I feel quite sure that neither practice helps in riding the forward seat; jumping without stirrups contradicts the principles of forward riding. I have seen as many skilled bareback riders fall off when learning to jump and at other times as riders who like to have their stirrups. The only thing I believe bareback riding, with a minimum of reliance on grip, will do is teach a rider to sit down. (It is always a good idea to warm up for a schooling session by riding for a few minutes with one's feet out of the stirrups.) But if the rider must depend chiefly on grip to maintain his seat, the practice does more harm than good. Then the rider becomes tense instead of supple. Occasionally I may suggest briefly riding without stirrups for novices who have learned to post wrongly and tend to bounce. If they enjoy it, they may do it frequently; if not, I never force it on them. Riders with an inferior sense of balance find it an ordeal; they tense up and do not benefit. Even as a beginner Linda enjoyed riding bareback and has done a lot of it. But I never told her to do it, and I doubt whether it makes any difference in her riding. If you learn to school, you will learn to sit down whether you have stirrups or not.

was riding the horse in a D-ring snaffle with a drop noseband, a bridle in which Corky could execute all school movements.

However, on this day things weren't going well. The pupil was trying to follow my instructions to "open and close the horse like an accordian"; in other words, to extend him, then collect him, then smoothly extend him again, sometimes at a walk, and with frequent changes to a trot, both slow and fast.

I say thing weren't going well, for Corky was obviously loafing. His walk was merely a stroll, his trot little more than a lazy jog. He simply was not taking the rider seriously. Even the best-trained horse will act this way under a rider who will let him get away with it. If ridden consistently in this inept way, any horse eventually will be spoiled.

After about twenty minutes of rather vain effort my pupil stopped to complain, "He just won't respond to my legs."

"Perhaps he feels lazy," I said. "Let me try him."

Corky did feel lazy, he was lazy, but I was on him hardly ten seconds before he woke up. He got the lead out fast. For me he did everything he had refused to do for my pupil. I rode the horse for only a few minutes, and he was light and responsive; then the pupil remounted to try again.

For a couple of circuits of the ring—about two minutes—Corky was on the bit, responsive and alert, as he had been with me; then, like a clock that needs winding, he began to relax, and in another minute he was slopping along again as before. His nonchalant lack of respect for the rider wasn't funny; it was insulting.

I exhorted the student to use his legs. He did. Corky broke into a shambling trot, stealing the reins by extending his head and neck. "Pick him up," I urged. "Fix your hands. Leg him into the bit."

Corky came to an abrupt stop, dropping his nose, and started to walk backward.

"You're hanging on his mouth! Use your legs!"

Corky continued to back, and now his ears were back, too. He looked angry, out of patience. Fearing that he would rid himself of the rider, I hastily ended the lesson.

I cite this typical example of how even a schooled horse—or I might say especially a schooled horse—will react when badly ridden, though the rider has hands that would commonly be called "good"—meaning merely light. Good hands by themselves are not enough. Good legs, educated legs, are far more important. For, I repeat, if the rider cannot create *and maintain* impulsion in the horse—free, energetic, flowing forward movement—the hands have nothing to work on. They can only stop the horse or make him go backward—and not the way he should rein back. This is how jibbers and rearers are made.

All riders must go through this awkward stage of learning to use their legs efficiently. The pity is that so many never get beyond this stage. They never know the pleasure of riding a horse that is truly light, a horse that will "work in the wind of the boot."

Thus, while Tonka was still on the longe line and even before Linda had reins to handle, she began learning to use her legs. This is how we did it:

With the stallion moving at a slow, relaxed walk, I'd tell Linda, "Squeeze him with your legs—just a little bit." Trying hard to do it just right, and not sure just how much "a little bit" was, Linda would close her legs in a squeeze that was practically infinitesimal—a mere zephyr of the boot. Tonka, however, wasn't *that* good yet. He'd continue at his leisurely walk. Then Linda would make a mistake that all beginners make: she would lightly close her legs again and keep them closed, maintaining a steady pressure while waiting for Tonka to respond.

"Relax," I'd say to her, and, "Whoa!" to the pony. "Linda, you must not keep a steady pressure on him. If you do, he'll soon become insensitive to your legs. Give him just *one* squeeze, then relax. If he doesn't respond, squeeze him again, harder; then immediately relax again. Each time you squeeze a little harder than before, but only a very little. And always after squeezing him, you momentarily relax your legs before you squeeze again."

Gradually, by repeated trial and error over a period of several days, Linda learned correct, elementary use of her legs. But, of course, she made mistakes, as we all do while learning (and later when we should know better, too). Perhaps her most frequent mistake was moving her lower legs to the rear when she applied the aids. Another was a tendency to raise her heels, pointing her toes down. She had to learn to apply her aids for straight forward movement where her lower legs hung near the girth in a simple pincer action that could be achieved merely by turning her toes out slightly; no displacement of the legs to the rear was necessary. The leg applied behind the girth serves a different purpose; we'd work on that later.

With the pony under my control on the longe line, Linda was free to concentrate on learning to use her legs without worrying about her hands at the same time. Co-ordination of hands and legs is a problem all novices must eventually solve, but I do not believe in asking them to worry about this when they first have to master something more basic. Here, as in schooling colts, one thing at a time means faster progress.

I believe that starting without reins and emphasizing leg aids also had a good psychological effect on Linda that she has never lost. Unconsciously she developed the all-important "urge to go," an unreasoned realization that the first step in solving most difficulties is to ride a horse straight forward, moving briskly, and then go to work correcting whatever the difficulty may be. This is something many novices—and all timid riders—never learn. In moments of difficulty they want to slow down and stop; they hang on the reins instead of pushing the horse straight into his bridle. This "go complex" paid off more noticeably when Linda took up jumping. She "threw her heart over the fence," and her mount followed it. Sticky jumpers with a tendency to refuse usually jump freely for Linda. Several contributing factors, such as good balance and co-ordination and light hands, are involved in this, but the paramount influence is the rider's "urge to go."

CHAPTER XVI

Hands: The Horseman's Touch

I N beginning to co-ordinate her hands and legs, I gave Linda two rigid rules to follow:

1. When the hands act, the legs remain passive; when the legs act, the hands are passive. Never use both at once.
2. Use the reins with a light pull and a quick slack—and use only *one* rein at a time.

The reason for the first rule needs little explanation. When a rider urges with his legs and checks with his hands, the two aids contradict each other. When this opposition of the aids is exactly as we intend it to be, on a schooled horse we can achieve practically any effect or movement we want—for example, to cite opposite extremes, the *piaffe*, a cadenced trot with no or almost no forward movement, requiring a very high degree of collection; and a fast gallop or a big jump that makes the horse extend himself to the utmost while still being fully on the bit. Correctly applying even one aid, however, demands a certain degree of skill. Simultaneously applying two or more with exactitude and correct timing requires a great deal of skill, the result of much practice. But this is precisely what the novice rider does not have; it is what he hopes to acquire. Until he does, he will create fewer difficulties for himself and less confusion for his mount by sticking strictly to the rule: *Hands without legs; legs without hands.*

To some of you the idea of using only one rein at a time may seem strange. Why only one rein, when you have two? How can you rein a horse to a halt and keep him straight if you don't use both reins? Persons who have never quite grasped how to use a hackamore and those who have only a hazy motion of how to develop a horse's mouth ask these questions all the time.

The simplest answer is that you do use both reins but you use them alternately, not together. Suppose, for example, you are riding straight forward at a trot; you decide to slow to a walk. You can, of course, do it by simply hauling straight back on both reins—and in self-defense the horse will almost certainly fling his head up and thrust his nose out in an effort to save his mouth which you have hurt. But this certainly is not the result we want. We want not only to slow down but to slow down smoothly and in balance, with the horse comfortable, mentally calm, relaxed, and completely under control, ready if we demand it to come to a full stop or even rein back.

This kind of slowdown, smooth and balanced, is achieved by the rider "giving and taking" the reins one at a time; and the principle is the same whether you are using a hackamore, a snaffle or a curb bit. You take the slack out of one rein for a moment or two, then you release it and do the same with the opposite rein. If the horse is wearing a snaffle or a bit, this gentle "sawing" on the reins, which horsemen call "vibrating" the bit, slides the mouthpiece slightly from side to side. This helps to keep the mouth sensitive and relax the jaw, whereas a steady pull on the reins impels a horse to resist the hands and will eventually make his mouth numb.

Perhaps at this point I should remind the reader that when beginning to learn how to use her hands Linda was working Tonka in the hackamore. That means that, except when actually reining, she rode at all times with the reins slightly slack. This is the only right way to use the hackamore; it is strictly a slack-rein instrument—which is one of its limitations.

Even after she had progressed to working Tonka in a snaffle,

Linda continued to ride with loose reins for a long time while she was learning. It takes time and diligent practice to develop a sensitive touch on the reins. Some riders never achieve it. They start wrongly and their bad habits become fixed. Having nobody to correct them—or being too bullheaded to admit their ignorance and take lessons—they usually are not even aware of their faults. They can ride for a lifetime without ever knowing what good hands really are, or what a good mouth is.[1] When, if ever, they eventually hear of "dressage" and perhaps see an exhibition of it, they regard it either as a kind of mysterious black magic or as something worthy only of their scorn because it isn't "practical." For such people, loose-rein riding is the only humane way of riding; anything less crude which they attempted would be merely torture for their unfortunate horses.

My insistence that Linda should ride with slack reins was simply a logical carrying out of Rule Number 1. Thus, to start Tonka walking or to accelerate from a walk to a trot, she simply closed her legs lightly; her hands merely held the slack reins. To slow or halt him she felt the reins, softly "vibrating" the bit, while her legs remained passive.

Gurus who like to make a black art of horsemanship will object here that this seesawing action of the hands on the reins, each hand acting independently yet in unison with the other, is too advanced and too difficult for a beginner to learn right from the start. At a trot, for example, the rider must have a fairly firm seat or his hands will jiggle up and down as well as back and forth, pulling on the horse's mouth. Certainly the rider must have acquired a quite firm seat. That is why I allowed

---

[1] It is my belief that automobile driving has much to do with the prevalence of poor hands among so many horsemen, both young and old. Today almost everybody drives a car; I cannot think of a horse owner of my acquaintance over the age of eighteen who does not, and many of them drive trucks as well as passenger cars. Most good drivers form the habit of gripping the steering wheel quite firmly; this is particularly true of younger drivers who have gone through driver training programs, such as those conducted by many high schools. Even with power steering, there is little reason to develop sensitivity of touch. This heavyhandedness, I am convinced, carries over when the experienced car driver mounts a horse. Generally, his hands are rarely as good as those of a younger rider who has not yet learned to drive cars.

Linda no reins in the beginning and why I stressed sitting down relaxed with never a mention of posting at the trot. That is how one develops a firm seat. The fact that the rider uses his hands alternately, one taking while the other gives, is no valid reason for considering the action difficult. One might as logically argue that a student driver should not be expected to keep a car on the road by moving the steering wheel from side to side. For the action of the hands, whether they are holding a steering wheel or reins, is practically the same.

Driving Aids Good Hands. Driving is one of the best preliminary skills to help a novice progress in the art of riding. It aids a pupil in developing sensitive hands without having to worry about his seat; which, on horseback, is the basis of good hands. Unfortunately, if wrongly taught, driving can also have quite the opposite effect, teaching a youngster to hang on the reins and to rely on heavy, pulling hands, two things that will ruin any horse's mouth. Today, relatively few horsemen understand the art of driving— without a steering wheel. This is why some trainers do not approve of driving green colts, while others who try it get poor results: they just don't know how to drive. Learn to do it right or not at all.

The longer I ride and the more I teach riding, the more firmly I am convinced that learning to do things correctly from the very beginning is the quickest and surest way to success. If certain basic lessons sometimes seem difficult, mastering them will almost never be as difficult as the later correction of entrenched bad habits. The old saw, "Practice makes perfect," cuts both ways—perfectly good and perfectly bad.

Linda's only difficulty in learning to use the reins resulted from her own forgetfulness. As long as she followed instructions, using both reins but only one at a time, and reined with light pulls and quick slacks, she had no trouble; Tonka responded as I had schooled him to do. But after about a month of work in the ring Linda began to take results for granted.

Growing careless, she fell into the habit of stopping on only one rein—after all, if one pull gets results, why follow up with another one?—and she forgot my repeated warning, "You must slack *quickly, instantly*." The pony's stops and turns slowed down; his halts became crooked as well as slower. Linda tried to correct him (instead of correcting herself) by pulling harder and by "holding" him with the reins to enforce prompter obedience—a fatal mistake, a flagrant violation of the vital principle of pull-and-slack. Almost before she knew it—even before I realized what was going wrong—Linda had "hackamore trouble," an affliction much more common than is usually realized, particularly by those who suffer from it.

One thing should be clearly understood here: The fact that a horse can merely be ridden in a hackamore—as he could be ridden in a halter or with a rope around his jaw—does not make him a hackamore horse. A true hackamore horse must be as light in the hackamore as later he should be in the bridle.

When Linda began riding him, Tonka was that light. I could handle him with the reins looped over my little fingers. However, you can make only a few mistakes before a pony realizes that he can "go through" a hackamore. Once he learns this and develops the fault, it's hard to cure. Usually he must be started all over, and sometimes that fails to work. Switching to a snaffle may be the only solution.

When I saw that Tonka had lost his lightness in the hackamore and was even actively resisting the reins, I called a complete halt to the schooling. Grounding Linda, I went back to work on the young stallion myself.

Discarding the hackamore, I worked him for several days in a snaffle. In addition to the regular reins, I also used draw reins. The only times I employed the draw reins, however, were at those moments when Tonka showed resistance. This is the only way draw reins should ever be used, always in conjunction with ordinary reins. Used as a powerful corrective, they reinforce the regular reins, not replace them. The trainer should use them as lightly and as little as possible, just enough to overcome the horse's resistance and not a bit more. If the rider relies on them to do the work of the regular reins, draw reins will almost certainly cause the horse to develop a faulty head carriage and to learn to get behind the bit, an error that can happen so quickly that the rider may not even be aware of it until the damage is done.

As soon as I had broken down the colt's resistance I switched back to the hackamore. In a week Tonka had regained his former lightness.

"You see," I told Linda, perhaps unnecessarily, "he wasn't doing anything wrong. You were. Now don't goof him up again. Do it right."

However, Linda, acutely aware of her own failure now and anxious to "do it right," developed a bad case of jitters. Tense and nervous, trying too hard, she began to do almost everything wrongly. My explanations and attempts to correct her seemed only to confuse her. Her confusion and nervousness conveyed themselves to the pony. Linda rode him only three times before Tonka was worse than ever; the young stallion showed very plainly that he was getting fed up with the whole business. During the third session in the ring his fermenting resentment exploded. Remembering how easily he had got rid of Sheilagh, the gray pony suddenly bogged his head and went to bucking. Luckily, Linda managed to stay with him for the half dozen jumps he got in before my bellowed, "No!" spooked him into throwing up his head and breaking into a gallop. "Pull him!" I shouted, and Linda hauled back on one rein, circling the pony and finally getting him stopped.

The girl was thoroughly frightened, and I didn't blame her. Riding a bucker is not the sort of thing that bolsters a novice's self-confidence. For her to dismount immediately, however, would have been the worst thing she could have done, harmful not only to her own self-confidence but to Tonka's notion that to get his own way all he had to do was pitch. Unless we ridded him of that idea, his usefulness as a child's mount would be ended before it had even begun.

"Stay with him," I advised Linda. "Never mind reining. Just keep him moving. Trot him around the ring a few times. If he tries it again, pull his nose around to your knee and spin him. But stay on him."

Linda obeyed. She was scared stiff, but you couldn't have guessed it watching her. One of her great assets as a rider is courage. She can make herself do what she is afraid to do—and anyone who has never been afraid on horseback either has very little experience or has very little common sense.

Then I mounted the stallion, with blood in my eye, determined to teach him a lesson he'd never forget. I *wanted* him to buck. I realized that the young stallion's bucking had been simply a show of resentment at the way my daughter had been handling him; I did not really blame Tonka. Nevertheless, I knew, he would have to learn to put up with something less than perfection by his rider, as every child's pony must—and every adult rider's horse as well. This is an imperfect world, and nobody can fit into it very well if, when things go a bit wrong, he can think of no better solution than throwing a temper tantrum.

Alas, I might as well have saved my blood and thunder for another day. A successful lesson needs two—one to teach and one to learn. Tonka cannily declined the role of learner. The instant I mounted he made it plain that he knew the complete score by heart. Undoubtedly he sensed my mood, for he was on his best behavior. I put him through every movement he had been taught, and he responded beautifully. No one has ever called Tonka a fool.

I gave him a good workout, and he wasn't so frisky when I stepped off and handed the reins to Linda. She mounted and put him through a repeat performance—and you may be sure that this time she was careful how she handled those reins.

This experience finally convinced me of something I had been reluctant to admit—that the hackamore is not a very suitable instrument for a novice rider. Though on the surface it may seem rather illogical, a rider has a wider margin of error when using a snaffle then he has with a hackamore; in other words, he can make more mistakes, have less trouble correcting them and still get good results in his training.

Superficially, this seems illogical because a snaffle works on a colt's sensitive mouth while a hackamore leaves the mouth untouched. This is why so many riders who lack real knowledge look on the hackamore as being very mild, merely a kind of halter that can be pulled on quite hard without harm to the horse and without detriment to his schooling. This conception of the hackamore, however, is completely false. When used without finesse, it is anything but mild. For, contrary to the common idea that the hackamore works on a horse's nose— an idea shared by some hackamore horsemen who do not have the capacity to reflect upon and analyze their own methods— the big "bite" of the hackamore is on the lower part of the sharp jawbones that jut out above the chin and taper upward toward the throat. A horse has only a thin layer of flesh here; there is little more than skin stretched over the sharp bones. It is this extremely sensitive area that must be kept in mind when fitting a hackamore. The more snugly the bosal is adjusted around the muzzle and the stiffer it is, the more severe is the effect on the sensitive jawbones of a pull on the reins. A rider's lack of understanding on this point is why so many hackamore colts are "skinned up" and eventually ruined. It takes only a few hard pulls to break the skin over those sharp jawbones.

If, as is commonly thought, the nose were the vulnerable part, a hackamore horse pulled too hard or jerked by the reins would not shoot his nose up; he would learn to avoid the punishment by tucking his nose in, overbending. But such an abused horse throws his head up to avoid the pain concentrated on his sharp lower jawbones. This pain can be much more severe than the discomfort of a thick, smooth snaffle pulled up against the corners of the lips. The soft lips give and stretch to pressure; the jawbones cannot. Thus, a good hackamore horseman needs extremely sensitive hands as well as great tact. And this is asking a bit too much of the average novice rider.

Therefore, I decided that there was no point, but there might be grave risk, in any further work toward developing Tonka into a finished hackamore horse.

If I had it to do over, I would not have put a hackamore on the gray colt at all, except to correct his faults on the longe. I would start him in the snaffle. I believe that this would have saved time—which is not important—and made the task of learning easier for Linda, which is important.

CHAPTER XVII

Bits: The Horse's Mouth

THERE is such a variety of snaffles on the market that a discussion of schooling is rather pointless unless we first agree on what a good training snaffle is, what types to avoid, and why.

There are snaffles with corrugated mouthpieces, twisted wire snaffles, rather thin triangular snaffles, Springsteen snaffles for strong-armed he-men whose horses mysteriously turn out to be hard to control, snaffles with thick hollow mouthpieces, and some with two mouthpieces designed to act like nutcrackers. I have seen a snaffle, designed by a self-styled "trainer" of jumping horses, with a mouthpiece that was simply a length of sprocket chain salvaged from a bicycle. As a mouth-mangler, it was almost as efficient as a ripsaw.

These various styles come in different sizes with mouthpieces of various thicknesses and rings of different diameters, some of them too small.

A snaffle suitable for training colts is above everything else, in my opinion, *mild*. If it isn't that, why use a snaffle at all? If you need a more severe bit to start a colt in, use a curb—and admit that there is something wrong with the colt or something wrong with you.

This pre-eminent quality of mildness automatically eliminates snaffles with corrugated, triangular, or twisted-wire mouth-pieces, as well as those that are so thin they resemble the bridoon of a Weymouth bridle. Very rarely, some of these types may be useful in reforming spoiled horses or ponies or in correcting certain faults of a poor mouth or a defective head carriage; but none of these faults should be found in a colt just being started.

Taffy, All Tied Up. This is how I tie a snaffle high in a colt's mouth to keep him from learning how to get his tongue over the bit or stick his tongue out one side of his mouth. The middle of the cord is tied at the joint of the snaffle; the ends are knotted midway up the colt's face, then tied to the browband of the bridle. I first do this when introducing a colt to the snaffle at feeding time; he learns to eat his grain with the bit in his mouth, which helps him to forget about it. I continue to tie the bit during the first few weeks of mounted schooling. After that I can confidently forget about tongue-over-the-bit.

The second mark of a good snaffle is that it is so designed as not to abrade the corners of a colt's lips or to slip halfway through its mouth when the rider pulls one rein. Either or both of these accidents can happen, however, if the rings are too small (less than two and one-half inches in diameter) or unless the bit has cheeks designed to prevent just this or is equipped with leather or rubber guards to protect the lips. Snaffles suitable for small ponies may have proportionately small rings, less than two and one-half inches in diameter, but should always have cheeks or guards.

Lacking either, a snaffle can be kept in position fairly well by running a curb strap through the rings and buckling it snugly, not tightly, under the jaw. Preferably, however, rings should be large. D-rings and eggbutts are less likely to abrade the corners of the mouth than plain round rings.

The Drop Noseband. Years ago a pupil brought me a mare that had a confirmed habit of resisting the bit by opening her mouth wide, twisting her jaw askew, balling her tongue, getting it over the bit and sticking it out the side of her mouth. Green colts often develop the same habits under a rider whose hands aren't very good. I told the pupil, "Get a drop noseband." He did. But at our next lesson he looked at me reproachfully. "Fifteen dollars for just two little straps!" he said. "Boy, I picked the wrong hobby!" A drop noseband, however, is a great aid in schooling, and there are economical substitutes quite as effective as the real thing. Here is Tonka wearing one that costs practically nothing. It is simply a rubber "O"-ring that happens to fit his muzzle just right—if it were too tight or too large, it wouldn't be any good. A leather curb strap makes a very practical adjustable noseband. Buckle it around the muzzle just above the bit snugly enough to admit two fingers—the bit will keep it on. A horse will soon give up trying to open his mouth when he finds out that he can't.

In the beginning the method of handling the reins is exactly the same as when using a hackamore—one rein at a time, with very light pulls and quick slacks. The colt is taught to go on loose reins, fully extended and quite relaxed, mentally calm. Then we depart from the hackamore method of reining: very gradually we take the slack out of the reins, beginning to ride on light contact. This riding on contact prepares the colt for the vital lesson of learning to go "on the bit," a lesson on which all more advanced training is based.

"On the bit" is a term from a foreign language, as far as almost all Western riders are concerned. There are stock horse trainers, professionals of long standing, who cannot put a horse

Draw Reins: Strong Medicine. On a few occasions early in his schooling Tonka showed a bit too enthusiastically that he liked to run, and he could really pick 'em up and lay 'em down. A couple of times he caught Linda by surprise. To remind him that she was the rider and that the rider sets the pace Linda rode him in draw reins a few times and let him know unmistakably when she wanted him to stop. As the picture shows, draw reins work like pulleys. The reins are fastened to the cinch rings and run up through rollers in the snaffle (or through the rings of an ordinary snaffle) to the rider's hands. A strong pull on either rein can haul the horse's nose all the way around to the rider's knee; a pull on both reins can draw his chin into his breast. He can't throw his head up to avoid the bit; the rider can easily pull it down. Polo horses are often ridden in draw reins. If overused, draw reins can teach a horse the evasive trick of overbending, a ruinous habit. Note that Linda has ordinary reins in addition to the draw reins. The draw reins are the emergency brake, used only as a last resort. At this time Tonka was still a stallion and not quite three years old.

on the bit. They not only don't know how to do it; they have no clear understanding of what being on the bit means. Reared in the cult of the loose rein, they are unable to analyze, for example, why a horse pokes his nose up or throws his head in resistance to the bit. Their only remedies for such faults are gimmicks—tiedowns, wire nosebands, draw reins, short running martingales—contraptions designed to *force* a colt to do what he should be schooled to do.

I remember one of these industrious gadgeteers who invented what he considered the world's best hackamore: in place of a heel knot it was equipped with a sawed-off doorknob. I have known riders to try to lower a high head by whacking a horse on the poll. Only the other day I read an article by a well-known professional on how to teach a horse to rein back. After airing some general theories on the subject, he explained in detail how he, as a judge, wanted to see a horse rein back. On the surface, his ideas seemed sound and sensible. But when he switched from theory to practice, explaining the various methods he often used with "difficult" horses—using the bit roughly "if necessary," whipping a horse across the forelegs, and so on—all his fine theories and lofty ideals came apart at the seams, the gaps revealing the mind of a commercially successful trainer who didn't know what he was talking about.

I am not against gimmicks if they are effective; that is, if they accomplish exactly and permanently the precise results we want. Strictly, almost every item of horse gear that isn't purely decorative may be termed a gimmick designed to help us achieve certain results. But the only really effective way to develop a horse's mouth, or to lower a high head or raise a low one, or to teach a horse to rein back, or to do anything else well is to put the horse on the bit. After a colt has been ridden enough to understand simple rein cues, this is the first task a knowing trainer sets out to do—and it cannot be done by staying out of the horse's mouth on loose reins while riding with your feet shoved forward to his elbows.

Putting a horse on the bit is greatly a matter of feel. It depends not only on the individual animal's responsiveness but even more on the rider's own sensitivity. With practice a rider can develop his hand and leg sensitivity to a very high degree, but an inexperienced rider is almost certain to meet a number of failures before he finally succeeds. Such temporary setbacks should not discourage a young rider; he should remember that the same thing happens to everybody. Patience and practice are necessary.

Linda found this step in training very difficult. Reflection leads me to believe that this was chiefly because she did not understand clearly the results to expect; somehow, I failed to put over in a way that she could grasp precisely what would happen, how Tonka would feel to her, once he started moving on the bit. This is not easy to convey to someone who has never experienced it, but as simply as I can put it into words this is what happens:

In response to the urging of the rider's legs, the horse extends, going up against the bit smoothly and softly. He yields to the resistance of the bit by relaxing his lower jaw, flexing as he "chews" on the bit. This soft relaxation of the jaw results in relaxation of the muscles along the spine from the poll to the croup—if the jaw is stiff, the horse will be stiff all over. In this state, the horse is soft and supple; he moves lightly, delicately balanced, the movements of the hindquarters unified with those of the forehand.

It is the rider's task to feel immediately when the horse responds like this and promptly to reward him with a momentary cessation of all hand and leg action. Then again the rider fixes his hands and urges with his legs to repeat the flexion. This fleeting process is repeated over and over. Neither horse nor rider is ever passive or static. It is a constantly changing state of flux as mount and rider communicate with each other, giving and taking, yielding and demanding. The more highly trained the horse is, the more readily he flexes and the longer his response lasts to a single demand, a mere closing of the legs and of the fingers, by the rider. When horse and rider are in almost-perfect accord (I realize the futility of talking about perfection), the horse appears to work entirely on his own with the rider completely passive.

It should be stressed here that riding a horse on the bit has absolutely nothing to do with riding in a high state of collection and even less with "setting" his head in a certain predetermined position. When a horse is light and supple, proper position of the head takes care of itself automatically; it depends on what the horse is doing and on the animal's individual conformation. A long-striding jumper galloping over a course of big obstacles or a stock horse sliding to a quick stop can be as well on the bit as a dressage horse performing the passage. Not to realize this must lead inevitably to errors in training.

The first preliminary to putting a colt on the bit is to teach him to *accept* the bit. While he learns to respect it, he should never be given reason to fear it. That is why we begin with a mild bit, a smooth thick snaffle that the most sensitive colt won't be afraid to go into. Contrary to popular ideas about "the velvet mouth," we want to teach the colt to go up to the bit, accepting a firm support from the rider's hands. A horse that won't do this has not been schooled to have a good mouth. He has, in fact, no mouth at all. He remains always behind the bit or over it. When reined to turn, slow down or halt, he does one or more of three things:

He shoots his nose out and flings his head up.

He forcibly thrusts his head forward and downward, boring on the bit.

He lowers his head, arching his neck, and tucks his chin in toward his breast.

Whatever evasion he resorts to, the horse will open his mouth, with the lower jaw stiff and contracted.

All these reactions are efforts to avoid the bit, which the colt has not been taught to accept. This is the outstanding fault of the loose-rein system of training. It explains why we so often see stock horses that are anything but soft-mouthed and that fling their heads up the instant they feel the bit.

In contrast, a horse that has been taught to accept the bit

can be ridden either on contact or with the reins slack. If loose-reined, when the rider closes his legs and takes up the slack, the horse knows what to expect, has no fear of the bit, and knows what to do.

The best gait at which to begin teaching the colt to accept his bit is a slow trot. At the trot a horse moves his head back and forth very little, hardly at all, whereas at a walk as well as at the lope or canter the back-and-forth movement of the head is considerable, so that to maintain contact the rider must move his hands correspondingly, opening and closing his elbow and shoulder joints as if his arms were springs or rubber bands. To do this well, maintaining a smooth, even contact with the horse's mouth, neither jerking the reins nor letting them slacken, is not quite as simple as it may sound; in fact, many other-wise good riders cannot do it consistently. So to keep things as simple as possible, begin this lesson with the colt at a slow trot.

Ride with loose reins until the colt is thoroughly warmed up and going well. Then gradually take the slack out of the reins until you feel the lightest contact with his mouth. At this point fix your hands: however much your body may move with the motion of the trotting gait, your hands should become ab-solutely fixed *in relation to the horse's mouth*. Tension on the reins should be unvarying. With hands thus fixed, leg the colt into his bridle, urging him to take hold of the bit.

The rider should use his legs not in a steady, constant pres-sure but by intermittently squeezing at about every second or third stride. The legs should remain in their normal position near the girth, not moved to the rear.

Precisely how a colt reacts when he feels this first light re-sistance of the bit depends not only on how skillful the rider is but on the animal's individual temperament and how thus far he has been "broken" or schooled.

A green colt, having a sensitive mouth, usually recoils from the bit; he may open his mouth and perhaps arch his neck slightly. The rider must not make the grievous mistake of taking up the slack in the reins by moving his hands back toward his

177

body. That is the easiest way to teach a colt to overbend, get behind the bit and eventually go over it—a ruinous habit very difficult to cure if a horse becomes confirmed in it. Instead, keeping his hands in place, the rider must vigorously use his legs to make the colt extend and "reach for the bit." In other words, the rider gets the slack out of the reins not by pulling the bit back to the horse but by urging the horse forward again to meet the bit.

This one fundamental of schooling cannot be over-emphasized: *All the action of putting the horse on the bit*—and later the action of collecting him in any degree—*works from the rear to the front;* never, never from front to rear. The principle applies even to stops and rein-backs. The rider initiates the action, creating impulsion, with his legs. His hands simply accept the impulsion created. A horse lacking impulsion (which should not be confused with mere forward movement) leaves the rider nothing to work on. Such a horse is as useless as an automobile without an engine. All he can do is coast.

A mature horse or pony accustomed to being ridden always on slack reins will, of course, probably pull down to a walk or even abruptly halt, for that is what he has been taught to do when the rider takes up the slack. Anticipating this, the rider should instantly and firmly push the horse on, if necessary making him trot a bit faster. He should *not* move his hands forward, giving the horse more rein. By slowing or halting, the horse has already slacked the reins and evaded the bit. The rider, with hands fixed, should push him back up to it.

If the horse, slowing or stopping, also flings his head up or forcibly thrusts his muzzle out and downward in an effort to take more rein, the rider must not give an inch. With hands and arms fixed rock-firm, he should let the horse bump himself in the mouth and energetically leg him back into the trot. The rule here is: unyielding hands and strong, active legs.

It took Linda only a few trials to get the idea over to Tonka; obeying her legs, he accepted the bit quite casually. You may achieve the same result even more quickly, or it may take you longer. Forget time; it doesn't matter. Only final results matter.

But however long it may take, if the rider is patient and persists, eventually any colt and even a spoiled horse will give in, accepting the light pressure of the bit without fuss. The rider should be satisfied with very little progress at a time; if a colt merely tries without fully succeeding in a lesson, the rider is doing well. Then he should be prompt to reward with a few moments respite from schooling, letting the colt relax. Then begin again. Repeat, repeat, repeat, but only for brief periods at a time. Never overdo it. Keep the colt fresh. Quit while he is still ready for more.

This vital secret of successful schooling, incidentally, was a difficult lesson for Linda to learn. When I told her to do something, she would go on doing it indefinitely with the monotonous regularity of a clock, waiting for me to tell her when to stop. It took her quite a long time to realize that Tonka could become bored repeating the same exercises over and over and that then the schooling ceased to be of any benefit. This is not uncommon among young pupils; they learn to rely too much on their instructor to do all their thinking for them, while they merely do as they're told. A good instructor must anticipate this; he should encourage independent thinking even if at times it goes contrary to some of his own ideas.

After the colt is confirmed in his acceptance of the bit at all gaits, even to the extent of possibly "going through" his bridle, beginning to pull a little, he is ready to be put on the bit.

Now the rider's hands, as already mentioned, must become more active. Our aim now is to get the colt to relax his lower jaw, not merely accepting the bit but yielding to its lightest pressure and to do this *without losing impulsion*. To accomplish this the rider must co-ordinate his hand and leg actions to a greater degree than when riding merely on contact. But we still follow our original rule: Hands without legs; legs without hands. Later, with practice, a diligent rider naturally learns to use his hands and legs simultaneously; but until that comes naturally we can forget it.

With the colt trotting along on light contact, the rider begins to move the snaffle slightly from side to side of the mouth.

"*Final Exam,*" *For Fun. Here are a couple of tests you might like to try on you own horse. They will tell you what kind of mouth he really has. The second test will surely reveal how good your own hands are. Remember that you must maintain contact.*

In the first photograph (above, left) Linda is riding Tonka in a mild snaffle; in place of reins she is using a rubber band—that's right, a rubber band. For the technically minded, and for sceptics, the rubber is an eighth of an inch in diameter and durometer tests 50±5. In plain English, that means it is elastic enough for any horse to do as he pleases while hardly feeling the bit, particularly a snaffle. In these "reins" Tonka responds to all cues at all gaits and will rein back.

The second photograph (above, right) shows Linda executing a volte at the trot in reins that are anything but elastic (page 181, left). These reins are made of brown paper and thread. A ten-inch length of thread about six inches from the bit connects the two portions of each rein. These

He does this by gently increasing the tension on one rein while letting the opposite rein slacken slightly, then reversing the action. The movement is a soft, gradual seesawing of the bit in the horse's mouth done by merely closing the fingers of one hand on the rein while relaxing those of the opposite hand. The bit moves less than an inch in the horse's mouth.

If these gentle vibrations do not induce the horse to relax his jaw, the rider may resort to half-halts, gently shaking the bit with little pulls and slacks. These light, repeated pulls-and-slacks move the bit up and down as well as from side to side in the

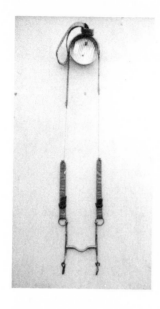

reins once belonged to Lt. Col. M. F. McTaggart, who used them to demonstrate what a schooled horse could do; they are pictured in his book The Art of Riding. *In these fragile reins Tonka will do anything he will do in leather reins. In fact, Linda was amazed to learn that he would do it better. The discovery quite deflated her. She had worked so hard to develop good hands—only to find out suddenly that Tonka was way ahead of her, much more sensitive than she had realized.*

The fourth photograph (above, right) shows Tonka reining back in the paper-and-thread reins.

Try this exercise with your horse. You may find the test an eye opener.

mouth. The rider must be very careful not to let these pulls degenerate into jerks. The reins should never fall slack.

Naturally, most horses when reined in this way tend to slow down. The rider should immediately relax his hands and urge with his legs to maintain the pace; then try again.

If the colt merely opens his mouth, he is not relaxing his jaw. On the contrary, a horse softly on the bit does not open his mouth at all. He "smiles." He chews softly on the bit, his lips closed but the lower jaw mobile, active.

Even riders of limited experience, if they have any sensitivity at all, can feel when a horse moves on the bit; it's a feeling difficult to mistake, similar to the feeling one experiences when riding a lively stallion as he sights another stallion or a mare. Suddenly, all the horse's movements become light, springy, almost as if he is hardly touching the ground. The movements of the hindquarters synchronize with those of the forehand. The horse moves in airy balance as if completely free.

At first, this lightness may last for only a few moments, and then you must begin again. But once you have achieved this, and can do it consistently, everything else becomes easy. You are in harmony with your mount, and you know at last what true horsemanship means.

CHAPTER XVIII

Do You Really Want to School?

"Most people do not ride; they are conveyed."

This weighty maxim, uttered by a great English horseman, Lieutenant Colonel M. F. McTaggart, condenses a whole philosophy into a single sentence.

I ask you to ponder this quotation, then reflect on your own horsemanship and the kind of horsemanship you see about you.

If you do, I think that you will soon realize a fact which is not always at first obvious: Schooling is not for everyone. First, it is a solitary task; it lacks any aspect of competition. You only complicate it, at least for the horse, by having company. It is repetitious and often routine, the sort of riding many persons would consider a drudging bore rather than fun.

The fact remains, however, that schooling and only schooling makes a finished horseman. No matter how good a rider appears to be when suitably mounted on a well-schooled horse, unless he can make a horse he is not a finished horseman. It's not merely a matter of natural aptitude or talent; it is even more a matter of temperament.

I recall a perfect example of this, an attractive young girl who came to me for riding lessons. A fairly experienced Western rider, she was determined to learn to "ride English." She wanted me to give her a quick cram course in the fundamentals of "flat saddle riding" so that she could show her half-Arab pleasure horse in a show scheduled nine days from the date of our first lesson.

I gave her eight daily one-hour lessons, covering as many points of "English riding" as I felt she and her mount could absorb. Rather to my surprise, that girl mastered every lesson. Her own riding, as well as her horse's way of going, improved 100 per cent. I have never had another pupil who listened so attentively, worked so hard, carried out instructions so well, and caught on so fast. She was that rare sort of pupil who makes teaching sheer delight.

With eight lessons to bolster her confidence, the young lady took her horse to the show and entered six classes. The pair brought home five ribbons. I am not implying that five placings in six classes is valid proof of the rider's skill or the horse's quality. The way shows are run and the way most classes are judged, I don't think ribbons mean much. But in one class an incident occurred that does illustrate how far this horse and rider had progressed as a result of only a week's concentrated work. The judge called for a canter and the horse got off on the wrong lead. My pupil was not experienced enough to feel this, but her fiancé at ringside spotted the fault immediately. As she rode past him, he called out, "Wrong lead!" Cantering on the straight, the girl cued her mount for a flying change, and the horse changed promptly. A week earlier neither one of them would have known what to do.

I congratulated myself on having acquired a most promising pupil. I took it for granted that, having had her appetite for knowledge whetted, she'd be back for more lessons. But that was the last I saw of her for weeks. Then one day we met again, and I was curious enough to ask why she had never come back. The idea had occurred to me that her reasons might be economic. I was prepared to cut my fees for a pupil of such promise.

Her reply flattened me. English riding, she informed me, was "too hard," requiring too much physical effort and too much mental concentration from both the rider and the horse. "When I ride," she said, "I like to just enjoy myself, relax. I want the horse to take care of himself so I can have some fun."

"Isn't it fun," I asked, "to feel your horse moving in perfect balance and instantly responsive to your lightest cue?"

She nodded. "But it's too much work."

"But no one rides on the bit all the time," I said. "Of course you relax and let the horse go on loose reins. The point is, if you have schooled your horse——"

"I know. But it's too much work."

"Then why," I asked, "did you want to learn to 'ride English' in the first place?"

"Just to prove to myself that I could do it," she said, "and to prove it to my boyfriend."

A few months ago I saw this girl at a show. Riding the same horse, she was competing in Western classes. As we were talking, she happened to mention that she was having a great deal of difficulty getting the horse to rein back. She and the horse, carefully avoiding "too much work," had backslid to their starting point.

I have dwelled on this incident in some detail because it is so tragically common, typical, among young horsemen, many of whom show real promise—which they never even come close to fulfilling because for them riding remains always only a physical exercise. Once they discover that skilled horsemanship must be learned the hard way and cannot be mastered merely by reading or listening to a few cure-all rules or using Ike Wizard's Special Superduper Gyroscopic Balanced Saddle or Louie Tamale's Peruvian Plated Bit, they lose whatever ambition they might have had. Happiness for them is attending short-cut "clinics" conducted by shrewd showmen who understand their featherbrained customers perfectly. Happiness is being the life of the weekend trail rides while the horse slops along with the reins dangling to his knees, "taking care of himself." Happiness is wearing out the seat of the breeches against the saddle while the brain remains dormant.

Such gregarious "fun on horseback" riders are hopeless as

far as fine horsemanship is concerned, for they refuse to give it the necessary time and thought. As a result, their horses are perpetually out of luck, never given the benefit of intelligent schooling. Often, the horses have nothing to do from Monday to Friday but loaf; then over the weekend they are ridden into the ground. The animals go through life in a state of constant confusion. For some mistake the rider chose to overlook yesterday the horse will be punished for repeating tomorrow. Riders of this type usually "love" horses and consider themselves kind masters, when actually they are heartlessly cruel. They make their horses' lives miserable.

I say such riders are cruel because they make "problem horses," horses that have problems and horses that *are* problems. With the exception of difficulties that arise from faulty temperament, practically all the problems we have with horses and ponies are the direct results of faulty schooling. Often we fail to realize this because when things go wrong, we are apt to attack the problem from two very common angles. Too many of us like to jump to the conclusion that the horse is stupid or stubborn. If we are less cocksure and more broadminded, we wonder, "Is my riding all right? Am I doing something wrong?" I would suggest saving both of these approaches until later. I think the first question always to ask yourself is, "How clearly am I *communicating* with the horse?" For it makes little difference how smart or how dumb the horse may be or how well or how badly we ride if we cannot clearly convey to the animal what we want him to do.

This approach often requires us to make some radical changes in our established pattern of thinking—not always an easy thing to do. Most of us, for example, think of the bit as an instrument of forcible control, though we may prefer not to admit it. We say that some horses have snaffle mouths while others are difficult or impossible to control without a severe curb or a halfbreed or a spade bit—then we can really "set 'em up"! In other words, we are thinking in terms of forcing a horse to obey. There are infrequent times in training when a certain amount of force judiciously applied may get good results—as when a horse knows quite well what we want him to do but decides that right now he doesn't want to do it, and he practically dares us to make him; or when we are up against a spoiled horse that has been allowed to have his own way because his bluffs have never been called. However, as a general rule, with most horses we shall get much better results if we quit thinking in terms of force and concentrate on clearly conveying to the animal's understanding what we wish him to do.

If we can train ourselves to do this, eventually our whole concept of what skilled horsemanship is will undergo a radical change; the results we achieve will convince us beyond any doubt. For in ultimate results there is no parity between the two methods. A horse strong-armed into obedience is nothing but an unwilling slave, and his whole manner shows it. But a horse schooled with patience, sympathy and good humor develops into a comrade willing to do almost anything you ask because you have built up his confidence in you.

To those who have never tried it, perhaps, this way of schooling may seem to be slower in getting results than the rough-and-ready way of doing things. Actually, however, in the long run it is much faster. Iron fists and strong arms can never achieve what finesse will.

Even if this were not true, ask yourself: What's the rush? When you consider that a healthy horse or pony might well live an active life of twenty years or even longer, and during that time he can give you either a great deal of pleasure or a lot of exasperating trouble, what is a little extra time spent in getting him started right?

Intelligent schooling is more than a matter of doing. It is first of all a matter of *planning*. In at least a general way, you should have a fairly clear over-all plan, a good idea of the final results you want. This plan should be flexible, tailored to suit the individual colt or horse. It should get to work on first things *first*. Here is an example: When I started Tonka, the first necessary step was to quell his over-aggressive cockiness, which inept handling had permitted him to develop to the point of being dangerous. Until this was accomplished—calling all his bluffs and trumping them and generally cutting him down to proper size—any systematic schooling was out of the question. Thus, if you have a very high-strung colt, your first task will be to calm him down. If he is sluggish (and you know he is in good health), you may have to get him up on his toes. How you handle these preliminary problems is an index to your grasp of pony or horse psychology and a test of your equestrian tact.

Some of the questions you should ask yourself at the beginning of schooling are:

Do you want a show pony or a practical "using horse," a specialist or a versatilist?

How far do you wish to carry the schooling? There are three general categories, though they may overlap to some extent:

Basic——This is as far as most horses and ponies ever get, because it's only as far as the average rider knows how to take them. The riding is crude, completely lacking finesse. The horse is ridden on loose reins, except when the rider pulls them to turn, slow or halt. Control of the gaits is limited to tapping, kicking, or spurring the horse into a faster pace and to pulling on the reins to slow down. Reining back is done by pulling, without leg aids, and the horse may or may not back straight. Starting a lope or canter, the horse takes whichever lead he prefers. Ideally, the horse should be calm and relaxed to the point of laziness.

Intermediate——At this level a horse will impress most riders, as well as most horse show judges, as an excellently schooled mount, much better than he actually is. He will go well on light contact and he can be rated; that is, the rider can decrease or increase speed at any gait by taking with his hands and squeezing with his legs. The horse will back softly and straight any number of steps the rider demands, but without flexions. He is responsive to the legs as well as to the hands, can be moved sidewise, and will do turns on the forehand, the center or the haunches. At the canter or gallop the rider can start him on either lead but must drop to a trot or a walk to get a change of leads. The horse can be moderately collected but not so much that he can do small circles without discomfort. Transition between gaits is fairly smooth but marked by a stride or two of the trot between the walk and the gallop; otherwise, it is likely to be jerky. A good horse schooled to this level can be shown successfully in performance and in horsemanship classes. The overwhelming majority of show horses in this country are schooled only to this level, and many fall well short of it. Often neither the riders nor the judges are aware of it.

Advanced—A horse schooled to this high level may be likened to a masterpiece of art: he is not for everyone. Even if you will be content with a very small profit, you won't find many buyers, or even connoisseurs who can appreciate him for what he is. He needs at least an intermediate rider—and the rider had better proceed cautiously at first and improve rapidly if he hopes to avoid an accident. "I can guarantee that a horse is perfectly schooled," Colonel M. F. McTaggart once stated. "I cannot guarantee that anyone else can ride him."

The wisdom of this statement was unhappily brought home to me only a few weeks ago. I let a woman—with years of experience in riding, she said—ride Tonka across country. For a few miles all went well; then with explosive suddenness everything went wrong. Even the unlucky rider is not certain about exactly what happened, but suddenly the gray pony burst into a gallop. I suspect that the woman unintentionally applied her legs or used them with a degree of force that she may have considered mild but to which Tonka reacted as he would to an electric shock. The surprised rider, thrown off balance perhaps a bit to one side, may have given an unintentional weight cue, reinforced perhaps by a tug on the reins. Tonka, at full gallop, swerved in a ninety-degree turn. The woman hit the ground with force enough to daze her, breaking her right arm. Tonka immediately stopped and came back to her—an action that convinces me he had not merely run away. No doubt to his understanding the whole accident was very puzzling; he had simply obeyed her aids, and the woman had inexplicably reacted by falling off.

A horse schooled to this degree is a supple athlete; his reactions are much quicker than the average rider's. At this level of training quality of movement is important, lightness imperative. The gaits are rhythmic, elastic, full of impulsion, and the rider can vary any gait from full extension to full collection. At any gait the horse can be halted in a stride, reined back, then resume the interrupted gait or change to another gait, as the rider directs. Horses of this caliber are best exemplified by those that compete in The Three-Day Event of the Olympic Games; they can do anything and do it well, yet they are not specialists in any one field, as show jumpers and dressage horses are. In my opinion, for those of us who enjoy horses and mounted sports for their own sake and aren't in "the business" only for money, this is the ideal to aim at. You may never fully attain your goal, but you'll have fun along the way; and even if you do fall short, you will soon have a horse or pony immeasurably superior to the average nag.

The reason you should ask yourself at the outset how far you want to carry the horse's schooling is simply this: If you wish to go beyond basic or elementary schooling you should from the very beginning train yourself not to *pull* on the horse's mouth, even if the horse is already accustomed to being pulled. If you have developed the habit of pulling on the reins, you must break the habit. Of course, there may be rare moments of emergency when, to save your own neck, you might have

Three Stages of Schooling. In each of these phases (see facing page) of schooling Tonka's mental attitude varies quite as much as his movements do, ranging from lazily relaxed to vigorously alert. At no time should a horse be pushed to a more advanced stage. He must work into it gradually. It takes time; a good trainer needs patience. In even the most advanced stage of schooling never neglect plenty of riding on loose reins, preferably across country. In the ring, work on the bit, even when only slight collection is demanded, should always be followed by brief periods of relaxation on loose reins. These are the "coffee breaks" that keep a horse from going sour.

Basic Schooling

*A slow trot on
loose reins*

Intermediate Schooling

*A medium trot on
light contact*

Advanced Schooling

*A semicollected trot
with the horse on
the bit*

to pull on the reins and pull hard; but, excepting such unusual circumstances, from the very first day of schooling train yourself to control your mount by repeatedly fixing and yielding your hands in conjunction with proper use of your legs. Even horses that have had their mouths abused learn with surprising quickness to respond to a fixed hand; in fact, once they understand what it means, they seem to be grateful to the rider for no longer abusing them. A green colt whose schooling is to go beyond the elementary stage should hardly know how it feels to have his mouth pulled on. If the rider does begin by pulling on the reins, he will soon have to quit it in order to make any progress. Therefore, it is simpler to rely on the fixed hand from the very first lesson.

A final reason you should ask yourself to what level of horsemanship you aspire is that an honest answer will enable you to enjoy horsemanship, in whatever degree you prefer, to the maximum, saving yourself—and your horse—a lot of possible unhappiness and maybe a good deal of money as well.

I dwell on this question, which on the surface may seem to be of less importance than it is, because I have known so many novice riders, mature men and women as well as young people, who liked to delude themselves into believing that they were willing to put in the necessary time and effort to become first-class horsemen when actually they had no greater ambition than to remain just novices or, at best, rather inferior intermediate riders, even though they refused to admit it.

Not long ago a novice horseman came to me with an excellent mare, his pride and joy. He wanted me to school the mare with the goal of developing her into a dressage horse, a specialty for which she showed real promise. At the same time I was to give the owner himself advanced riding lessons so that eventually he would be able to ride her.

He was a man I liked, a personal friend, and he seemed so earnest in his ambition that my desire to help him got the better of my scepticism built up over the years. I warned him, however, that the job would take a long time and that he would have to be patient. He realized that, he said.

Exactly two months after I had started schooling the mare, however, my friend called the whole project off. For a number of reasons, none of them insurmountable obstacles or even really important, he became discouraged, perhaps impatient would be more accurate. I think that one day he suddenly realized that the goal he had set himself was so far off and entailed so much more painstaking work and time than he was able or willing to put into it that the whole idea seemed hopeless. Abandoning his lofty dream, he was content to settle for an ordinary pleasure horse.

This man was lucky. He admitted his error; he had the maturity to face facts squarely. Many young would-be horsemen, however, are not so fortunate because they refuse to face reality. They persist in confusing genuine ambition and determination with their own wishful thinking. Deluding themselves all their lives, they never really enjoy horsemanship as much as they could—and they almost never achieve what should be every true horseman's aim, having a happy, contented horse. Quite the contrary, their horses suffer much abuse through the riders' demanding more than the horses are schooled to give—because that is more than these riders have ever learned how to teach them. It is an unhappy, futile circle circumscribed by self-delusion and wishful thinking.

A couple of years ago I received the following letter from a young woman:

Dear Mr. Young:

The Schooling of the Western Horse to me is a very impressive book. Because you are its author, I decided to write to you for help. You see, I've been interested in horses ever since I can remember. I haven't had any real professional training in riding, training or handling of horses; but I have spent eight or ten years working around them. Horses are the first interest in my life. However, I attended college, received an A.B. in Physical Education and I am now a professional worker in the field of Recreation. I still want to work with horses. I am not financially able to drop everything to attend an academy of horsemanship even if I could find one—and believe me, I wish I could! Is there any such thing as apprenticeship where one could live, work and learn? I wish I could make horses my life. That has been my dream and still is, but I figured that now is the best time for me to begin. I just don't know where or how to start. Please know that I am serious.

This young woman, though she might resent the knowledge, is only one of many. I have received similar letters from, and have talked with, other young dreamers who wanted to make horses their life work—but for various reasons have not. The great majority of them, I know, never will, and that is probably for the best. They can make better livings in other fields and still enjoy horsemanship as a healthful hobby—indeed, they are likely to enjoy it much more as a hobby and as a sport than they would if they had to *work* at the job. But that is of less importance than the fact that almost all these dreamers are kidding themselves. Why I am convinced of this I tried to make clear in my reply to this young woman:

Dear Elizabeth,

Your great desire to make horses your life work is an old problem and one which few people solve; for the solution is as difficult as it is simple, so difficult and simple that it usually seems impractical and sometimes almost impossible. It can be summed up in one sentence: If horses are the first interest in your life and your greatest ambition is to work with them as a profession, subordinate everything else to that one end and follow your heart. That is the only way.

You don't say how old you are, but since you have finished college I assume you are in your early twenties. You have earned a bachelor's degree in physical education, and you say you are "not financially able to drop everything" to attain your goal in life. These facts lead me to doubt that it is your great goal in life. I believe, from experience, that if it were you would already be well on your way to achieving it, or you would have achieved it by this time.

Elizabeth, when people tell you that they want to do something more than anything else in life but have not done it, you can rest assured that they are kidding themselves. For almost all of us accomplish only as much as we really want to accomplish. No matter what we say our big ambition is, we do only those things which we truly want to do. If we never come close to achieving our big ambition, invariably it is because the price is too high and we are unwilling to pay it; the sacrifice is greater than we are willing to make.

When you finished high school you decided to go on to college. Why? Why didn't you go looking for a job with horses? If you had, and had stuck to it, today you might own your own stable. Or did you try, only to find out that being a hired hand in somebody else's barn doesn't pay much? You know the answers; I don't. But I do know that whatever you did, and regardless of your reasons, going to college was a thing you wanted to do more than you wanted to work with horses. This is obvious, for otherwise you would now be working with horses. Others have done it. They had to face the same choice you faced.

I know an old horsewoman who let her marriage and everything else go to pot because they interfered with her one consuming ambition—to own and train horses. Today in her old age she has nothing except her horses. You and I might consider her life barren and lopsided. But she is content. Her horses are all she wants.

I do not think you made a mistake in choosing college. Your degree in physical education should help you to land a job as an instructor at some school that stresses equestrian sports.

When you speak of working with horses, I wonder whether you mean schooling horses or teaching riding. Have you pondered this? In this country it is practically impossible to earn a decent living just schooling horses. To make any profit, or merely break even, you must charge more than most people are willing to spend on or for a horse. You must have a sideline or several sidelines, such as boarding, giving lessons, and so on. Those who have the best angle on this, I believe, are the trainers of cutting horses; they make a lot of their income competing on the horses they have trained for clients. Working with horses really boils down to working with people. Horses are owned by people. You may be an excellent trainer or a poor one, but if you don't satisfy the people who send you horses you can't stay in business.

Finally, but by no means least important, have you objectively and clearly appraised your own talent for this work you say you want to do? Yearning and dreaming, even when based on real determination, are not enough to get by on. You must have some natural talent and you must develop this talent until you have acquired skill. Thousands of young people are "crazy about riding," but relatively few of them ever rise above mediocrity. Merely riding a horse and schooling a horse are very different things, as different as just listening to music and composing it.

Think back and ask yourself what have you accomplished in the past ten years that might prove you have real talent for horsemanship. What have you achieved with your own horses? Have you ever taken a poor horse or a spoiled one and developed him into a better one? If, as you say, you have always been interested in horses, "have spent eight or ten years working around them" (whatever that means), and like the work enough to want to make it your profession, surely you must have accomplished something —but what?

I know of no competent instructors who would take you on as an apprentice. To work with any of the good teachers you would have to pay for the privilege, not expect them to pay you. Afterward, when you faced the problem of making your new knowledge pay off and finding a job, you would be on your own.

I hope that I have not sounded too discouraging and that you will write again and tell me your plans.

But I must have been too discouraging, for I never heard from her again.

CHAPTER XIX

Schooling Clarified

I FIRST thought of calling this chapter *Schooling Simplified*. That has such a comfortably
familiar ring. Americans are so receptive to the simple and
leery of the difficult—*Riding Simplified*, simplified sex, Six Simple Lessons in Kangaroo Boxing, Pogo Stick Jumping Simplified,
and so on. But then I wondered: How can you simplify something that is a simple business to begin with? What I really
want to do is clarify the simplicity of schooling for those who
think it is difficult and complicated.

I have said that schooling, an essential for every horse, is not
for every rider, because so many people enjoy riding as a social
recreation not much different from dancing or picnicking.
However, there is also a large group of riders who shy away
from schooling because they don't really understand how to
go about it. They are rather hazy about what they should do
and would be at an even greater loss if asked to explain why
they should do it—whatever it is.

This chapter is for them. If effective, it should help to put
some professional trainers out of business—including maybe me.

The traditional term for a schooling ring is *manège*, a French
word that can be used in a wider sense than as a place to school
horses, but for our purpose that is sufficient. *Riding school,*

meaning the same thing, connotes usually an indoor ring. Most Western horsemen reflect the rodeo influence in their preference for the term *arena*—and the way some of them proceed with a green horse they should have hungry lions roaming about to provide authentic atmosphere.

Though I habitually use the word *ring*, I am aware that it can be misleading. Who hasn't seen "riding academies" where the enclosure for beginners actually was a circular ring? Sometimes the ring is an oval, like a miniature racetrack. I still sadly remember being asked to inspect a new ring which the proud owner had built by his own hard labor. The board fence, freshly painted, gleamed white in the sun; there were two excellent gates—and no corners. A running track could not have been laid out more carefully.

"How do you like it?" my friend asked, beaming.

I looked at him glumly. "Why did you have to make it oval?"

"I thought it was supposed to be rounded at each end. Most show rings——"

"You wanted a schooling ring. It should have corners." He looked so crestfallen that I tried to cheer him up. "You can correct it easily. Just straighten out the ends."

"Tear 'em down? Dig more holes? After all that work!"

"Then square the corners with a couple of logs placed at right angles on the ground."

But he never did. I must have been too discouraging. The ring still stands, beautifully white and picturesque as seen from the highway, but the oval track inside the fence is covered with grass, for no one ever uses it now. Shortly after our unhappy conversation my friend sold his horses. His hobby now is gardening. I hope no one ever tells him that his tulips look like cowslips. Anyone so easily discouraged could never school a horse, anyhow, no matter what the shape of his ring.

The schooling ring is not to be confused with a breaking pen, a rather small circular enclosure with a high wall and sometimes with a snubbing post in the center. The breaking pen, common on large ranches and used by many Western trainers, is primarily for gentling colts and green horses that have not

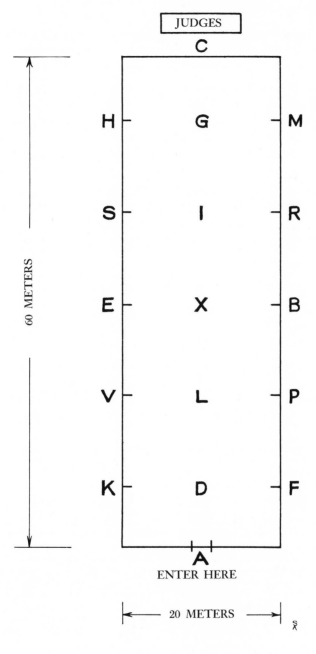

Olympic Games Dressage Ring

been handled much and for working them with a minimum of effort and risk the first few times they are saddled. Such a pen is excellent for giving a frisky horse his first lessons on the longe. He can go only around and around with no corners to duck into, and if the line is long enough he can't pull the trainer's arm off.

The size of the dressage ring used in the Olympic Games is 60 by 20 meters (approximately 195 feet by 65 feet). Since precision is essential in this type of riding, the ring is marked at various points by letters (see page 199). The program to be followed by each contestant is the same. Cantering into the ring at A, he rides to G, halts and salutes the judges, who are outside the ring beyond C. From G the rider walks his horse to C, turns right to M, proceeds to K, and so on throughout the whole ride exactly as the program specifies. The rider, having memorized the program, must change gaits and directions as and where the program calls for each change.[1]

---

[1] Here is a good example of how thoughtlessness can lead us into accepting ideas and practices simply because they are common or have always been done that way:

While writing this chapter I wondered, for the first time in my life, why the standard dressage ring used in the Olympic Games and in international dressage competitions is marked the way it is. I was chagrined to realize that I hadn't the faintest idea. It was something I had unthinkingly accepted.

Having recently read *Horseman's Progress*, a splendid book that should be in every serious horseman's library, I wrote to the author, Vladimir S. Littauer, confessed my ignorance and asked him to enlighten me. I thought that the question would be so simple to Captain Littauer, a former Imperial Russian cavalry officer, that he would probably laugh at me. Imagine my astonishment to receive the following reply from this most knowledgeable expert:

"I have delayed answering your letter because, since I myself did not know the answer to your question, I wanted to consult certain people. Neither Bill Steinkraus [captain of the United States Olympic jumping team], nor two outstanding riding teachers, nor an Austrian High School rider, could tell me why the letters in the Dressage arena are placed the way they are.

"You probably know that Dressage competitions are rather recent, and that in the nineteenth century High School horses were merely demonstrated, primarily in circuses. This is why, in the first equestrian Games of 1912, the conditions for the Dressage test were very different. The arena was smaller (forty meters long) and not lettered. Within ten minutes time limit the rider, at will, had to demonstrate certain school movements at the three gaits. . . . Five jumps were included as well as an obedience test. . . .

"In the Games of 1920 for the first time a lettered arena was introduced. It was shorter than today's (fifty meters) and the time limit was ten minutes.

If a ring of these dimensions seems rather small to you, particularly too narrow—it is. For advanced dressage it is adequate; most of the movements require that the horse be ridden in a state of high collection. Only two gaits in advanced dressage might be described as moderately fast, the extended trot and the extended canter. (Extension at these gaits refers to the swing of the horse's limbs, not to the forward speed at which he moves.) At neither gait will a highly schooled horse under a skillful rider cover ground as fast as a green horse or a reasonably well-schooled hunter moving at a brisk trot or canter. For any real work at a gallop, the standard dressage ring is much too cramped, except perhaps for a very small pony (under 13 hands).

For general schooling purposes, in my opinion, the most practical size for a ring is approximately thirty yards wide by at least sixty yards long; a length of seventy or eighty yards would be an advantage, though more than that maximum would not be. In a ring of about this size you have plenty of room to work at extended gaits and in large circles; you can let an eager young horse go without the grave risk of constantly cramping him (which many riders do without being aware

In Berlin, in 1936, the time limit was seventeen minutes. I am inclined to believe that this time more letters were added.

"I am mentioning the above data to point out that no matter what the original reason for the arena marking was, the order of following the letters was bound to be upset by changing programs—they [the programs] changed, I believe, several times. . . .

"Although probably some very precise Dressage riders may place great emphasis on the official distribution of the letters (through sheer habit), I think in your life and mine the matter is not worth bothering about."

The matter may not be worth bothering about, but the fact that I had never before thought of asking the question did bother me. Even the distinguished company my ignorance put me in—several excellent teachers, an Austrian dressage expert, and an Olympic gold medal winner—could not sooth my bruised ego. It seemed almost incredible that for years I had blindly accepted this oddity simply because it was. It still amazes me that apparently nobody else has ever asked the question. Finally I turned to that fount of equestrian knowledge, my good friend Carson Whitson. His answer flattened me.

"I don't know," Whitson replied. "And I don't know anyone else who knows."

Let this be a lesson to you. The next time anyone tells you something about horses or riding be sure to ask him, "*Why?*"

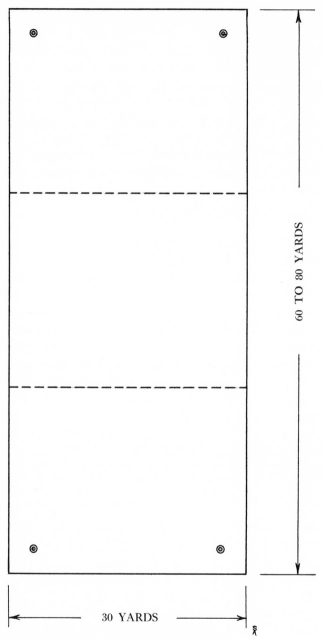

60 TO 80 YARDS

30 YARDS

Preferred Size Ring for Cross-country Horses

of it). If you are developing a hunter or a jumper, you have plenty of room to lay out your jumps. And remember there's no law requiring you always to use the whole ring. There will be times when you may want to work at slow gaits with frequent turns. Then mark off twenty yards at one end of the ring with a couple of poles or logs laid on the ground and use the width of the ring as the long side of your restricted area. A ring of this size can thus be divided into three or four zones for slow work, enabling several riders to school their horses without interfering with one another (see page 202). The experience of having to work regardless of the presence of other horses nearby is good discipline for a young horse—and for the rider!

There is nothing complicated or abstruse about schooling exercises. All are based on the *natural* movements of the horse. In the ring we ask no more of him than he can do when free in a field without a rider on his back. We simply teach him to act on command or cue. Any forced, artificial movements such as the Spanish walk and the sort of "dancing" some circus horses are taught have no more place in schooling than the stunts of kneeling down to "take a bow" or lying down to "play dead." These are mere exhibition tricks for the amusement of the childish and the ignorant.

The purpose of schooling exercises is to develop a calm, obedient, athletic horse. They may be divided into three general categories:

1. Movement on straight lines, including halting and reining back.

2. Movement on curves: circles, including figure 8's; half-circles, reverse half-circles, serpentines, quarter-circles (as when turning a corner of the ring); and all turns—turns on the forehand, on the center and on the haunches, this last including pirouettes (spins), pivots and rollbacks.

3. Lateral movement or movement on two tracks: side step, half-pass, head-to-wall, tail-to-wall and shoulder-in.

Two-Tracking. Lateral movements, or movements on two tracks, are often the most difficult to master. The difficulty is in doing them well. Correctly positioned, the horse moves forward diagonally, sidestepping slightly. He must not lose free forward impulsion as he crosses one foreleg and one hindleg in front of its opposite member. In other words, the movement though on a diagonal must always be predominantly forward, not predominantly sidewise. If the horse loses impulsion or leads with his hindquarters while facing away from the direction of movement, the exercises are worse than useless. This is what makes them difficult. The horse must have reached a certain stage of schooling before the rider can hope for success, and the rider must learn to co-ordinate rein and leg aids.

In the top photograph, Tonka is starting a turn on the forehand in a corner of the school, moving his quarters around to the right. In the middle photograph he is moving to the right with his head to the wall. In the bottom photograph he is starting a turn on the hindquarters to the left. Perhaps by this time you can judge how well the movements were being done. Linda's expressions suggest that she was not, perhaps, completely satisfied.

With the exception of the last exercise, shoulder-in, a movement I regard as a purely gymnastic embellishment not at all necessary to a well-schooled horse and quite easy for a horse that *is* schooled, all these are natural movements. Any horse can and will move straight ahead and halt straight, or move on a curve or sidewise. Any green colt can step backward if he has to, though it is more natural for him to turn away from anything he wants to avoid.

Viewed in this way, what is forbidding or mysterious about schooling? Only, I think, that the average rider doesn't have a clear concept of the over-all schooling process; he has not grasped the fact that schooling *must begin at the beginning.* Seldom can a particular fault in a horse be isolated so that it stands as a problem completely by itself, unconnected with anything else. With practically no exception, it is based on something else, something more fundamental than the fault itself. The fault is merely an effect; the deficiency it is based on is the real cause. To realize this is to understand the art of schooling.

Let's consider a few common examples of this misunderstanding. Probably the best source to examine is the typical advice-to-the-readers column to be found in some horse magazines. Month after month and year after year frustrated rider-readers moan for help in their troubles, which follow a general pattern:

"My horse neckreins fine to the right, but he won't turn to the left. How can I make him?"

"I can't ride my mare away from the stable. She rears and whirls, trying to go back. What can I do to break her of this?"

"When I ride alone my horse is fine, but with other horses he always wants to run."

"If I let her canter, she starts galloping. I almost have to pull her head off to stop her."

Et cetera ad infinitum.

Horsemen exasperated by such problems as these actually are admitting just one plain fact: "My horse is not schooled."

(Text continued on page 223)

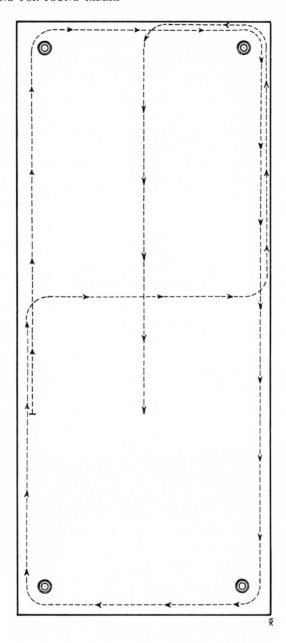

*Riding the Corners and Change of Hand. Remember that the first
step in schooling is to get your horse moving freely, briskly, straight
ahead, with regular, cadenced strides. A moderate trot is, as a rule,
the best schooling gait.*

Ride straight *down the fence. Watch for wandering and weav-
ing, faults that indicate lack of impulsion.*

Before *you reach a corner anticipate the horse slowing down.
Drive with your legs or touch him with the whip.*

*Ride deeply into the corners but keep in mind that the sharpness
of a turn increases with the speed of the gait. Thus, a turn with
a ten-foot radius is easy at a walk, more difficult at a trot, and too
much to expect of a green horse at a canter or gallop. This also
depends on the size of the horse. You must use horse sense. A safe
rule is to begin big and gradually work down.*

*In turning, watch for inward drift, "slipping," or cutting the
corners, as well as overbending and head-tilting.*

*Check anticipation. Change directions frequently. Never follow
a routine.*

*Start the canter in a corner to be sure you get the correct lead.
How much cantering you can do depends on the horse's age and
development. There is no set rule.*

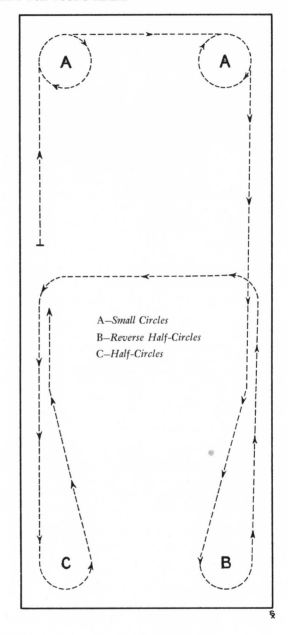

A—*Small Circles*
B—*Reverse Half-Circles*
C—*Half-Circles*

Small Circles, Reverse Half-Circles, and Half-Circles. You can begin these movements after you have your horse moving freely on straight lines without constant urging. Surprising a horse with unexpected circles is a good way to check his anticipation and keep him alert.

A *designates small circles called* voltes. *A volte is a circle with a radius equal to the length of the horse—about nine feet for an average horse and proportionately smaller for a pony.*

B *represents a reverse half-circle.* C *shows a half-circle. The only difference in these is that in the former you ride at an angle away from the fence and turn back to it, while in the latter you turn away from the fence and then angle back to it. In both, the horse's course away from or back to the wall should be a straight line until he begins to circle.*

Do a lot of circling and make the circles of different diameters. If your horse seems less supple on one side than the other, work more to that side—for the fault is probably yours. I am skeptical of the common idea that most horses naturally have favorite sides or prefer one lead to the other. Free in a field, they will turn or gallop either way with equal ease. One-sided horses, I am convinced, are made by one-sided riders. I think you will find that your horse turns more easily to the side you find easier. An important part of schooling is constantly checking yourself for faults. Don't always blame the horse.

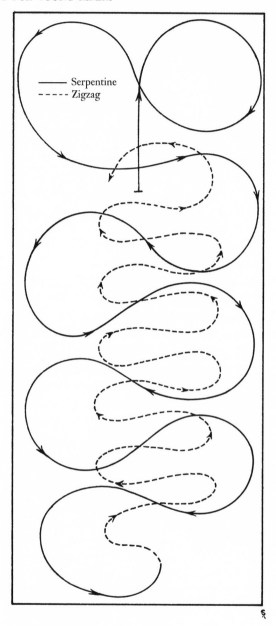

Serpentine
Zigzag

Serpentines and Zigzags. These movements are a continuation of the cornering and circling exercises shown in the diagrams on pages 206 and 208.

Notice that in the serpentine there are no straight lines. The horse is always moving in an arc, changing from side to side. The loops of the serpentine should be large, at least half the width of the ring. The movement is best done at a brisk trot. Don't try it at a canter unless you have a mature horse that will automatically change leads.

The zigzag, having sharper turns, should be done more slowly. Begin at a walk; then trot. The bends of the zigzag should have at least the same radius as a volte. Anything smaller becomes a turn on the quarters or a rollback, which we should not expect of a green horse. When riding a zigzag watch for overbending at the shoulders. Remember that the horse's whole spine from poll to tail should form one true arc.

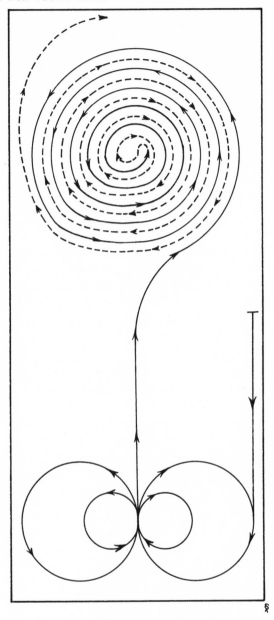

*Figure 8's and Spirals In and Out at the Canter. Many horsemen
use the figure 8 almost exclusively to teach a horse to change leads.*

Take the canter coming out of a corner; this will put you on the
correct lead (left lead on a circle to the left, right lead on a right
circle). As you near the center of the figure 8, drop to a trot for
three or four strides; then resume the canter on the opposite circle.
Change direction before you ask the horse to resume cantering.

Cantering in a large spiral is an excellent exercise for slowing
down an impetuous horse. If he's really hot and a big mover, you
might work him outside the ring, in a large field. A wet saddle
pad solves many schooling problems, if you don't overdo it. Spiral
gradually into a predetermined center; then, changing directions
(and changing leads), spiral back out.

As the spirals get smaller most green horses will break, dropping
to a trot. A good rider can prevent this by "rocking" with the
horse's cantering motion, besides urging with voice and legs. The
smallest spiral at the center, just before you change directions and
start back out, should not be less than about ten yards in diameter.

A horse that won't stay on a circle without constant reining and
without fighting the bit is either insufficiently schooled or overworked. If the latter the trainer is always to blame.

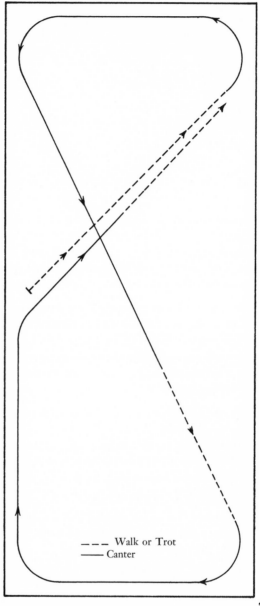

———— Walk or Trot
———— Canter

Teaching Change of Leads on Cue. To teach a horse to change leads and take a specific lead on cue I prefer this pattern to the figure 8. It gets results more quickly and the horse rarely learns to anticipate the change.

As the diagram shows, you ride at a walk or trot diagonally into a corner of the ring and start the canter on the turn. Approaching the third corner, you drop to a walk or trot, then do the same thing but this time on the opposite lead.

Very gradually you demand the canter farther and farther from the corners and decrease the number of strides at the walk or trot until the horse will change on the straight with only one stride interrupting the gait.

The aids used are almost the same as those for riding the corners and doing half-circles. For the left lead, feel the left rein and apply the right leg behind the girth; for the right lead, reverse the aids.

When the horse will consistently and smoothly take either lead on the straight with only one trotting stride to break the canter, you can try for a flying change. Apply the aids as the hind legs leave the ground. To time this precisely you must develop "feel" through the seat of your pants.

I do not believe in teaching the counter-gallop (i.e., circling to the left on the right lead)—unless you have nothing else to do. I consider that an exercise beyond the scope and purpose of this book.

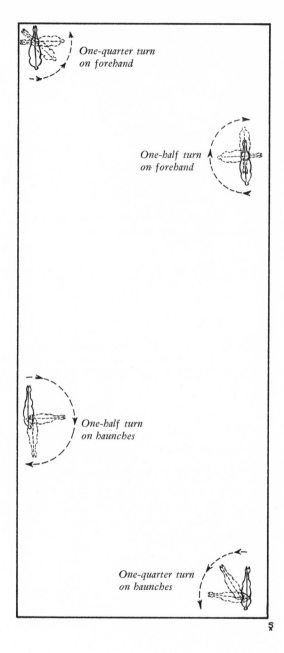

One-quarter turn on forehand

One-half turn on forehand

One-half turn on haunches

One-quarter turn on haunches

216

Turns on the Forehand and on the Haunches. Some Western train-
ers like to begin "putting a leg on" a young horse soon after they
have begun riding him. I have yet to see one who could do it
correctly in such a short time. Invariably these horsemen are satis-
fied with any way of side-stepping as long as the horse moves away
from the leg. Some trainers even believe that the rider should move
his inactive leg away from the horse. In my opinion, work on lateral
movements should be postponed until a horse is very good on
straight lines and curves and goes well on the bit.

Turns on the forehand are easier to do than turns on the haunches.

It's usually a good idea to begin with a quarter-turn in a corner
of the ring. The walls help. Eventually you should be able to do
half-turns without the aid of the walls, and then full turns (360
degrees).

In these two lessons, hurrying the horse and applying the aids
too forcefully are the surest ways to failure. Ask for only one step
at a time; then pause and collect the horse before you ask for the
next step. Once the horse has learned and obeys well, the pauses
are almost imperceptable.

Except in advanced dressage, the horse's feet near the center of
the circle, or the pivotal point, need not remain stationary, but
the rider should check any tendency to step backward.

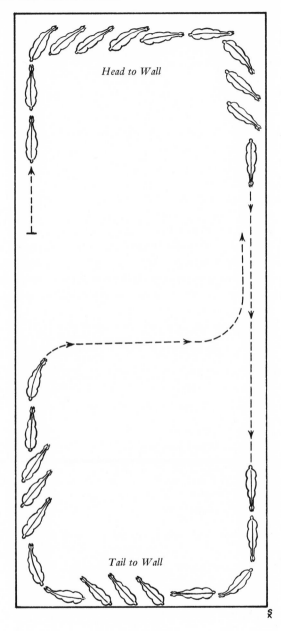

Head to Wall

Tail to Wall

Head to Wall, Tail to Wall. These are valuable suppling exercises, for to do them correctly the horse must reach out with both legs on one side and cross over in front of the legs on the opposite side, toward the direction of movement. If the outside legs do not cross in front of the opposite limbs, the movements are worse than useless. The exercises can be done at any gait, but begin at the walk. It is important to remember that the horse should face slightly toward the direction he is moving; never away from it. The hindquarters should not "lead" the forehand. In effect, the movement is straight ahead, parallel with the wall, but the horse moves on two tracks with either the forelegs or the hind legs farther away from the wall.

Head to Wall—*Ride deeply into a corner of the ring. When the horse is bent in the middle of the turn, feel the inside rein (away from the wall) and push with the opposite leg. In other words, try to hold the horse on the arc of the turn as he leaves the corner, moving parallel with the fence. Be satisfied if you get only one or two steps at first; then let the horse straighten out.*

Tail to Wall—*To execute this movement you hold the horse on the arc of the turn as if about to execute a volte in the corner. As the horse veers away from the wall, feel the opposite rein (near the wall) and with your leg push his hindquarters toward the wall. This is a bit more difficult than head to wall. The horse has a stronger tendency to face the wrong way. You must check this tendency with the reins, but never use force.*

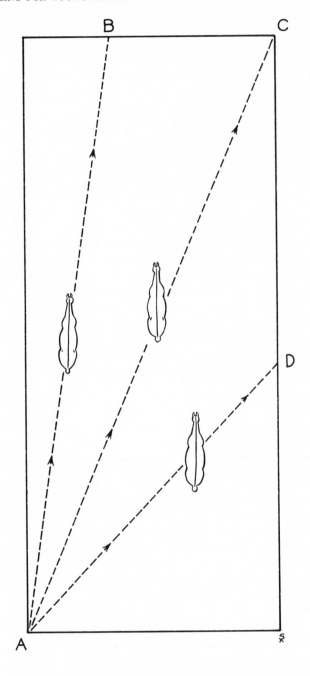

Side step. The sins that have been committed in attempting this movement are legion. Show-off parade riders are the worst offenders. It is very easy to do this deceptively simple movement the wrong way—by emphasizing side movement more than forward movement. Movement forward must always be predominant. *Even when the horse moves directly sidewise without advancing to the front, he must have the* impulse *to go forward. He must always "be ahead of the legs"—both legs.*

To benefit from this exercise you must clearly understand that the horse does not merely sidle, moving diagonally while taking mincing little steps to the front. On the contrary, he steps forward freely with long smooth strides, but crossing the left legs in front of the right or vice versa. The gravest faults are to lose this free forward impulse and to let the hindquarters get ahead of the forehand.

The horse should be either straight, facing directly to the front, or be inclined slightly toward the line of movement. He should never even slightly face or bend the opposite way.

The exercise can be done at all gaits, but work gradually, beginning at a walk. Be satisfied with only a little lateral movement (A to B) before you demand more (A to D). Keep in mind that the more acute the sidewise movement becomes the easier it is to let the hindquarters take the lead.

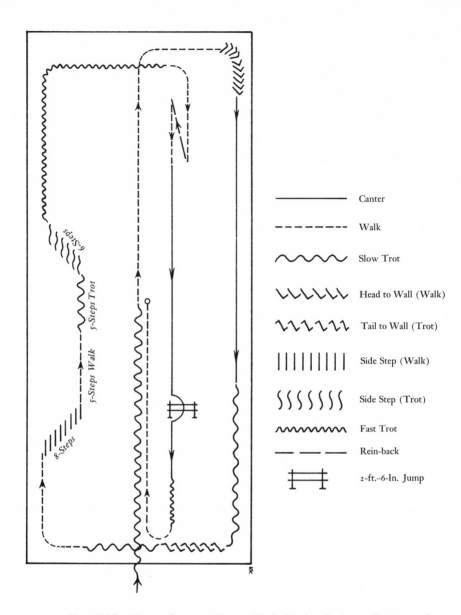

Legend:

——————————— Canter

– – – – – – – Walk

~~~~~~~~~~~ Slow Trot

∨∨∨∨∨∨ Head to Wall (Walk)

⌇⌇⌇⌇⌇ Tail to Wall (Trot)

||||||||| Side Step (Walk)

∫∫∫∫∫∫ Side Step (Trot)

ⱽⱽⱽⱽⱽ Fast Trot

— – — – — Rein-back

╫ 2-ft.–6-In. Jump

Test Ride. If you have really studied this book, instead of merely reading it, and have practiced, there is nothing in this simple test ride that you should not be able to do.

If you have difficulty with anything, the solution is simple—and it never changes: Study some more, practice some more. There is no shortcut to success.

But instead of recognizing the fact and beginning from scratch with simple fundamentals, they try futilely to correct effects when the only real solution is to eliminate the causes.

For example, a horse that cannot be ridden away from its stable has never been confirmed in obedience to the leg—and no lesson in all schooling is more basic than that. A horse that rears or is difficult to stop is not on the bit—poor schooling, poor riding. You can't "put a stop" on a horse unless you first "put a mouth" on him, and you can't develop his mouth unless you first "put a leg" on him; that's elementary schooling. And so it goes, fault by fault, right down the line to the ultimate end —basic work, necessary, unavoidable work in the ring.

Unfortunately, the sages who give the advice the magazines print too often do nothing to dispel the inexperienced horsemen's muddlement. Reading between the lines, one can easily see that some of these experts must surely know that the remedies they suggest will, in the long run, prove quite ineffective; but they do it, anyhow, just to "get the job done." Their attitude is understandable, if not entirely ethical. After all, they don't have to carry out their own advice, and it isn't their fault that some nag they never saw and never will see has been spoiled. The frustrated novice who seeks advice is generally bothered by just one specific problem; that's what he wants to solve. It seems too discouraging, entirely too drastic, for the expert to reply in one sweeping statement, "Your horse isn't schooled, and obviously you don't know how to school him. Either turn him over to a professional or get rid of him."

Any Voice of Experience who answered in that vein would be ruthlessly censored by the editor; editors want to sell magazines, not antagonize readers. Yet most of the time that would be the only really sound advice if the unhappy recipient could bring himself to follow it. The particular fault in the horse that the novice rider can't cope with is a result of poor schooling or lack of any schooling, and the only way to eliminate a result is to remedy the cause.

However, with rare exceptions, the equestrian Dear Abbies don't come right out and say this, emphasizing that the only place to begin schooling is right at the beginning. There are no easy short cuts.

Thus the myth that schooling is complicated and difficult persists. The professionals, cannily giving away no secrets, flourish. Publishers get richer; editors get fatter; magazines get bigger; circulation climbs; and the endless stream of letters from frustrated riders flows on with the same perplexing problems. "Dear Editor: Hope you can read this. I'm writing with my left hand. The problem is my horse bites. . . ."

The accompanying diagrams illustrate basic school exercises. These are the movements professionals work on when schooling a horse. They do them over and over, though not in any set routine and not with equal emphasis on all exercises. Which exercises a trainer stresses depend on the individual horse. The rule to be followed is simple: Whatever the horse finds most difficult you spend most time on—without overdoing it, tiring the horse, and eventually making him stubborn and sour. Lessons should be brief, with frequent rest periods when the horse is allowed to relax on a free rein. Whenever possible, work in the ring should be followed by exercise across country, mostly on loose reins.

It seems self-evident that work on straight lines is the simplest, therefore the point to begin. What is not always so clear to many novice trainers is that this simple work is also the most vitally important. "Ride your horse forward and hold it straight." I don't recall who first said that, but the rule has been repeated a thousand times and with good reason. For every well-done movement, even reining back, is based on impulsion to *go forward*. Without that you have nothing, you can accomplish nothing; everything your horse does he will do badly. Don't worry about change of leads, straight stops or anything else until you have confirmed your horse in the habit of obediently moving straight forward with energy and snap.

This apparently simple work on straight lines merits more time and more careful attention than most riders usually give it—particularly those who "ride Western." It takes time for a colt to develop cadenced gaits, but this quality, cadence, is critically important in schooling. Until you achieve it, you haven't accomplished much. Jerky, irregular gaits, with a tendency to weave and wander instead of moving vigorously straight forward, are sure signs that the horse lacks impulsion or "drive." They indicate also that the horse is not mentally calm, physically relaxed.

An easy way for the rider to check on the cadence of his mount's gaits is to listen attentively to the hoofbeats. Whatever the gait, the footfalls should follow one another with metronomic regularity.

A rider who has a good ear for music might find helpful a stunt I very often do, though I've never heard of anyone else doing it. When the horse is moving well at a brisk working trot, I think of a tune that "fits" the rhythm of his gait. If you can't think of a musical air that seems to "fit" your horse, you may have to make up one. When you have found the right tune, "think" it or hum it as you ride. Then you'll know instantly when the horse loses cadence.

Years ago I schooled a young Arabian stallion, a very high-strung colt, whose disorganized gaits at first simply wouldn't "fit" any tune I could recall. I thought I'd never find what I came to think of as "Aravic's tune." But one day during a workout I finally hit the right chord—a really weird variation of "California, Here I Come." By coincidence, the colt was from California, and after schooling he returned there.

When turning, practically all horses have a natural tendency to slow down or to make the turns too wide; some horses will do both at once. When turning the corners of the ring, don't let your horse do either. Approaching a corner, drive with your legs. Ride deeply into the corner so that the horse must bend as he turns. That's what the corners are for and why a ring without corners is of little value in schooling.

Since most beginners are uncertain about how deep is deep, I like to place an old automobile tire on the ground anywhere from six to twelve feet out from each corner post and tell the pupil to turn the corner between the tire and the post. The exact distance of the tire from the corner doesn't matter much,

Cantering in a Small Circle. In riding turns and circles, a very common fault of many riders is their failure to stay in central balance with the horse. They either overlean in toward the center of the circle or turn or let their weight slip to the outside, forcing them to prop on the outer stirrup. Either way, they are out of balance with the horse; their weight throws him off balance and adversely affects his performance. Some riders do this even when riding on the straight, particularly when applying a leg aid. They collapse one hip. In finished riding this is a grave fault. Pupils who drive cars, I have noticed, seem to be more prone to this fault than younger riders who do not drive. They have habit against them. Rounding a curve in a car, you must balance from the seat; on horseback, you balance from the foot. Some novices not only bend at the hips but sharply tilt their heads to the inside as well; they look as if they have stiff necks. In this picture Linda and Tonka are doing pretty well on a small circle at the canter ("Nobody is perfect!"). Both are leaning at the same angle and looking along the arc of the circle. Linda's weight is predominantly over her inner seatbone and stirrup. Her outer leg is passive because Tonka now responds to weight cues, but a green horse would need an active leg just behind the girth. Photograph by Msgr. J. Graham

except that the faster the horse works the farther from the post the tire should be. We can hardly expect an untrained horse to do almost a ninety degree turn at a gallop.

Remember this principle: The sharper a turn or the smaller a circle, the more difficult it is for the horse to work at speed. Be very moderate with a colt or with a green horse. Give him time to learn, time to develop.

Virtually all novice riders find circling difficult; even some experienced riders do. The difficulty is in visually judging whether the horse is following a true circle, an egg-shaped course, or even a roughly triangular one—or just meandering around in vague changes of direction. This is true of riding figure 8's also, for a perfectly executed 8 is simply two connected circles. There are two ways of overcoming this difficulty. Select a certain mark or place an object on the ground as the center of your circle; then try to maintain the same distance as you ride around it. An easier way is to mark a true circle on the ground with barn lime and ride exactly on the line.

A common mistake most novices make in practicing circles is to try to hold the horse on the circle by constant rein pressure. Enough of this will ruin any horse's mouth; it certainly won't improve his disposition. Our ideal should be to school the horse to go on his own: once we have put him on the circle, he should follow the arc with little or no further guidance.

The Volte. This picture is a front view of basically the same exercise seen from the rear in "Cantering in a Small Circle." Here Tonka is at the trot and he is turning around a tire in a corner of the schooling ring in a very small circle, called a volte. Linda is looking in the direction of the movement, Tonka is bent on the arc and both are at virtually the same angle.

Therefore, in circling the rider must give and take, riding with legs as well as hands. If the horse tends to drift out, take; if he veers in toward the center, straighten him. ("Straight" in this exercise means bent on the arc of the circle.)

Generally speaking, the aids in schooling a horse on turns and circles are as follows, and they are applied in the sequence given:

1. Looking the way he intends to turn or circle, the rider very slightly shifts his weight to his inner seat bone and stirrup.

2. He applies his outer leg just behind the girth.

3. He lightly feels the inner rein, giving and taking. He may or may not bear the outer rein against the horse's neck. (When both reins are used, one is dominant and the other supports it. Thus, in neckreining the bearing or outer rein is dominant.)

Eventually, as the schooling progresses, the rider's slightest shift of weight will be enough to start the horse turning.

CHAPTER XX

The Hunting Set

WHEN Tonka was three years old we moved to a new neighborhood, a very "horsey" locality that boasted an imaginary hunt club. The Brandybibbers Hunt never existed except in its members' bemused minds. There was neither a clubhouse nor a club stable, and nobody owned any closer relative to a hound than a Saint Bernard or a cocker spaniel. If any foxes ever had roamed the area, sharpshooting farmers with distinctly un-English notions of sport had taken care of them long before we arrived on the scene.

The Brandybibbers Hunt Club, in short, consisted of a loosely raveled group of neighbors who liked to jaunt about the countryside on Sunday afternoons playing follow-the-leader on horseback over—or more often around—a few low simple jumps. About once a year they persuaded some newspaper society editor to send a photographer and a reporter out from the city to cover one of their houndless foxless "hunts." The pictures invariably showed the local gentry enjoying a stirrup cup before setting out on the chase. One memorable year somebody showed up with two couples of hounds that had never been trained to hunt. That was a red letter day. The hounds were in the foreground of the most important photograph; then the bewildered beasts were hustled back into their crates while the "hunt" got under way.

To a newcomer, these autumn Sunday "hunts" were astonishing spectacles. The riders included a number of grandparents loosely mounted on nags to match; children on weedy ponies bitted in Western curbs either too large or too small for their tough mouths; a swarm of teen-agers, mostly girls, whose chief asset was enthusiasm; and the leaders of the hunt, the landed gentry, sedate businessmen, and middle-aged matrons galloping in their imagination over the turf of their own private Leicestershire.

Not one of our sporty new neighbors—with two or three possible exceptions—was well-enough mounted to clear a four-foot obstacle safely, assuming that there had been a jump that high in the "hunt's" territory and that anyone would have ventured to try it. Yet practically all of them rode with stirrup leathers so short you would have thought that they were going to ride in a steeplechase. They "rode English"—or what they thought was the English style—to a degree that made them look grotesque. I have never seen so many ugly seats among any other group of riders.

Since most of their riding, even on the Sunday "hunts," amounted to little more than hacking about the countryside, with a good deal of walking and trotting, the Brandybibbers' exaggerated "jumping seats" naturally became uncomfortable. Yet it apparently never occurred to any of them to lower their stirrups to a sensible length. Instead they sought relief from their cramped positions by lolling back on the cantles, which didn't make their horses too happy. To keep the unfortunate beasts from slowing down to a crawl the riders habitually swung their lower legs back and forth like pendulums. They seemed to think that they were legging their horses along. All they actually did was rub the hair off their mounts' barrels just behind the girths and make the animals so insensitive to precise leg aids that they might as well have been dead. This—in addition to lack of quality—was the mark of the typical Brandybibber "hunter."

I once tried to explain to a Southern friend of mine, a retired

Master of Foxhounds, what the Brandybibber Hunt was really like. The poor fellow refused to believe that I wasn't exaggerating or pulling his leg. It seemed incredible to him that such a preposterous organization could exist.

However, if these frustrated fox hunters seemed weird to us, I'm sure that the feeling was soon mutual. How disparate our ideas were may be illustrated by two incidents:

The first time one of our neighbors, a pillar of the local set, saw me riding a horse in a hackamore, she asked, "How does that thing work?"

One day Linda, exercising Tonka across country, met several of our new neighbors on horseback. They looked startled. "You're *riding* him!" one of them exclaimed. "A stallion!"

It had never occurred to Linda that she might have been doing something unusual. She rode along with them for a while, but they kept well clear of her. The little stallion's presence quite plainly made them nervous.

The Brandybibbers' attitude toward stallions was the same as their attitude toward tigers. With one exception, a girl friend of Linda's, they would not have dared to enter Tonka's stall. Most, indeed, would not get within arm's length of him. We learned without delay from some of our neighbors that they "wouldn't have a stallion in their barn."

After seeing some of their barns, I could agree with that, if the stallion had any choice in the matter. From the outside, most of their barns looked neat and trim; inside, the stalls were usually filthy.

We had just about settled down in our new home when I bought a Morgan stallion. The news was all over the neighborhood even before the horse arrived. Shortly after we had him installed, the local experts began drifting in to look him over. I think that they were attracted mostly by his reported price and the fact—if any of them knew it—that he was a show horse, a stallion in his prime that had never been defeated in a breed halter class. Linda and Sheilagh almost choked suppressing their laughter as they listened to some of the typical comments:

"He's beautiful—but with all that muscle he looks almost like a draft horse." (Corky was the first Morgan most of them had ever seen at close range.)

"How will he go in a group if he's a stallion?" (This, about a horse that had been in innumerable shows and led parades!)

"Two stallions in the same barn—and with mares! You'll have nothing but trouble. *I* wouldn't have a stallion in my barn!"

The Sunday after his arrival I rode Corky in his first "hunt." He took it in stride as casually as if he had been doing the same old thing every Sunday for years, and though he was in sleek show condition he had no trouble matching strides with the "hunters."

On this ride, however, I first noticed something that troubled me. Two young girls were riding mares in heat—and the youngsters had not the foggiest idea that their mounts *were* in heat. When I asked one girl she looked surprised. "I don't know," she said. "*Is* she?" Neither showed the slightest concern about riding directly in front of my stallion.

I encountered the same blissful ignorance on later rides, and it wasn't only the teen-agers who were ignorant. We rode in a veritable miasma of ignorance.

I warned Linda to be on the lookout for this when riding Tonka in company, and it was fortunate that I did.

It is, of course, no more than reasonable to expect the rider of a stallion to be always alert and in full control of his mount, but it seems equally reasonable as a matter of ordinary safety and courtesy to expect the same of any rider in a group.

Impressing rules of safety on young riders, however, is often difficult. Constant vigilance when riding in company is one of the hardest things to teach youngsters. They chatter; they daydream; they clown around; and reckless show-offs are to be met in every group. Even if you teach your own child good company riding manners, he will often find himself with others who have been taught nothing. When many of their elders, who should set an example, show little common sense, consistent enforcing of safety rules becomes a major task. Most of the time it is only sheer luck, coupled with the ponies' good sense or lethargy, that prevents more accidents than there are. But sooner or later somebody is almost certain to be hurt.

"I think," I told Linda, "Tonka should be gelded. He is simply too much horse for you to ride safely among these nitwits. What do you think?"

It didn't take her long to agree. She had had some nervous moments on cross-country rides with her new friends. "They just don't know," she remarked, "how it feels to be mounted on a stallion."

This was one of the most difficult decisions I've ever made. I liked the gray stallion just as he was—a miniature war horse, full of fizz and vinegar. If pinned down, I might even admit that in sheer spunk and devil-may-care dash he was the best little horse I ever rode. On his back, I would have attempted with confidence any task a horse can do. I hated to think of quenching forever that cocky Prince Valiant spirit.

Facts, however, are facts, and the foremost fact was that Tonka was not my horse. Logic had to prevail over sentiment. A common mistake many pleasure riders make is overmounting themselves—buying a horse or pony that catches their eye, then finding to their dismay that they can't handle him and being too proud or too stubborn to admit it. That's how accidents happen, and how many promising colts and young riders are ruined. Ignoring sentiment, we called the vet.

"What a beautiful pony!" the vet exclaimed. "It's a shame to cut him."

The doctor knew horses, and his unbiased professional opinion hardly cheered us.

Tonka's changed outlook on life was not immediately evident; it was several months before he began to act like a gelding. But the fact that he was now "like other horses" made Linda a more popular riding companion among the neighborhood teen-agers. This is something I never did look on as a great asset.

In the first place—by this time, I probably need hardly say it —none of this social "hunt" club set had even a glimmering notion of what educated riding was. One gentleman, whose company I found most congenial, was fairly well read on the subject, but his practice fell a good deal short of his theory. Excepting him and possibly another gentleman, whom I never got to know very well, the "hunting" set was a rabble of equestrian illiterates. A few I wouldn't rate even that high, like the clucking hen who gave "riding lessons" to local youngsters by mounting them on her own nags and shooing them around a small ring with a buggy whip.

Naturally, the junior riders were as ignorant as their elders. As a rule, they were better riders simply because they were younger and more athletic and rode much more, but their ideas and methods were just as primitive. I can recall only one of them who ever showed any equestrian tact or an understanding of equine psychology. But this girl, Jo, an intelligent, likable teenager, was an exception, a rider whose potential promise none of the others could even approach. The rest were merely acrobatic young clowns on nags no better than they deserved.

Almost from the first day, however, Linda fitted in with this gang as if she had organized it. She has a great—and sometimes unfortunate—gift for making friends easily and quickly, as well as without a great deal of discrimination. She fits in because it is instinctive for her to conform. She must have the approval of her peers. She often did the most idiotic things just to be "in" with the group. Perhaps one example will make this clear:

Shortly after we had settled in this fox-free "hunting" country, Linda was out riding with a group one day when they stopped at Jo's home. While talking with the young riders, Jo's father happened to mention that his standing offer of a new pair of spurs to any rider who would jump a horse over his stone wall was still good. The wall he referred to—a real stone wall solidly built, not the collapsible show-ring variety—was about three and one-half feet high from one side and a few inches higher from the opposite side where the ground was lower. It was an obstacle the Sunday "hunt" leaders discreetly ignored. I suspect that this might have been one reason why Jo's father had made his standing offer. The number of spurs he didn't have to buy probably tickled his sense of humor.

This was the first time Linda had ever heard about the stone wall. She hadn't even had a good look at it yet, merely a glimpse from the driveway leading to the house. But she spoke up.

"Tonka has never had any jumping lessons yet. May we use any horse, or must we ride our own horse?"

"Any horse."

"All right," Linda said. "Then I'll jump it."

She did not bother to explain that, like Tonka, she had never had a jumping lesson in her life, either. She knew no more about jumping a horse than about pole vaulting.

While someone held Tonka, Linda mounted a nag appropriately named Lemon. From what I saw of this animal, I'd nominate him as probably the clumsiest brute in three counties. I'd think twice before asking him to hop over a log. But Linda galloped the crock pell-mell at the stone wall, soared over it—her first jump—then turned Lemon around and jumped back from the sunken take-off side.

The valor of ignorance!

I have paused in this writing to ask my daughter, "Why did you do it?"

"To prove to myself that I could," she tells me, "and I wanted to make you proud of me."

I can't argue against that, for a few weeks later when she received her new spurs she proudly presented them to me. She has never worn them. Yet I feel sure that the presence of an audience and their untutored reaction to her exploit ("You've got guts," one of them said admiringly) had a lot to do with her impulsive daring.

I think that Linda would almost rather die than risk being "out of it." If the junior Brandybibbers had galloped about and leaped fences standing on their saddles, Linda would have broken her neck if necessary to master the stunt. I could have talked myself blue in the face arguing that it wasn't good horsemanship. That would not have mattered as long as Linda was "in."

I say this deliberately and with great regret because, almost before I realized what was happening, Linda had unobtrusively adopted the ridiculous Brandybibber "jumping seat." She

Linda—Before the Brandybibbers. This was the balanced seat Linda had acquired before she took to skylarking with the foxless fox hunters. Note the span of empty cantle behind her, the vertical stirrup leather, the pointed knee, the forward inclination of her torso. Compare this seat to Carson Whitson's seat when he was at the Cavalry School (see page 307). The two might have been poured from the same mold.

You School in Winter, Too. These pictures were taken during a schooling session shortly after I had made the discovery that Linda was acquiring the Brandybibber seat. It was not exactly a completely happy lesson. The chill winter air was warmed several degrees by some of my remarks. In the top photograph notice the forward position of Linda's foot. Her shin is vertical, but the stirrup leather is not; it is considerably ahead of the vertical, and Linda is well back in the saddle, close to the cantle. The picture was taken as proof to convince her of how she was riding. The bottom photograph was taken a short while later, after—with a good deal of urging—she had begun to get forward in the saddle where she belonged.

    At this time Tonka was three years old and still a stallion.

omitted only the pendulum swing of the lower legs because (she tells me now) this would have made Tonka as insensitive to the aids as any Brandybibber plug and she did not want that to happen. But the too-short, forward-pushed stirrup leathers, the rump on the cantle, the sloppily slouched, rounded back, the overlong reins, and the puppy-dog way of holding them with knuckles up and close to the waist—in no time she had it all down pat. And the first time I noticed it and realized what had happened, I almost exploded.

In an early chapter I have referred to the harmful influence of successful youthful show riders who have been taught to ride a safe pony or horse in a stereotyped way; their young friends copy their styles and thus the bad influence spreads. Linda provided an excellent example of a youngster's susceptibility to the same sort of influence but with a reverse twist: for the dubious privilege of being one of the "in" crowd she temporarily abandoned her own high standards and most of the ideals I had tried to instill in her and adopted the Brandybibbers' inferior standards.

It's a matter of personal individuality, I suppose, or the lack of it. For the Brandybibber crowd had quite the opposite effect on Sheilagh. "I didn't need to prove myself to them," she tells me now. "I saw from the very first that they didn't amount to anything." Their self-satisfied ineptitude and their unconscious, habitual abuse of horseflesh angered and repelled Sheilagh. She had absorbed enough principles of horsemastership to know—as Linda also knew, but chose to disregard—that the quality of a horseman can more accurately be gauged by the appearance and manners of his animals and the cleanness of his barn than by his expensive clothes. Sheilagh did most of her riding in the ring on my Morgan. If when riding across country after a schooling session she sighted any of the natty group, she speedily put distance between them and herself. She saw them clearly for what they were and had only contempt for them, while Linda, an extrovert, was happy to socialize with and imitate them.

As a natural result, Sheilagh's riding improved while Linda's gradually fell apart.

When, cracking down, I made Linda work alone in the ring

with me, she proved that she could still do things right if she wanted to—and had to. But if I corrected her in the presence of any of her pals she felt humiliated, became stubborn and sullen. The instant I turned away she reverted to the sloppy style. She would rather be "in," even with her inferiors, than right.

That was several years ago; we have long since left the Brandybibbers to chase their imaginary foxes over kindergarten jumps, carefully avoiding that solid stone wall. But even now traces of the pernicious influence can still be seen in Linda's seat —little details, sloppy habits, that weren't there before. Deliberately and foolishly, for the sake of a fleeting popularity that her sister was wise enough and proud enough to scorn, Linda formed certain bad habits—and habits can be hard to break.

Well, the move seemed like a good idea when we made it.

Looking back, I can regard it only as a minor catastrophe, unless the experience has taught Linda a constructive lesson.

About that I still have some doubts.

CHAPTER XXI

Jumping: Hard Hats and Soft Heads

I AM not a staunch believer in that little gem of village idiocy, "You ain't a horseman until you've had a hundred falls." I have had more than my share of falls, and I'm not breathlessly eager for the next one, though I'm unworried about when it will come. I particularly dislike falls that bring the mount down as well as the rider. A rider, if he is lucky enough not to break his neck, can usually figure out the cause of a fall and resolve to be more careful the next time, but to a horse or a pony a bad fall is a terrifying accident that is likely to set back its schooling weeks or months and undermine its confidence in its rider.

I believe in doing everything within reason to avoid falls, but having ridden my share of rambunctious colts, green jumpers and just plain clumsy nags, I am well aware of the ever present possibility of falling. It is a risk of riding that can be minimized by intelligent schooling and common-sense precautions but never completely eliminated—just as it can't be eliminated from skiing or skating or other sports.

Children, as a rule, do not worry unduly about falling, but some nervous parents more than make up for this. I have known several fond fathers to become so upset after learning that their darling daughters took their first fall while learning to jump that they laid down an ultimatum: Quit jumping or get rid of the horse. Such jittery spoil-sports should strive for a more sensible perspective. Riding over jumps is less hazardous when properly done than football or skiing or driving a car. Why magnify the risks?

Only a few parents go to the opposite extreme. These like to pretend that riding a horse is a feat of daring almost on a par with the charge of the Light Brigade. In fact, most of them really believe it is because, being inferior riders themselves (if they ride at all), they always had trouble with their own horses and never progressed far enough to learn the first elements of putting a horse at a jump. I recall in particular one woman whose teen-aged daughter was a jumping fanatic. Mama never overlooked a chance to remind whoever would listen that jumping is "a *gutty* sport" requiring great courage and daring. I know stock horse trainers who won't jump a horse over anything higher than a thick log if they can avoid it. One such trainer told me with an unabashed grin why he disliked jumping: "My head is too soft."

I submit that both of these viewpoints are unrealistic and quite as cockeyed as the notion of some jumping fanatics that any form of riding which does not involve jumping is mere "equitation."

There are few things in life I enjoy more than riding a well-schooled jumper, but I am not a fanatic on jumping; I can take it or leave it. I believe, however, that at least moderate jumping —jumping over obstacles up to three and one-half feet—is an essential part of the education of every horse and pony schooled for use outdoors. I am ignoring here those lopsided specialists kept exclusively for use in the show ring. These, having as their only purpose in life the winning of trophies and ribbons, do not come within the scope of this book.

In this chapter I propose to tell how Tonka was schooled to jump and how Linda was taught to ride him over obstacles without either of the youngsters ever getting the idea that jumping was a big deal meriting medals for bravery or additional life insurance. For the two of them, jumping was merely a phase of schooling, which—with no pun intended—they took in stride.

Tonka's first tiny steps toward becoming a jumper were taken over the cavalletti, long before I should have dreamed of asking him to jump anything. Walking and trotting over bars a few inches off the ground is not, of course, jumping—but it is a step toward that goal because it helps to develop in a colt willingness to *go over*, instead of around, whatever happens to be in front of him. Hopping over puddles, gullies, ditches, logs and small fallen trees serves the same purpose.

I know of people who think they are using intelligence in schooling by urging a yearling colt—or even a weanling—to hop over small jumps, even if the urging must be done with flicks of a whip or the pressure of a rope against the colt's rump. Their reasoning is that this doesn't hurt the colt and the sooner he learns to jump the better. I think this practice is utterly stupid for two principal reasons: first, a colt's soft leg bones are so susceptible to injury that even this mild form of hopping over a rail, with all the animal's weight momentarily supported by one foreleg, *can* quite easily result in an injury; second, a young rider, whether through ignorance, thoughtlessness or lack of supervision, is almost certain to take it for granted when the colt is only two or three years old that he is a fairly capable jumper, and that therefore it is quite all right to jump him fast and frequently. Nobody knows how many colts have been blemished and injured in this way.

I never let Tonka jump anything except an occasional small ditch until he was almost four years old, even in spite of the fact that he was always so exceptionally strong and durable. If he had been a big colt—16 hands or more—I'd have held him back until he was about five, for the bigger they are, the more liable colts are to injury.

I realize that quick-money trainers and commercial breeders will think me too conservative or will envy the vast wealth which enables me to ignore the economic facts of life. However, I'm not ignoring facts, economic or otherwise; I am vitally concerned with facts—and the foremost fact I am concerned with is that the horseman who makes haste slowly progresses faster and farther in the long run. He may wear patched jeans, but he will ride a better horse.

Tonka was introduced to the cavalletti on the longe line and without a rider. Then I saddled him, Linda mounted, and we repeated the first lessons. The pony wore a cavesson and Linda had no reins. I controlled Tonka with the longe. I instructed Linda to rest her hands lightly on the pony's neck just in front of the withers, leaning forward slightly and keeping her seat clear of the saddle so that almost all her weight was in the stirrups. This position put her forward over Tonka's center of gravity, enabling him to carry her weight with the least effort, and it introduced her to the jumping position she would later use over obstacles without giving her anything else to worry about—no reins, no need to control her mount, nothing to jump. She was able to concentrate entirely on maintaining a good forward seat and on developing her balance.

After about a week of this—with some riders it may take longer—I replaced the cavesson and longe line with a snaffle bridle and reins. Then Linda rode him over the poles while I merely watched. I watched to see that she maintained a correct jumping position and that she did not hang on the reins. She had to ride over the poles with the reins completely slack, doing absolutely nothing to interfere with Tonka's efforts to balance himself and move forward with complete freedom. If she had any trouble keeping her balance with her seat clear of the saddle, I told her, she could place her hands on her mount's neck to steady herself; but, if possible, she was to keep her hands low, forward and clear of the horse, about ten inches apart.

We worked on this for about two weeks, not as a special exercise but simply as a part of the regular schooling. Thus, Linda might be working on circles and figure 8's and transitions from one gait to another when I'd say, "Take him over the bars." Without halting or making any special preparations that might have given Tonka the idea that something unusual was coming, she would head for the cavalletti at a trot, and as Tonka neared the first pole she would rise in the stirrups, move her hands forward, and over the grid of poles they would go. Then Linda would sit down in the saddle, take the slack out of the reins and resume what she had been doing, or perhaps do something else. No sweat, no big deal, nothing out of the ordinary; just part of the daily work.

The next step was to give Tonka something to jump. I started him on a heavy bar resting on blocks, with another pole on the ground as a take-off bar; the jump was only about eighteen inches high. A weanling could have hopped over it. But I put Tonka on the longe again and I let him look the jump over from all sides first. Then I started longeing him in a big circle well away from the obstacle. As he trotted around me, step by step I edged closer to the jump—and suddenly Tonka found himself going straight at the middle of the bar. And naturally, being Tonka, he refused. He slid to a sharp stop just in front of the jump, then backed away, snorting his false alarms and suspicions. I've seen many colts, brought along this way, pop over this first little jump without a moment's hesitation; I have seen others, without benefit of cavalletti or any other preparation, take their first jump as if they had been doing it for years. But Tonka, introduced to anything new, has always had to be different. He is the perpetual country boy, the rustic wise guy, who won't be taken in by the city slickers. In some ways this suspicious alertness is a godsend; for example, on treacherous ground he is the safest mount I've ever ridden. But in other ways it is sometimes laughable and sometimes a nuisance. We have learned to live with it.

Sweet-talking him, I drew him away from the jump and started him circling again. This time as I moved within range of the obstacle I gave him the command to canter, "Hup!" He obeyed, but as he went at the jump he faltered. I repeated, "Hup!" and flicked the whip. Tonka seemed to bound about four feet straight up, shoot forward in the air, and come straight down. Landing, he exploded into a headlong gallop. I had all I could do to hold him. He almost pulled me off my feet. But I held him to the circle, and he soared over that insignificant jump a second time, clearing it by about three feet.

Around and around he went like a maniac while I, dropping the whip, took a hip-lock on the line and dug my heels into the turf. Each time he went over that insignificant jump as if he were leaping the gates of Hell with the Devil after him. I think he did it about a dozen times before he began to slow down and his leaps flattened out and the terrific pull on the line lessened. By that time my legs were rubbery and I was more than ready to call it quits, but I stuck it out until he had slowed to a canter and was popping over the bar with no more than a couple of feet to spare. Then I told him, "Whoa!" and Tonka stopped. Flicking sweat out of my eyes and wishing only to sit down until my heartbeat got back to normal, I walked up to him, patted him on the neck and told him how good he was.

And you can believe me that I meant what I said. I knew that I had a natural jumper on my hands, and horses like that, big or small, are rare.

After I got my wind back and my heart quit trying to knock a hole in the top of my head, I turned the gray pony around and had him jump the obstacle from the other side a few times. This he did quite sensibly, even casually. And that was the end of the first jumping lesson.

Every day for about a week we went through this same routine, minus the race-horse antics. Tonka seemed to enjoy jumping, and I had to repress his tendency to go too fast, but he never repeated his mad galloping of the first day. As I've said, he always had to be a little "different," but no one ever accused him of being dumb. He took to jumping with zest.

I checked his tendency to rush by making him walk or trot up to the jump. Sometimes I even halted him with a sharp, "Whoa!" just as he was about to take off. Whenever I did this I always made a point of walking up to him and patting him for his prompt obedience to my command. Then I'd start him circling again and the next time around I'd let him jump.

He learned to jump out of a trot and even a walk by my adaptation of the gallop command, "Hup!" Now it took on another meaning besides to gallop; it also meant "Jump!" I never let him get too close to the jump before I gave the com-

245

Agility Exercise: Air-O-Batics. Most horses can jump quite well if they hit the take-off zone with plenty of momentum. They may jump with their heads in the air, their backs caved in, and their legs dragging; but momentum gets them safely over. However, depending on agility and spring rather than momentum to get over an obstacle is a different matter. A good jumper should be very agile; in emergencies he'll need all the agility he has. To develop his agility and spring, I often put Tonka on the longe and made him jump out of a trot, or, increasing the spread of the jump, I'd hold him to the trot until only two or three strides before the take-off, then let him speed up into a gallop and jump. This picture shows him doing that. Some horsemen do not approve of longeing over jumps since the horse is usually on at least a slight arc. This jump measured sixteen and one half feet broad. Note the variety of "junk" it's made of—cavalletti, drums, timbers, logs and old tires. It looks crude, but it serves its purpose.

mand. I wanted him to learn to stand back and jump big before he ever found out that there was any other way of jumping. A sticky jumper—one that goes at an obstacle timidly or with plain lunkheaded laziness and has his head a foot beyond the jump before he finally bucks over—is a most unpleasant animal to ride. Tonka was naturally bold and I did everything to encourage this.

As our second week of jump schooling began I added another low obstacle, placing it directly opposite the first jump on the longeing circle, so that as Tonka moved around me at the end of the line now he had two jumps to clear. As I had done with the first obstacle, I let him examine this new jump from all sides at close range before sending him over it. He took both jumps boldly, but as he started the second time around he did what I had guessed he would do. He put on speed; his easy canter became a brisk gallop. Not to discourage him, I let him fly both jumps at this pace once before I checked him with a sharp, "Whoa!"

Ordering him to walk, I quickly shortened the line so as to draw him away from the jumps. After a couple of circuits inside the jumps I put him into a slow trot. As he passed one jump I gave him more line, enlarging the circle. When he came to the next jump he was facing the middle of it, in jumping position, and I said, "Hup!" and over he went from a trot.

Quite often I frustrated his tendency to jump at greater speed than necessary—a tendency I wanted to have completely under *control* without actually discouraging—not by checking him but by stepping back and shortening the line, drawing him closer, so that he would pass inside the jumps. With the line thus shortened, I would revolve on one spot while Tonka galloped in circles with nothing to jump. That pony caught on fast. I don't think he ever made two complete circuits inside the jumps before slowing down. Then I'd give him more line, move along with him and let him jump again.

By such various means I simply refused to let Tonka get the idea that jumping was a daring feat to be rushed into at steeplechase speed. I insisted that he must take the jumps at whatever pace and speed I set. This is a way of jumping you seldom see in most open jumping classes at shows, where more often than not many riders, even with the "help" of severe bits and strong arms, have all they can do to control their mounts.

Probably some readers who will undertake the schooling of a young jumper by the method explained here will wonder how much of this work was done every day, how many times at each lesson I asked Tonka to jump. I cannot answer that; there never was any exact figure. I never began a lesson with a daily

Use Your Cavalletti in Jumping. These pictures illustrate only two of a number of ways cavalletti can be utilized in jumping lessons. One jump is composed entirely of cavalletti. If more were added, the obstacle could be made higher. If they were turned over ninety degrees, it would be lower but broader. In the other picture the cavalletti are used as takeoff bars in front of a timber jump. If a couple of bars were added on each side, all elements would make an excellent broad jump, which could be jumped in either direction. Placing a few cavalletti in front of a jump, which forces a horse to approach at a trot, is an excellent way to reform a rusher—unless, of course, he is able to match Tonka's feat of blithely galloping over the bars!

"quota" of jumps in mind. In fact, I never even thought this important enough to keep any count of how many times he jumped. To school horses successfully you often have to play things by ear—never mind what the books say. If you overplay or underplay, you are lacking in equestrian tact. You must understand your own horse and adapt your procedure to get the best results from him.

Looking back, however, I don't think I ever had Tonka jump more than, at most, twenty times in any one day. If this seems like a good deal of jumping for a colt not quite four years old, even an exceptionally strong pony colt, bear in mind that the jumps were less than two feet high. He could pop over them from a walk—occasionally he did it from a standstill. Instead of counting how many times he jumped, I concentrated on *how* he jumped. I never let him get hot or tired, never pushed him for an extra effort. Usually he jumped on thick, springy turf. If I thought the footing poor, too hard or too sloppy, we skipped jumping that day. Often after a series of four or five jumps we might have a break, Tonka cropping grass while I explained something to Linda or instructed her to observe this or that point. Tonka's schooling may have been strict, but it was never strenuous. He was always still fresh when we quit.

Horses don't mind jumping if it doesn't hurt them or if it isn't prolonged until they are tired.

When Tonka was going the way I wanted him to go—jumping freely, calmly and attentive to oral commands—it was time for Linda to put into practice what she had rehearsed in dry runs over the cavalletti.

CHAPTER XXII

Jumping: Soft Hands and Firm Legs

U P to the elementary stage the schooling had progressed thus far, Tonka had learned more about his end of the jumping game than Linda—in spite of her lucky fluke over the stone wall—knew about hers. While the pony had been actually jumping Linda had only been watching and listening. Now it was time for her to put theory into practice.

We followed the same general procedure as when starting work over the cavalletti. I put Tonka on the longe; Linda had no reins. She was to concentrate, I told her, only on her position in the saddle. She had to learn to synchronize her movements with Tonka's, staying in rhythm with him during the take-off, the flight and the landing.

Her first attempts, of course, were pretty awkward, mostly, I think, because she was tense and nervous—she was not afraid of falling; she just wanted to do everything right. But of course she didn't—nobody does at first.

Her biggest fault was the common one of "jumping ahead of the horse." Knowing that she should be forward with her weight off Tonka's loins, she would rise in the stirrups as he approached the jump. At the moment of take-off Tonka had to check slightly to lift his forehand over the obstacle. This sudden check, though relatively slight over a low jump, would throw Linda, balanced in the stirrups, farther forward than she intended, or expected, to be. This movement was instantly followed by a forward surge as Tonka, thrusting his head and neck down and out, sprang off the ground, flinging Linda back into the saddle with a thump.

This quick check-and-thrust at the take-off is probably the hardest thing for a novice rider to learn to synchronize with. If not firmly seated, a rider needs a built-in gyroscope to maintain his balance.

Linda's sense of balance was good, but not that good. More than once she had to grab Tonka's mane to keep from falling. When she plopped back into the saddle on landing Tonka would often lay back his ears at the unintentional abuse.

Explaining this check-and-thrust of the take-off, I instructed Linda:

"Three or four strides before the take-off *sit down* in the saddle. Get forward by leaning from the hips and pushing your rump back toward the cantle. This will lower your upper body closer to Tonka's withers; your center of gravity will be closer to his. When he rises to the jump the sudden check will throw you forward. As he goes up and over keep your torso low and grip firmly with your legs. Try to keep your seat off the saddle until *after* he has landed."

By doing it over and over—and with no reins to worry about—Linda learned the various movements that make up a smooth jump, but she had great difficulty learning to return to the saddle softly after landing. Her tendency to plop back into the saddle should have been easy to correct if she had always remembered to keep her loins hollow, taking the impact on her feet in the stirrups, with her knees acting as springy hinges. Unfortunately, her "fashionable" Brandybibber slouch was still with her, more than she realized. Having developed the bad habit of slouching with her back rounded, she often didn't know when she was doing it and did it even when she tried not to. Only persistent practice will enable her to break the habit completely.

First Jumps. Here are two of the earliest pictures of Linda and Tonka learning to clear obstacles together. They were taken, I believe, only the second or third time I let Linda jump the young stallion off the longe. At this early stage, with the obstacles (formed of heavy cavalletti) low and not very broad, I emphasized forward impulse, going at jumps boldly. If occasionally Tonka, naturally bold, went a little too fast, I cautioned Linda to sit down, keep

In the last two lessons on the longe I attached reins to the side rings of the cavesson, and Linda held the reins as she would when jumping free. Even had she hung on the reins, she could not have hurt Tonka's mouth, but I wanted to be sure that she wouldn't hang on the reins. She didn't. We put the longe line and the cavesson aside and bridled Tonka with a smooth, jointed snaffle. I moved the two jumps we had been using so that they were in line and set about thirty yards apart.

"Go ahead," I told Linda. "Try it. Start at a trot, then canter.

*her hands still and let him go—and never to pull him up sharply
after a jump. A bit too much speed is a lesser fault than not enough;
with speed you have momentum. I also wanted to develop boldness
in Linda. A jump rider who is timid about riding fast must overcome his nervousness or he will ruin every horse he rides. Linda's
open mouth in one picture suggests that she might have been busy
with this problem.*

Hold him straight at the middle of the jumps. During the last
three strides use your legs; ease off on the reins, so that when
he takes off you have no pressure on his mouth at all. If you
must, let the reins go slack; but give him complete freedom to
jump. After you get over the second jump slow down gradually and halt. Don't turn around. Pat him and praise him."

It worked precisely. Linda rode well and the gray pony
jumped willingly and calmly.

"Now turn around." I was standing near a wall of the ring,

well out of the way. "Wait a few moments. Keep him calm and relaxed. Then jump back. Stop where you started."

Linda cantered him back and forth over the two jumps half a dozen times, and that was all for that day. As soon as he was unsaddled and turned into his box, Tonka got a feed of oats.

We followed this easy schedule for several days. I never missed a chance to impress on Linda the importance of going at a jump with gradually increasing momentum so that the final stride just before the take-off is the longest, the horse "jumping off his hocks" as he uncoils like a giant spring. I illustrated the point I was trying to get over to her with a diagram:

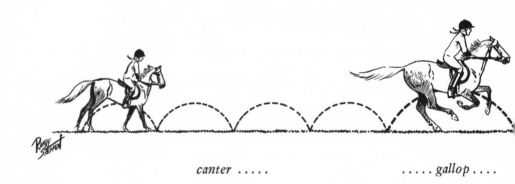

canter . . . . gallop . . . .

These last three strides are the most important. It is in these final moments that a horse decides whether to run out, refuse or jump. And if the rider is timid, nervously freezing to the reins and not urging strongly with his legs, it is almost a certainty that the horse will run out or refuse or, at best, jump badly. Bold riders make bold horses. This is not to imply that one must ride at a fence with a whoop and a holler, reckless as a drunken Indian. He should ride calmly but urgently with light hands and firm legs, determined to clear the obstacle.

Contrary to what most novice riders think, there is absolutely no reason to get back from a jump, even a big one, fifty to one hundred yards, then ride madly at full speed. If a horse is obedient to the legs, as a jumper should be, all the speed and momentum necessary can be generated in the last three strides. Years ago I watched a noted high-jumping horse at an exhibition in a small indoor arena. To clear a jump about seven feet high he cantered only five strides before taking off. He approached a jump so casually you wondered until the last moment whether he would jump or stop. But when he jumped, it was like watching a compressed spring suddenly released.

faster . . . .   *fastest . . . .*   *JUMP!!*

These last three strides are the most important!

The higher or broader a jump is the more restricted the take-off area becomes. Over a three-foot jump, for example, a horse can safely take off anywhere from three feet away to as far back as, say, twelve or fifteen feet. But if he is going at a four-foot abstacle he doesn't have this much leeway. If the jump is five or six feet he has even less. This principle can be graphically illustrated in diagram form:

3-ft. High Jump   Safe Take-off Zone . . . . 9 ft.

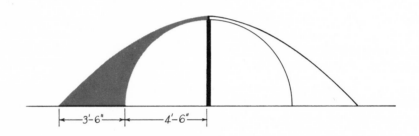

4-ft.–6-in. High Jump   Safe Take-off Zone . . . . 3-ft.–6-in.

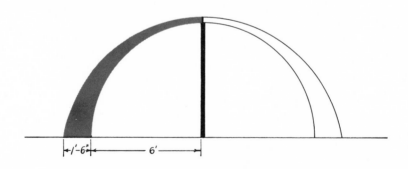

6-ft. High Jump   Safe Take-off Zone . . . . 1-ft.–6-in.

(The distances given in these diagrams are not to be taken as mathematically exact either in relation to one another or for all horses without exception. No figures can be exact or final because horses vary in jumping capacity—and riders in skill. Jumping capacity encompasses such individual variables as balance, spring, agility, willingness, and so on; and all these factors may be altered by such influences as the condition of the ground and how much weight the horse is carrying, as well as by how well the rider rides. Thus, a jump that proves difficult for one horse under a particular rider may be quite easy for another horse of superior ability or with a better rider. Naturally, the superior horse or an average horse excellently ridden will have a larger safe take-off zone; he can make a mistake, yet successfully get over an obstacle that under the same circumstances would prove disastrous for an inferior jumper or even a good jumper handicapped by a poor rider. The figures given are only approximate, for the purposes of illustration.)

In other words, the higher or broader a horse jumps the more accurate must be his, or the rider's, judgment of exactly where to take off. This can be developed only by experience, and as a rule the horse learns it before the rider does. Only the most expert riders can accurately "place" a horse. Even the best of them can't do it every time. They must put a great deal of trust in the horse. After all, he is the one that does the actual jumping.

Only a horse that develops this nicety of judgment to a high degree can be called a safe, reliable jumper. And the only way to develop it is by practice over a wide variety of different obstacles. In jumping particularly, no amount of theory can replace practice.

CHAPTER XXIII

Jumping: Adding the Spice

I T is at this stage of a young jumper's education that many riders, even experienced trainers, make what I consider a serious mistake. Instead of immediately introducing the young horse to a gradually increased variety of low jumps, they stick to the usual bar jump and merely add more bars to make it higher. Bold young riders, impatient to see "how high he can go," are usually the worst offenders. Linda herself furnishes an example.

One day while out hacking, she passed near our sporting neighbor's stone wall, the first obstacle she had ever jumped. She wondered whether Tonka could clear it, in spite of the fact that his jump schooling had only recently begun. No sooner thought than tried! Though he had never faced anything so formidable, Tonka leaped the stone wall. Fortunately, Linda had sense enough to let him look it over from both sides before putting him at it.

I knew nothing about this until Linda told me recently, long after we had moved away from the Brandybibber country. She added that later on different occasions she had put Tonka over this stone wall repeatedly from both sides. Undoubtedly, this belated knowledge will help to shorten my life at least six months. It is an excellent example of why venturesome young riders often need closer supervision than timid ones—and of the impossibility of always seeing that they get it.[1]

Personally, I am never in a hurry to find out how much higher a young horse can jump beyond the low limits I have set for him at this stage. Common sense tells me that he can, if necessary, jump perhaps three times higher or even more, but having to prove it won't teach him anything, except possibly to dislike jumping. If a young horse raps his shins a few times knocking down a heavy pole the experience can make him very jittery about jumping. Horses don't knock down poles because they enjoy rapping themselves. Trainers who deliberately rap them by "poling" lack imagination and understanding. If all these Fearless Fosdicks were rapped on their thick heads with sledgehammers, the world would suffer no great loss.

The best experience for seasoning a green jumper is facing him with a wide variety of obstacles of different shapes and materials so that very soon, long before you have found out "how high he can go," almost no obstacle you can show him, and certainly none he is likely to meet in the field or in the show ring, will surprise him or spook him.

For the average amateur owner keeping one or two horses at home this fundamental requirement often seems to be a stumbling block. Solidly constructed jumps, even if you build them yourself, can run into a fair amount of money. Building them takes time—and we aren't all skilled handymen. Once set up, the jumps are heavy and cumbersome to move about—but it won't be long before we'll want to move them because in a short time, the take-off and landing areas will be pretty well cut up, hoof-pocked and hard-packed. Having learned these facts of life the hard way, it seems, most people with only one

---

[1] This is just one of the Linda-Tonka team's exploits I knew nothing about until long after the event. Another one was Tonka's victorious race against a speedy Quarter Horse. This occurred when the gray colt was three and still a stallion. In spite of my warnings never to let him run all out, Linda accepted a challenge to race. The stakes were two ice cream cones—one for the rider and one for the horse. Though he got off to a poor start, Tonka came from behind to win by a couple of lengths, then went another quarter-mile before Linda got him stopped. His cone was a five-scoop superduper, each scoop a different flavor, and he begged for more.

The Phases of the Jump. These five photographs illustrate a complete jump. Though for discussion purposes we commonly speak of each phase of a jump as separate, of course it is not. It cannot be. Jumping is movement, fast movement. The phases flow and blend into one another. Each one influences those that follow. At every split second the balance of the horse and of the rider is dynamic, changing. When the flow is even, the blending smooth, we have a good jump.

Above left: The Take-off. Undoubtedly this is the most important phase of a jump. If it is wrong, everything that follows will be commensurately wrong. It is a critical moment not only for the horse but for the rider, for it is when so many riders get off balance, thus hindering their mount's effort throughout the jump. Approaching at a gallop, the horse checks momentarily; to raise his forehand he must shift his weight to the hindquarters. This check —slight if the horse is well balanced and has good momentum, abrupt and jerky if he misjudges—tends to fling the rider forward out of the saddle. That's why it is so important during the last few strides of the approach for the rider to be firmly seated.

About middle: The Thrust. As the horse springs the powerful thrust of the hindquarters tends to push the rider back into the saddle. If Linda had been off balance a moment before, this surging, upward thrust would now throw her "behind the horse." She might even completely lose her seat—this is the moment when so many falls begin. But with her weight balanced in the irons, supported by a firm knee grip and by her hands lightly on his crest, she leaves Tonka's hindquarters free to do their work of propulsion efficiently.

Above right: The Ascending Flight. Tonka is still going up. As he extends fully, thrusting his head forward and stretching his neck —a combination of movements known as basculing, *which a horse whose mouth is abused will not do freely—Linda follows his mouth with her hands. With the horse in full flight, obviously there is nothing helpful the rider can do except remain as still as possible and allow the horse complete freedom. There should be prac-*

tically no tension on the reins. Hands and arms should be as elastically yielding as rubber bands. Ideally, each of Linda's forearms and each rein should form a straight line from her elbow to the bit. Ideals are good things to have. Hang onto them.

Above left: The Descent Begins. Linda's weight is still off the saddle; her hands are still yielding. Tonka, wisely, is looking down at the landing, but Linda has finally learned to look ahead to see what's next. Always let the horse take care of the landing. There is absolutely nothing you can do about it. Looking down only shifts your center of balance; it also causes you to round your back so that on landing you'll bang down into the saddle. The first fault is anything but helpful to your horse and the second won't exactly fire up his enthusiasm for jumping.

Above right: Pay Attention to Landing. If your take-off was poor, it is unlikely that your landing will be much better. But even though you have safely cleared an obstacle, don't think that how you land is unimportant. It is very important to your horse. This picture illustrates why wise horsemen jump with moderation and tend to be fussy about the hardness of the ground they ask a horse to jump on. Notice here that the shock of landing over even this relatively small jump has bent Tonka's left pastern at almost ninety degrees. A fraction of a second before the shutter was snapped, his right leg, the leading leg, had been subjected to even greater strain: at the moment of impact all his weight, plus Linda's weight, was supported by that one leg. This picture shows better than words could why so many overworked jumpers break down prematurely while others turn sour on jumping. A good rider absorbs the force of landing in his knee and ankle joints, sinking softly back into the saddle as the horse resumes the gallop. Horses whose backs are abused by clumsy riders don't "land going away" from an obstacle. They often falter before getting back into full stride and frequently show their resentment by laying back their ears. People who let their children jump two-year-olds and ride yearlings can ruin their colts through lack of understanding the great strain which jumping entails.

or two horses try to make do with a couple of simple bar jumps, or even a single pole laid atop two oil drums—one of the most deceptively difficult-to-judge jumps a green horse can face.

Of course, if you board your horse at a stable that specializes in the training of jumpers, you'll probably have all the variety your horse needs. Assuming, however, that you prefer to keep your horse or pony at home, you can make your own jumping course at very little cost, a course that you can easily change to suit your needs and move to fresh ground whenever you wish. All you need are imagination and ingenuity. Then make your jumps of whatever materials you have available.

There are certain common items to be found around practically all stables and farms, even the most modest one-horse suburban barn. These are baled hay, baled straw or shavings,

Logs, Stuffed Sacks, and Drums.

and empty grain sacks. Most of us also have a few fence poles or posts, perhaps a few oil drums, old automobile tires and miscellaneous lumber. All these things can be used to put together some quite serviceable jumps; they may not look fancy like some of the equipment you'll see in big operations that specialize in white paint, but they will serve their purpose just as well.

I refer you to the accompanying sketches. These are merely suggestions to illustrate what you can do with whatever materials you have on hand if you use imagination. Jumps such as these have the advantages of being easily movable, they can be jumped from both sides, and the materials can be changed and combined to form an almost endless variety of different-looking obstacles.

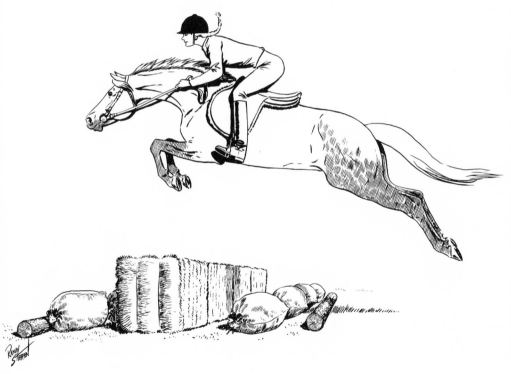

Logs, Stuffed Sacks, and Bales.

I would guess that Linda and Tonka have jumped a greater variety of miscellaneous "junk" than any other girl-and-pony team in the world. Nothing Linda points him at surprises Tonka any more.

You will notice that all these jump sketches omit any mention of wings. I don't believe in using wings. Intelligent schooling makes the use of wings unnecessary. A schooled horse well ridden will rarely try to run out, and then only for a good reason.

Here we revert to our fundamental principle of schooling. The rider, not the horse, makes all decisions. I believe in actually teaching a horse to go through the motions of running out and refusing when that is what the rider wants. It is the only way that a horse with a tendency to rush can be made a safe, reliable jumper. A good part of Tonka's schooling, as well as an

Triple Bar of Concrete Blocks and Bales Topped with Cavalletti.

essential part of Linda's training as a rider, consisted of the following exercise: She would ride at an obstacle at any gait I specified; perhaps during the approach I would give her the order to change gaits, say from a walk to a canter. At the last moment before the take-off I might give her any one of these commands: "Halt"; "Rein back"; "Circle away"; "Jump." Linda never knew which command I might give. She had to be firmly seated and in full control, ready for anything; and Tonka learned that, whatever Linda cued him to do, he had to obey promptly. This exercise is invaluable in teaching control.

In schooling a young jumper I find very little use for a whip. Long before we put a horse at even the smallest obstacles he should have learned obedience to the rider's legs, and for this basic lesson a whip is often necessary. In competition a

"Stone Wall"—Bales Covered by a Tarpaulin with the Ends Weighted Down by Logs or Timbers.

rider should usually carry a whip but only to be used in an emergency, as when a horse might bungle a difficult jump by faltering or hesitating at a crucial moment and perhaps spoil a good round or be disqualified. But in schooling, if a horse persistently refuses or runs out, it's a safe bet that for some reason he is afraid to jump—and the reasons may be as divergent as lack of practice, natural timidity, physical soreness or a slippery take-off. A crack with the whip is no solution to any of these troubles. The reasonable thing to do is to lower or shorten the jump, do something else for a while and then go back to the jump, or even quit jumping for a few days. Good jumpers, I am thoroughly convinced, are never made with the whip.

You will notice in the accompanying sketches that most of the jumps are relatively very low but that they are broad. These are the kind of obstacles that will safely and surely reveal to you "how high" your green jumper can go. There is almost

Bales of Straw or Hay and Drums.

nothing for the horse to knock down, or if there is he's not likely to hurt himself. But to get over such broad jumps a horse must jump high. It's a simple matter of trajectory. I refer you to pages 246 and 271.

The less his momentum at take-off, the higher the horse will have to spring to clear a spread of, say, fifteen feet. Conversely, the greater his speed at take-off, the flatter can be his trajectory; then the spread of his jump will be correspondingly greater. When great momentum is combined with powerful spring, the height and distance a horse can leap are astonishing. People who haven't given the matter any thought have to see a good jumper soar to believe how high and how far he can go between take-off and landing.

One day when Linda was working Tonka over a series of broad jumps, a couple of her friends arrived on horseback to watch the schooling. While Linda dismounted to chat and let Tonka graze, I rearranged one of the jumps. I made it bigger.

Oil or Feed Drums with Timbers or Logs.

At the highest point it was no more than thirty inches, but the spread was about fifteen feet or a bit more.

I invited Linda's friends to try it.

The girls looked at the obstacle; then they looked at me as if I had lost my mind. My assurance that their horses, considerably bigger than Tonka, could clear the jump without trouble failed to break down their refusals even to try.

"Let's see you jump it, Linda," one said pointedly.

Stationing one girl on each side of the obstacle, I told them to mark carefully the exact spot where Tonka took off and the exact spot where his leading forefoot touched the ground on landing. I myself stood directly beside the jump to check the height of the little gray's flight.

Linda rode fast and Tonka took off in good balance. As he sailed over, at the highest point of his flight the underside of his belly passed my line of vision approximately on a level with my shoulders or roughly about five feet above the ground. The distance from take-off to landing measured close to twenty-two feet.

The girls were amazed but completely convinced. After a few warm-up jumps over lesser obstacles, both of them ventured to try the larger jump. Their horses had no difficulty clearing it with room to spare.

An interesting sidelight is that neither of these two horses, though otherwise fairly experienced jumpers, had ever been put at a broad jump before; yet neither refused or tried to run out. It seems that most horses will face a low broad jump with more confidence than they will go at a high jump, even though they have to leap higher over the spread. I suspect that the reasons for this might be that they can clearly see the landing area even while approaching the broad jump and that they have no fear, based on painful experience with high jumps, of knocking anything down.

The distinguishing mark of a reliable jumper is his ability to get over a demanding course of varied obstacles without losing his nerve. Many horses that can jump big and sometimes brilliantly over a couple of obstacles cannot complete a course.

The Water Jump.

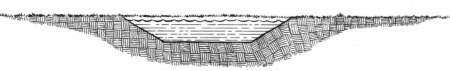

This is the only safe way to dig a water jump—with sloping banks on all sides! Twelve to eighteen inches is deep enough.

Never dig it like this!

Start with a narrow ditch. Flank it with logs to induce the horse to jump—not wade! Widen it gradually.

Two Spines, One Arc. Observe that Linda's spine is approximately parallel to Tonka's. In jumping, this is a good general rule to keep in mind. For if you can observe it in practice you will seldom either be left behind or find yourself "jumping ahead of the horse"—with a good chance of ending up on his neck when he lands. This ideal position is attained not merely by leaning forward but by pushing your rump to the rear and lowering your torso from the hips. This brings your own center of gravity nearer to that of the horse. The more closely the rider's center of gravity or balance coincides with his mount's, the less effort the horse must expend to clear an obstacle and to recover on landing and the more secure the rider will be. Compare this picture to the next one.

This Can Happen to Anyone. At this jump Linda was "left behind" at the take-off. Tonka may have jumped a moment sooner than she expected; Linda may have had her weight too far back at the take-off; or she might have been slightly off balance. The reasons this can happen to any rider are varied. If the horse is an erratic or "sticky" jumper, he can make the best rider look bad. The important thing to remember is: try your utmost not to pull on the horse's mouth by hanging on by the reins. Let the reins slip through your hands so as to give your mount freedom of his head and neck, his balancier. If necessary, give him all the reins while you grab the pommel. If you don't interfere, your horse will usually get you over the obstacle. Over this conglomeration of miscellaneous "junk" (timbers, cavalletti, drums, logs, old tires) Tonka soared about five feet high and a good twenty feet from take-off to landing. He was able to jump big in spite of Linda's poor position because she did not cramp him by hanging on his mouth.

They may start out like sure winners, but with each successive jump their "nerves" rapidly go to pieces. Unable quickly to adjust to different types of obstacles, they cannot jump calmly and consistently; they cannot be rated. By the third or fourth obstacle—if they've got that far—they are practically out of control. The rider becomes little more than a passenger hanging on to the reins. Such horses are frequently to be seen in open jumper classes. They regain their normal calm only when they have left the ring.

Sometimes this sort of erratic performance may be traced to faulty temperament, but much more often, I believe—because the fault is so common—it can be laid to defective schooling, a way of training and riding that upsets a normal horse's good disposition and is absolutely ruinous to a sensitive, high-strung animal. Too much haste, too much high jumping and too much of the whip have a lot to do with it. To avoid such unpleasant results, particularly with high-strung horses, much early schooling over low broad jumps as varied as the trainer can make them is, in my opinion, the best solution.

I have seen it work with other horses. I'm sure it will work with yours.

CHAPTER XXIV

Jumping: A Last Word

THESE facts are clearly evident; yet most of us, at least sometimes, are prone to forget them or disregard them:

Your horse will be happier, healthier and stay sound longer if you treat him as an athlete. Don't coddle him. Keep him in sensibly good condition. Work him into peak condition gradually but don't try to keep him at a constant peak; he'll go stale. Let him down as gradually as you worked him up.

Don't expect a colt, no matter how big and husky, to do the work a mature horse can do. That's how many jumpers and race horses are broken down years before they have even reached their prime.

Don't be a jumping fanatic. Jumping should be sport and fun. As a way of life, leave it to the professionals. They are paid to work at jumping. Their horses are specialists, never called on to do anything else.

We like to speak of "natural jumpers," but this is a very relative term. Never forget that your horse, no matter how good he is, is *not* a natural jumper. Proportionate to his size and strength, he is a very poor jumper compared to any ordinary house cat or to a dog. Jumping is an acrobatic feat for which your horse is physically ill-equipped. If you force or permit him to overexert himself just once, that moment of care-lessness can cost him a permanent injury or a serious blemish that may start him on his way down in the world.

Therefore, in jumping particularly, be moderate. Use horse sense. You cannot go too contrary to nature without penalty.

CHAPTER XXV

Barn Business

T HE field of horsemastership is so cluttered with antiquated rituals, customs, taboos and one-track-minded yahoos that I have at times wondered why any of us care to keep horses at all.

Take the matter of stable management and daily routine. We all agree that for the sake of efficiency there must be some sort of routine—but why should it begin at five or six o'clock in the morning, often before daylight in winter? Why should it be—as the old cavalry experts like to tell us—as rigid as a prison routine? I have never noticed that it makes any difference to my horses whether they are fed at five or seven or nine o'clock, either in the morning or the evening. If they're healthy and hungry, they'll eat. But they'll eat better, the military-minded martinets would have us believe, if they are fed at the same hours every day; their digestive juices start bubbling and all that sort of thing. I don't believe it. My horses eat heartily when they are fed. I think if they ate any "better," I'd end in the poorhouse. I feed them as I myself like to be fed—when I'm hungry. I don't have to look at a clock to know when that is. The all-important thing is that you feed your horse adequately, nutritionally, and at least twice a day (because of his small stomach). But rigidly following a timetable is of no importance whatever.

If this book does nothing else, I hope that it will lead young horsemen and horsewomen to *question* every bit of stable lore they hear. Accept nothing merely because someone says so. Make a habit of asking, "Why?" You'll be amazed at how many ridiculous answers you get.

A common example of horsey hocus-pocus is the "correct" way to mount a horse. Not one rider in a million today has any need to wear a sword, which was the original reason for mounting and dismounting a horse from the left. But if in a horsemanship class today you were to mount or dismount on the "wrong" side, every hidebound judge in the land would mark you down. Yet practical horsemen agree that any horse or pony should be accustomed to being mounted and dismounted from both sides—and either side is as good as the other.

A good grooming, according to one moss-hung bit of stable lore, is worth a feed of oats. Presumably this is straight from the horse's mouth, but I've never learned who the horse was. I suspect a jackass. If I were a horse, I'd prefer the oats. I enjoy a good steak dinner more than a massage. I've never seen a horse that would leave his oats unfinished when you showed him a curry comb and a brush. But I have seen many well-groomed horses that weren't worth their oats and others that hardly knew how it felt to be groomed that were worth every cent you could afford to pay for them.

"Grooming puts muscle on a horse." Of all absurd stable myths this one surely ranks near the top. You might as well say that a daily rubdown will turn a runt into a Charles Atlas or that rubbing hair tonic on your head will improve your brain. God, adequate exercise and good feeding put muscle on a horse. Massaging his hide has nothing to do with it.

Don't get the idea that I'm against grooming. I'm for it. Indeed, when I can get someone else to do the job for me my enthusiasm knows no bounds. I like the look of a well-groomed horse as well as anyone else. Grooming is a necessary chore. Horses in training that sweat should be groomed every day.

But many people who don't work their horses hard, ordinary pleasure riders, make a fetish of grooming. They pay more attention to how a horse is trimmed than to how he is exercised and fed. They fuss about the appearance of his mane and tail and pay only casual attention to the condition of his legs and feet, a matter of much greater importance.

Shoeing is another common fetish. Millions of horses are shod whether they need it or not—and thousands of them don't. Fat halter horses that have little more to do than look pretty and pleasure horses that seldom or never work on hard roads or over stony ground are often shod all around for no better reason than that their owners have been led to believe that all horses *should* be shod. Well, they shouldn't. The constant wearing of shoes is responsible for more poor feet than common neglect. One of the first things I do when taking a horse for training is to inspect his feet. If the animal is shod, I ask the owner, "Why?" About nine times out of ten I don't think that the answer makes much sense. I usually have the shoes pulled and the feet trimmed, or I trim them myself, before any schooling begins. With very rare exceptions, the horse's feet improve.

To shoe or not to shoe depends on the individual horse, the work he is required to do, and the terrain. The only general rules I recommend are these:

If a horse has good feet, give him a chance to do his work barefoot. If he can, don't shoe.

If he can't, try tips first.

If tips are not enough to correct whatever is wrong, then shoe. But don't keep the horse shod any longer than necessary. At least a few months of the year he should go unshod to let his feet expand and develop naturally.

To shoe a sound horse merely to let him stand in a stall most of the time is absurd.

The importance of closely checking a horse's feet can hardly be over-stressed. "No foot, no horse." Few people realize how easily a horse's foot picks up things that can cripple or even kill him. Years ago a well-known breeder hired a new ranch manager, who checked all the pastures the first day he was on

Grooming: The Feet. I take a dim view of doting amateurs who say that they "love" to groom a horse. I'd never hire one with any optimism that his enthusiasm would last very long—once he had a string of horses to do. Grooming a horse well is hard work. A skilled groom works with vigor, energy and speed; he wastes neither time nor motions. Outdoors on a chilly day, stripped of jacket or coat, he can work up a sweat; on a cold day his exertions will keep him warm. A poor groom, on the other hand, can fuss over a horse for hours without getting the animal more than halfway clean. It's all in knowing how. Remember that the efficient way is the easy way. Learn to be intelligently lazy.

Opposite left: To pick up a forefoot, pinch or squeeze the large tendon at the rear of the leg below the knee. If necessary, press forward with your arm behind the knee to bend the leg.

Opposite right: As the horse lifts his foot keep a firm grip on the leg and grasp it with the other hand, too. Step forward and rest the bent leg on your thigh or grip it between your knees.

Above left: To pick up a hindleg, stand beside the horse with your near hand pressed against his hip. Slide your hand down to the point of the hock and squeeze the large tendon just above it (the hamstring). The horse will raise or relax his leg. Grab the front of the foot with your other hand as you step forward, stretching the leg out to the rear.

Above right: Keep your grip on the foot as you rest the leg on your thigh with the hock firmly clamped under your armpit. This position gives you maximum control. Be careful to draw the leg straight out behind, not to one side, which might unbalance the horse. In cleaning the foot, pick from the heel toward the toe.

Brushing. The best way to brush out a tangled or a dirty tail is to do it in sections, one lock at a time. Grasp the whole tail in one hand just below the dock, lift it away from the horse and let some of the hairs fall. Brush with a full-armed sweeping motion, then let down some more hairs and continue. Change hands frequently so that the tail is brushed from both sides. If the hair is tangled or matted with burrs, use your fingers. A stiff brush is preferable to a comb. Too much combing can ruin a full tail.

Never use a metal curry comb on a horse's tender skin. About the only exception to this rule is when you use it lightly here and there to break up and loosen thick gobs of dried mud. Even for this, however, don't use a metal comb on the face or the lower legs. Use only a flexible rubber curry comb on the horse; save the metal one for cleaning your brushes. Curry with brisk, rotary motions, pressing hard to loosen the dead hair and the

the job. What he found shocked him. From one field of only twelve acres he gathered and hauled away more than two truck loads of rusty wire, tin cans and miscellaneous junk. Yet that breeder considered himself, and was generally acknowledged to be, a first-class horseman, when only dumb luck for years had saved many of his valuable mares and colts from serious blemishes or possible death by lockjaw.

Far too many stables are run in this slipshod way, with great attention paid to trivialities and surface veneer while really important matters are neglected. Amateur horsemen, those sentimentalists who want you to know how much they "love"

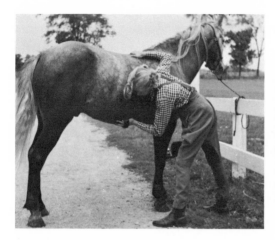
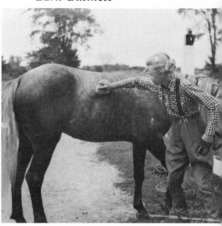

dirt. Begin behind the ears, work down the neck and back to the tail; then do the belly and legs. Move around to the other side and repeat.

The secret of brushing a horse to a high gloss and stimulating his skin is to brush vigorously. Use short, quick strokes and lean on the horse. Put muscle into every stroke. Stand well away from him so that, with your arm braced, you can put your back into the task. Follow the lay of the hair. Every third or fourth stroke take a quick swipe at the brush with the curry comb in your other hand. Set up a regular rhythm and stick to it. You'll be surprised at how quickly you can finish the job, and at how much your own circulation has stepped up. When you have finished, run your fingertips over that glossy hide, pushing against the lay of the hair. If your fingers get dirty or raise tracks of dandruff—start over and do the job right!

horses, are more guilty than the hardhearted professionals to whom horses are merely a livelihood.

Yet the pros have their faults, too.

I have often walked down the aisle of one of these horse palaces where everything is done on schedule and where all the horses are beautifully groomed and usually wear sheets to keep them that way, and I have had the sad feeling that I was walking down Death Row—a depressing death of the spirit. All the boxes are solidly walled up from floor to ceiling; each stall door has only a small grill through which the horse can look out— and see practically nothing. Each horse is, in effect, a prisoner.

For no just reason whatever, he is condemned to what amounts to solitary confinement. Except when taken out for exercise, he never sees any of his stablemates. Horses are curious, gregarious animals. They like to see what's going on and they need company. To shut them up in this way is nothing less than cruelty.

Yet people wonder why a colt or a stallion is difficult to control when led out of his stall without a chain twisted around his muzzle.

I realize that what I say here will have little influence with older horsemen. They will continue to do things as they always have done them, with or without reasons why the old ways are the best ways. But I am not writing for old-timers set in their ways. I am writing for *you*, the old-timers of tomorrow. In your hands lies the power to change the world of horses for the better. You need follow only one simple rule:

Treat your horse as you would like to be treated yourself.

CHAPTER XXVI

"The Show Game"

Tonka was four years old and had made a start at learning polo when he and Linda made their debut in the show ring. He might well have waited until he was fourteen or twenty if I had left the initiative to Linda, for though she had plenty of self-confidence and almost too much confidence in Tonka outdoors, the thought of riding before a judge and an audience filled her with acute stage fright. My repeated hints and suggestions that it would be interesting to find out how she and Tonka would look to a presumably impartial judge fell on deaf ears, even though I was careful to emphasize that winning was of no importance.

I knew, of course, that Linda thought otherwise. In any athletic competition she has always exerted herself to win; and, perhaps not so fortunately, being greatly gifted as an athlete, she always has been a winner. In school she won the nickname "The Roadrunner" for her speed afoot; in physical fitness tests she set records nobody else even came close to. Linda had yet to learn the hard lesson that to win you must risk losing and that losing is no disgrace. In her experience that was only a theory that applied to others. She shrank from facing the actuality applied to herself.

This disturbed me, not merely as an aspect of her equestrian education but as an important facet of her outlook on life in general. Life is a competition from beginning to end, and no one can get through it successfully who expects it to be always a sure thing. Linda had to learn to lose.

When a horse show to be held a few miles from our home was announced, I saw my opportunity. Naturally, we planned to take it in. While I was pondering how to get Linda over there with Tonka without arousing her suspicions, Linda herself solved the problem for me. She decided to ride along with some of her friends who were going to the show on horseback.

At the show ground, I wandered off by myself. Studying the program, I decided to enter Linda in Western Horsemanship. I picked that class simply because Linda had left home wearing blue jeans and riding Tonka in a stock saddle. If she had been wearing jodphurs or breeches and had put a flat saddle on him, I'd have chosen English Horsemanship or some similar class. What class she competed in did not matter. All that did matter was that she should learn that winning or losing is not a matter of life or death.

I made a post entry, shoved the armband into my pocket, and said nothing. But I kept track of Linda, who was riding about on Tonka and chatting with her friends. I knew just where she was when the class was called. Standing near the gate as the

first riders started filing into the ring, I beckoned to her. Linda rode over to me at a trot.

"You and Tonka are in this class," I told her. "I've entered you. Stick your arm out. Put this on." While she stared at me dumfounded, I slipped the numbered band onto her arm.

"Wait!" Linda found her voice. "I'm not going to ride——"

"Oh, yes, you are. I've paid the fee and I'm not going to waste it." Seizing the reins, I led Tonka into the ring. "Relax, baby. There's nothing to get excited about. You don't have to do anything you haven't done a thousand times at home. Just give him a slack rein, don't change hands, and be sure he takes the correct leads. Nothing to it!" I slapped Tonka's haunch. "Get going. Luck!"

Tonka fell into line with the other horses, I stepped out of the ring, and Linda was on her own.

Her sudden calmness surprised me. After the first circuit of the ring, she showed no sign of nervousness at all. She rode well Tonka went well. There were twenty-eight horses in the class, and the riders were of all ages, including adults. The judge, an experienced horseman and show rider himself, worked them thoroughly. When he finally lined up the class, I could see that Linda, if not actually enjoying herself, was certainly free of any feeling of nervousness. She was chatting with a girl next to her in the line-up and hardly noticed the

Linda and Tonka at a "Punkin Roller." A "punkin roller" is a small, informal show usually sponsored by a local riding club to add a few dollars to the club treasury—and to give everybody a day of sport and fun. It's a form of come-as-you-are neighborhood get-together, with informality the prevailing rule. Entry fees are small, ribbons numerous and trophies—if any— insignificant. Competition, however, can be keen. Many people bring their best young horses to get them used to show conditions. One judge handles all classes—he is supposed to know everything. The term "punkin roller" stems from the idea that you have only to roll the pumpkins off a field and there's your show ring. But don't think you can't be beaten at a "punkin roller." You may find yourself competing against a future champion being prepared for the big time by a seasoned show rider.

judge until he was standing before Tonka. "Rein back, please." Tonka, flexing slightly, moved straight back as if on rails, halted in balance, then stepped forward to his original position. Linda's movements were hardly discernible. The judge moved on down the line, and Linda resumed her conversation.

That was when I began to get nervous. I hoped that I was prejudiced, but as impartially as I could view the proceedings it looked like another one of Linda's no-competition contests. There was not another entry in the class that came even close to her performance and Tonka's on that particular day.

The judge agreed. Linda was still chatting with her neighbor when the announcer called her number to come forward and receive the blue. Her thoughts were so far away from the possibility of winning that she actually did not hear the announcement. "They're calling your number," her friend had to tell her. "You've won."

I'll never forget the look of astonishment on Linda's face. For several moments she just sat there on Tonka while the realization of her victory gradually sank in. Then with a grin that dimmed the sun she rode forward to accept the prize.

A great way to teach her how to lose, I reflected wryly. Her first show, her first class—and she wins! It might as well have been a foot race or a rope-climbing contest. Linda Young first, as usual.

The next day, however, I realized that my pushing her into the ring had succeeded in its purpose. The fact that she had so quickly calmed down and had neither considered nor worried about the possibility of winning proved that. Linda had learned to accept the risk of losing.

It was fortunate that she learned this lesson in her first show and was lucky enough to win under a competent judge, for her and Tonka's second show was a real disappointment. It added considerably to Linda's education in the facts of horse-show life.

This time she was up against a Quarter Horse judge. In my considered opinion based on years of observation, there is nothing so utterly hopeless for a non-Quarter Horse rider to show under. I am convinced that nine out of ten judges who are Quarter Horse fanciers, once they step into a show ring, can't see any other breed.

I realize that I'll be castigated by Quarter Horse fanciers for expressing such a view, but I have seen too many clearly biased decisions by Quarter Horse judges to be convinced that I am wrong. Not long ago, for example, at a predominantly Quarter Horse show I watched an open trail horse class in which a registered Morgan completed the course without a single fault. He was closely followed by an Appaloosa and a grade-Arab, each of which had two minor faults. Their competitors, all registered Quarter Horses, were not even close to these three fine horses—but the trophy and every ribbon went to Quarter Horses.

Among Appaloosa fanciers it is a common complaint against Quarter Horse judges who also judge Appaloosa classes that they do not know, or deliberately disregard, the Appaloosa standard. Too many of them seem to think that an Appaloosa should be just "a Quarter Horse with spots."

I cite these facts as facts, not mere personal opinion. I certainly do not mean to imply that I doubt every Quarter Horse judge's integrity. There are honest men in all fields, and some judges wouldn't give their rich uncle a ribbon if they thought he didn't deserve it. What I do doubt is most Quarter Horse judges' knowledge of good horsemanship, their standards. This appalling ignorance, of course, is not peculiar to Quarter Horse judges only, but it is, I believe, most predominant among them. To this general ignorance the female Quarter Horse experts add an extreme, nit-picking fussiness about irrelevant minutiae that have absolutely no relationship to any reasonable standards of horsemanship.

For example, at one show the judge immediately set about reducing Linda's class by disqualifying all riders whose mounts did not look like Quarter Horses. Though the class was Junior Western Horsemanship, half the youngsters were eliminated without being given a chance to show what they could do. Most of them never got their mounts out of a walk before they were headed for the gate. Linda survived the summary eliminations through walk, trot and lope; then the autocrat of the ring waved her gateward with the remark:

"Your horse looks too much at other horses."

Since there were about fifteen other horses still in the ring, this was not a difficult feat, but how much was "too much" and what Tonka's glances had to do with Linda's horsemanship the judge didn't say. Apparently the judge preferred a horse that stared straight ahead at the horizon as if wearing blinkers. (I have schooled such horses and every one of them was not only clumsy but stupid. I have had them fall with me on level ground where a blind person could have walked with safety.) Tonka's way of going was no different from his performance in the first show. Only the judges were different.

I have gone into some detail about these two very different show experiences to stress an important point. The show ring is not the ultimate testing ground for a performance horse or a rider that some horse-show adherents would have us believe. Except in speed events, which are settled by the clock, and in such classes as knockdown-and-out, the way the ribbons are tied in any given class in any given show is merely an expression of that judge's personal opinion. If a judge likes your type of horse or your style of riding, you'll win; if he doesn't, you won't. It's as simple as that, and it makes no difference how good your horse really is or how good a rider you are. This is particularly true in horsemanship classes.

The fact that the A.H.S.A. spells out specific standards for the various classes makes very little practical difference. A judge is free to interpret the standards in his own way and he is responsible to no one for his decisions. You can't even protest a decision. Show managements will always back up a judge. Why not? They hired him for his opinions. For them to admit that he is either ignorant or crooked would necessitate admitting their own mistake in having invited him. This is something show managers don't like to admit, no matter how often they prove it.

Accordingly, the first rule I would give any young show

rider is this: Unless you plan to turn professional and wish to be the sort of trainer whose business success is in direct ratio to the number of show winners he turns out, *never* take showing too seriously. Enjoy it as a game or a sport. Accept the fact that only a few can win while the majority must lose. If you win, feel lucky; when you lose, even if you think you got a raw deal, forget it. And never, never fall into the trap of accepting success in the show ring as a true measure of a horse's merit or a rider's skill. The conditions of show riding are of necessity too artificial for success in the ring to be an accurate yardstick —except for show riding. Outdoor horse trials and combined training events provide a much more accurate index.

The second rule I would give a young rider is this: Before you show, you owe it to yourself and to your horse to learn the rules of the classes you plan to enter. I don't mean that you should try to memorize the rule book, but you should clearly understand all conditions of your classes even before you mail your entry fees. You may think that some of the rules are stupid—and there's at least a fifty-fifty chance that you'll be right—but if you don't want to play the game according to the book, stay home. Every game has its rules and the "show game" is no exception. When you send in your entry you automatically agree to abide by those rules.

As you get around from show to show, gaining experience, form the habit of studying judges. Professionals make almost a fine art of this. Observation will teach you what a particular judge likes. If he isn't your type of judge, don't waste time showing under him; save your money for other shows. In spite of my nasty remarks about the breed in general, there are some good judges—even Quarter Horse men! Each has his own pet ideas, even as you and I have ours. You must find the judges whose ideas are similar to yours. If after repeated trials you can't find *any* judge who thinks you deserve a ribbon, you'd better stay home and practice for a while or switch to another mount.

Always remember that in a show you are *showing*. Every moment you are in the ring you and your mount are on display.

The Complete Show Horse. Photograph by Araby Colton

Showmanship is the art of making everything you do in the ring *look easy*. What you do actually may be difficult. With a young horse or a temperamental one, you may be sweating blood, expecting the horse at any moment to blow up and make both of you look foolish. But while the judge has his eye on you, you have to pretend that your blood is ice water and that you and your mount are in perfect accord. If even the set of your face gives the impression that you are having difficulty, an observant judge will see it, and he will mark you down.

Fitting a horse for a show begins months before the day of the show because, whether you have a halter horse or a performance horse, condition begins with proper feeding and judicious exercise; both take time to show effect. In my opinion, these two factors of conditioning make daily grooming practically unnecessary. Good health makes a coat shine. If your horse doesn't shine after a lick-and-a-promise with a brush and a rub rag, then you have reason to worry. In these days of horse vacuum cleaners—and even if you don't have a vacuum—thorough daily grooming can be commenced only a few days before the show. If the feeding and the exercise have been right and the horse is healthy, he will step into the ring as full of bloom as any competitor that has been groomed practically to the bone every day for months.

CHAPTER XXVII

Cavaliers and Hayseeds; or,
Who Needs Boot Garters?

ABOUT a year ago I published a piece on the use of cavalletti in schooling. Among the photographs illustrating the article were the pictures of Linda and Tonka found on pages 132, 133, and 135 in this book.

The article drew a letter of mixed praise and criticism from a woman in California, who described herself as a trainer of hunters and jumpers and a riding teacher of children. She liked my article but considered the pictures "deplorable." She disapproved of them because Linda had not been wearing boots and breeches. "If any of my students," the lady wrote primly, "attended class dressed the way the young woman in the photo was, they would not be permitted to ride."

She also condemned the saddle pad shown in the pictures: "Using any type of blanket other than that made for the saddle is taboo!" But she didn't explain why.

While admitting the obvious fact that clothes don't make the rider, this instructor reminded me that boots and breeches *look* better than jeans and moccasins. She concluded with the suggestion that hereafter I should have my models "properly dressed."

The editor, precariously balanced on his editorial limb, hazarded the completely wild guess that as a trainer of horses I am probably less interested in "the formalities" than a riding instructor would be. "We agree with you," he assured his subscriber, "but from a standpoint of safety—boots should always be worn, and a helmet when jumping."

I found this issue of the magazine thought-provoking for other reasons as well. The cover reproduced a photograph of a winning show horse with its juvenile rider and its adult owner. Both the young rider and the proud owner were splendid in colorful outfits described as "Western equitation suits." In fact, their outfits were so splendid that the editor saw fit to identify not only the horse, the rider and the owner but even the designer of the suits.

The magazine contained an article on Western styles in clothing that quoted Oleg Cassini, the renowned men's dressmaker, as proclaiming the cowboy "the most elegant dresser today." Another feature, spread over three full pages, instructed readers how to clean and reshape their favorite cowboy hats. Of eight articles in the magazine only two dealt directly with the riding and training of horses.

Saying nothing about the letter deploring our unstylish pictures, I left the magazine on a table where the rest of the family would be sure to see it.

My wife discovered it first. She studied the cover. "Look." She held the magazine up for me to see. "A blue hat. Even blue chaps. What won't these clowns think of next?"

Linda's reaction was different. She studied the cover without any comment, then began leafing through the magazine. She stopped skimming to study some pictures.

"Take a look at this," she told me. "It says here this girl placed first in a bareback riding class. Just look at her horse!"

The photograph she indicated showed a girl impeccably attired in an "equitation suit" similar to those on the cover. She had a graceful seat, but her bridle hand looked stiff. Her horse was overbent, its neck arched, its face well behind the vertical. The pictures were excellent examples of false collection.

"They judge only the rider," I said.

"If the rider isn't responsible for overflexing the horse, who is?"

"Would you like one of those equitation suits?"

"Me? You wouldn't catch me dead at a dog fight in one of those outfits."

When Sheilagh got hold of the magazine, her expression suggested that she might have been looking at pictures of the Brandybibbers. "Equitation suits? I thought they were leftovers from a bankrupt circus auction."

I set down these observations and remarks to point up some facts—facts which many people of influence in the sport of riding would ignore.

Personal tastes differ. Individual ideas of style are shaped by various factors. Those earnest show exhibitors pictured in the magazine had spent considerable money and had gone to a good deal of trouble to be properly turned out in what amounts to a regulation uniform. Yet to my wife and to Linda and Sheilagh they looked garish, circusy, ridiculous. Linda, hardly noticing the fancy uniforms, cut straight to the essence of the pictures— the horsemanship displayed. If that was wrong, of what importance was the rider's clothing?

The field of equestrian fashion, however, is big business. Readers of horse magazines are constantly exposed to a barrage of snob-appeal advertising that adroitly confuses style in apparel with skill in horsemastership. The implication is that you aren't fit to associate with a good horse if you don't wear the right clothes. If you do wear the right clothes, however, you will automatically become a better horseman. Incredible as it may seem, more than one book on riding has pretended to "prove" this with photographs—a picture of a sloppily dressed rider on a horse that looks half-asleep, then another picture of the same rider smartly turned out on the same horse looking alert and eager to go, presumably because he is proud of his rider's snappy attire.

If this were merely a phase of the publishing business, it would hardly be worth mentioning. Publishers have to live. Advertising is vital to them. Without it they could not stay in business; and it is to our benefit that they should stay in business, for on the whole they do a tremendous amount of good. By disseminating ideas and providing a medium for the exchange of opinions on a national, even an international, scale, they can claim a great deal of the credit for the general improvement of horsemanship. The same cannot be said of the people who run horse shows and those who control the American Horse Shows Association. These are the people who make the rules which imply that clothes *do* make the rider, and if you don't have or won't wear the right clothes you will not be permitted inside their show rings.

Of course, as with everything else that isn't all white or all black, there are some good reasons for this clothes consciousness —up to a certain point. A horse show, after all, is a public spectacle; like any sporting event, it's a form of show business. Few spectators at a horse show really understand what they see. They look at it as they would view a circus or a parade. Unconcerned about the fine points, they like the color, the action, the beauty of fine horses in motion. But what sort of spectacle would a horse show be if class after class were filled by riders who wore any old thing, the sort of clothes they might wear when working in the barn at home?

Unfortunately, there are slobs of this type. Without some rules to keep them in line, they would wear anything. They wouldn't even bother to clean up. They would come to a show looking like bums, with their horses looking and smelling as if they had bedded down in manure. The minority I'm talking about lack any semblance of good taste or personal pride. They're the Hell's Angels type, addicted to horses instead of motorcycles. They need rules, rigid rules. Though they are a minority, show managements cannot afford to ignore them.

That is one side of the picture. Unfortunately, there is a darker, gloomier side.

Even without the slovenly Hell's Angels types to keep in line, too many of the people who run horse shows and most of those who control the A.H.S.A. would change horse shows into style shows because they themselves have been so thoroughly brainwashed by slick advertising that they really believe in this exaggerated importance of clothes. The A.H.S.A. Rule Book spells out in specific, trivial detail exactly what sort of clothes exhibitors in approved shows *must* wear. Consider, for example, Rule XVII, Sec. 2 (a) governing personal appointments in hunter seat equitation classes:

Exhibitors and judges should bear in mind that at all times entries are being judged on ability rather than on personal attire. However, riders should wear coats of any tweed or melton for hunting (conservative wash jackets in season), breeches (or jodhpurs) and boots. Dark blue or black hunting cap and black or brown derby is mandatory. . . . Judges must eliminate contestants who do not conform.

Notice the contradiction. First we are told that riders are to be judged on ability only, not on their clothing. Then we learn that all riders must wear coats and even what kind of coats, as well as boots, jodhpurs, hats and caps, and that a judge *must* eliminate those who are not dressed right.

The rule for saddle seat equitation classes is even more specific. Approved colors are listed. One's jodhpurs must match one's coat. If the class is in the evening, a rider must appear in *formal* dress. This includes a tuxedo-type jacket of conservative color with matching collar and lapels, a top hat and gloves. Should you fail to conform to these style dictates, the judge has no choice but to "eliminate" you without allowing you a chance to show what you can do. You can always console yourself that, with the right clothes, you *would* have been judged on your ability.

In Western, or stock seat, equitation we are spared the hypocrisy about all riders being judged on their ability only; otherwise, the rigamarol has the old familiar ring. All riders must dress the part, wearing Western hats and cowboy boots. If the management prefers, they must also wear chaps. If you use closed reins with a romal, you must carry hobbles on your saddle, whether your horse is hobble-broke or not—the idea being to pretend that he is. The saddle, says the book, "must fit" the rider—and the judge decides whether your saddle fits you, not you.

The rule book is crammed with this sort of nonsense applied to all classes right down the line. Probably the acme of idiocy is reached in hunter appointment classes. A lady member of a hunt, if mounted sidesaddle, may wear a veil; if astride, she may not, but then she must wear a hat guard. Gentlemen in top boots must wear boot garters that conform to the color of their breeches and the garters must be worn just so, no other way. A Master isn't properly turned out unless his sandwich case contains "a sandwich suitably wrapped," and he'd better be sure that his flask isn't empty should the judge decide to inspect it.

All this realism in the artificial atmosphere of the show ring! All this picayune detail about personal appointments in what is supposed to be a horse show! Is a hunter to be judged by the color and the placement of his rider's boot garters? Are we to assume that the wearing of a tuxedo-type jacket, a top hat and gloves qualifies a rider as a horseman? Is a stock horse's worth to be measured by whether the rider wears a cowboy hat and chaps? Would anybody but misguided souls unduly concerned with mere surface details presume that a stranger knows more about how a rider's saddle "fits" him than the rider does?

I say that such rules are the work of picayunish minds. Those who formulate them and those who endorse them are snobs much more than they are horsemen. Riding, in their view, whether they admit it or not, is less a sporting activity than a social accomplishment. The horse show is merely their display window. They would eliminate all those who do not conform to their petty dictates. This is right and that is wrong for no better reason than that they say so.

This shallow fussiness over fashions in style and mere surface appearance is one of the main reasons why so many intelligent horse owners do not show and have no interest in showing. As these people see it, the purpose of a horse show is to exhibit one's horse and to demonstrate one's horsemanship. The functions of a judge is to judge these things—and only these things. When (with the exception of costume classes) what a rider happens to wear can influence these ultimate ends, people interested in pure horsemanship are repelled by the blatant phoniness of "the show game." They do not object to high entry fees and the general expenses showing entails; they do resent having to buy an expensive wardrobe for which they have little practical use, merely to win a judge's approval—or even to be allowed into the ring. As one experienced horseman said to me, "I can do without some half-baked hick from Horny Corners approving or disapproving of what I wear and presuming to decide what tack is best for my purpose and for my horses. I wear what I like and I know what my horses like."

Twenty years ago if you wanted to show your horse in a Western class in an approved show, you had to use a spade or a halfbreed spade bit. The A.H.S.A. Rule Book said so. The rule was written into the book by a small but influential minority. But thousands of horsemen all over the United States had no use for such bits and bitterly resented the rule. I spoke for these horsemen when I wrote "Calling a Spade a Spade," an article in which I analyzed the action of the spade bit and the logic of those who use it. [1] Horsemen all over the country bombarded the A.H.S.A. with copies of the article, demanding that the rule be changed. Over the protests of the minority, who wanted the rest of the world to do things *their* way, the obnoxious rule, after many years, was finally scrapped.

If nobody had ever spoken up, however, if things had been left to those who hide their dimness behind the status quo, you would still have to show your Western horse in a bit that somebody else, completely regardless of your ideas, proclaimed to be the only *right* kind of bit.

I mention this matter as an example of what I hope you will train yourself to do. This is the one vital idea above all else that I would leave with you. Never hesitate to kick the status quo in the teeth. Never, never accept things as they are merely because that's the way they are. Think. Question. Analyze. Test everything. Experiment. Take nothing for granted. Never mind who tells you (including me), "That's wrong," or "You must do it this way." If you think you know a better way, try it. Your horse will soon enough let you know how right or wrong you are.

If this preoccupation with fads and fashions (which constantly change) were confined only to the show ring, it would

[1] *The Western Horseman*, March, 1950.

be at least tolerable. All competitions must have some rules; the horse show is no exception, though the rules governing attire are usually the least important. However, as my California critic clearly proves, this fashion fetishism is not confined to the show ring. It emanates from the show ring. It insidiously pervades the thinking—one might say the nonthinking—of those persons who control horse shows, as well as of those who regard success in showing as the ultimate criterion, to an extent that reaches far beyond the show ring. Most of these people who attain positions enabling them to impose their own standards on others, and to a less extent those veteran exhibitors who unquestioningly accept the standards, have spent the greater part of their lives exposed to the subtle influence of the advertising experts. Unconsciously they have absorbed the belief that clothes do make the horseman, though if you challenge them to admit it they indignantly deny it—just as they set out denying it in their written rules, and then give themselves the lie by explicitly dictating what kind of clothes show exhibitors must wear. This is why their influence is so pernicious to the very sport they would foster. They are in position to impose their artificial standards on the uncritical young, thus perpetuating false ideals from one generation to the next—ideals which have absolutely no connection with genuine horsemastership.

Apologists for the present horse-show system with all its style-oriented rules and regulations have a favorite argument: Things are done in a certain way because long experience has proved that these are the safest and most efficient ways. But this facile argument cannot stand up to even the most casual critical scrutiny.

Consider, for example, the safety-first statement: "Boots should always be worn, and a helmet when jumping." But just when is a boot not a boot? Nobody would argue that an English-type boot reaching up to the knee is truly a boot. But what is to be said of the popular cowboy boot with a soft top a mere ten or twelve inches high? Does it qualify as a true boot or is it merely a high-topped shoe? The answer hardly matters;

call it what you will. The real question raised is: What is so "safe" about either style of boot? What is either capable of saving you from?

Saddle Horse riders in conventional attire never wear boots. They wear jodhpurs with ankle-length shoes that can be called boots only in the English sense. Are we to infer therefore that Saddlebred fanciers have no regard for personal safety?

I doubt that any horseman with experience in riding both jumpers and cutting horses would ever say that a jumper is more difficult to sit. Even when you are "screwed down tight" in a deep stock saddle and have a firm grip with one hand on the horn, an agile cutting horse can sometimes dodge right out from under you. Yet has anyone ever dared to suggest that cutting contestants should wear safety helmets? A rider who showed up at a cutting wearing a helmet would never live it down.

Rodeo bronc and bull riders need protective equipment much more than jump riders do. But nobody has ever suggested this, for, if they very sensibly wore safety helmets, what would happen to the rough, tough cowboy image?

If a bronc rider in a hard hat seems improbable, try to imagine an exhibitor in Western attire, including chaps, competing in a gaited Saddle Horse class. Even if he were mounted on the finest Saddle Horse since Wing Commander, without the right clothes, under the present rules, he would get the gate.

A rider who dared to compete in a jumping class wearing a Saddle Horse exhibitor's outfit would be laughed at as an eccentric.

The point I am stressing here is not what is right and what is wrong. My point is that what those in authority say is right and wrong reflects merely their ideas of style—and those ideas are based on customs and conventions elaborated by horsemen of bygone eras whose wealth and leisure made it possible for them to be fastidious about trivial details. This is a pernicious way of thinking, an archaic state of mind that distracts us from what should be our only ultimate goal—better horsemanship.

Only when we put this goal paramount to everything else,

relegating personal appointments to the inconsequential status that they deserve, then and only then will success in the show ring approach the criterion of skill that horse-show proponents now claim for it.

I hope that I have not given anyone the impression that I am a self-appointed spokesman for equestrian hippies. On the contrary, I am entirely in favor of smartness, elegance, spit-and-polish—when it's voluntary. I can't help it that my daughters often prefer to ride in moccasins and jeans, and sometimes even barefoot and in shorts and without a saddle; nor do I intend to try. I think that they are old enough to know what they prefer. Myself, I prefer boots and breeches, and I can't recall how many times I have advised pupils to get them; nor can I think of any who ever regretted following the advice. But it was advice I gave, mere suggestion; I did not presume to dictate or to take advantage of my position to force my personal preferences on pupils. I care little what a rider wears, not because I approve of haphazard attire, but because I am concerned with his horsemanship. That and nothing else is the important thing. Whatever a pupil may want to wear, the lessons go on.

I am quite aware of the historical fact that horsemen as a class have always been dandies. From the befeathered Indian brave on his painted pinto to the crusty colonel of an imperial regiment of hussars, men who ride horses have always liked to dress up. Until comparatively recent times horseman was almost synonymous with soldier. The cavalry was the elite branch of most armies. The officers usually came from the "best" families, those with the most influential connections and the greatest wealth. The infantry may have been "the queen of battles," but the cavalry was the haven of the nobility and the aristocracy. These coddled bravoes were not at all bashful about considering themselves superior to mere foot soldiers, and they went out of their way to advertise their conviction. They had the wealth and the leisure and the supreme self-assurance to be dandies. They rode into actual battle wearing elaborate uniforms fine enough for a dress ball. They would have made a peacock envious or shamed a Mexican charro into hiding.

We are the heirs to this tradition of equestrian dandyism, and I would be the last to scorn it. I have never cared for the Puritan tradition. I much prefer Cavalier elegance, even when it takes the rather crude form of equitation suits and blue chaps. My personal tastes may be a bit on the conservative side, but I'm inclined to be fussy about even minor details of quality and fit. I have a pair of breeches almost thirty years old that have withstood more than their share of hard usage; they are still good because they were the best obtainable, when I paid more for them than I could really afford. I can never appreciate cheap

The Gray Old Pro. The system of schooling presented in this book aims at developing an all-round mount for practical outdoor riding. By this standard, how do we judge the excellence of a finished horse or pony? The key is that term all-round. *Versatility is the criterion. The more things a horse or a pony can do well and the better he can do them, the greater is his worth. With additional, specialized schooling he may become tops in any one field without losing his versatility, but if he isn't versatile mentally as well as physically he is not, by our standards, a top mount.*

This happy blend of mental, temperamental and physical abili-

boots, even for picture purposes. In some pictures Linda is wearing boots that are older than she is; before she grew into them, her older sisters wore them; before that, the boots belonged to their mother. Boots of this excellent quality are, in my opinion, the only kind worth buying. And the same goes for hats, breeches, saddles, bridles—you name it. I believe in having the best.

These are my personal preferences. But I do not insist that they must also be yours. If you are satisfied with less, I do not say that I am right and you are wrong. I would never refuse to give you a riding lesson if you showed up wearing clothes that did not win my approval. You could wear moccasins and jeans, tennis shoes and shorts, or even your grandma's favorite bikini

ties depends mainly on two factors—finding the right material to work with, then making the most of it; or, to repeat what we stressed in the beginning, picking the right type of horse or pony and handling him with intelligence. If either of these requisites is missing, the finished product will fall short of the highest standards.

This is the day of the specialist, the age of the artificial, a time when we want everything done in a hurry. To some, the ideal we strive for may seem impossible. But I think the development of Tonka proves that it is not—and that good horses and ponies are not made in a hurry or by artificial means. Today, there is hardly anything a horse should be able to do—fast work or slow, extended or collected, under saddle or in harness—that Tonka can't do, or quickly learn to do, and do it well. He can calmly and smoothly switch from fast galloping and jumping to precise school work in paper-and-thread reins; then he can be trusted for a lesson with the greenest beginner, adapting himself to the pupil's awkward efforts —and he knows to the minute when the hour is up!

This picture shows him working at a new job—teaching Linda's younger sister, Kristen (who is the same age as he is), the elements of jumping. When Kristen is ready, he will jump as fast and as big for her as he now jumps for Linda. Some day he will have my grandchildren to teach, and he will get the job done. Tonka, once a harum-scarum colt, is now the finished product—the versatile, trained horse.

topped by an Eskimo parka; I wouldn't care. But if your horsemanship proved to be inferior I would care, and the kind of clothes you happened to be wearing would not excuse your mistakes.

Within bounds, equestrian dandyism is a harmless vanity, merely a matter of personal taste. But this meticulous attention to dress gets completely out of bounds when horse shows degenerate into style shows. When petty dictators and nit-picking snobs can formulate and enforce rules which decree that a rider may not compete unless his attire and gear meet arbitrary standards imposed by an autocratic minority, then we have lost all sense of proportion, have forgotten what should always be our foremost goal, and have distorted the horse show into something it was never intended to be.

In my opinion, any riding instructor who, with a job to be done—a pupil to teach or a horse to school—is so spinelessly subservient to what *"They Say"* that he or she would waste time on such trivialities as clothes is to be pitied even more than scorned.

The unfortunate pupils of such an instructor are to be pitied even more. Pupils reflect their teacher. If they absorb what they are taught, eventually they conform to the teacher's mold. Then we have another crop of prissy little peacocks convinced that what they wear on horseback is just as important as what they can do with a horse. The pupils never learn, because their teacher never learned, to strip away the superficialities and get down to the bedrock principles of true horsemastership.

I do not expect that what I say here will have any effect on the brassbound minds now in authority, except to antagonize them. "One of the greatest pains to human nature," wrote Walter Bagehot more than a century ago, "is the pain of a new idea." The Old Guard doesn't want to be bothered with new ideas. They just want to have everybody do things their way. Today they would have us believe that the wanton mutilation of Hackneys, Saddlebreds, and Tennessee Walking Horses is not what every intelligent horseman knows it is—barbaric cruelty perpetrated in the unholy name of fashion. Twenty years ago the Old Guard insisted on the spade and halfbreed spade bits. Fifty years ago they scoffed at the forward seat. Before that, they objected to women riding astride; it was contrary to nature, they said. Always with unerring ineptitude, the Old Guard proclaimed as right what later proved to be wrong. The only thing they have ever succeeded in proving right is the wisdom of Mark Twain's observation, "The man with a new idea is a crank until the idea succeeds."

So I am not writing for the Old Guard. I couldn't care less about what they think. I am writing for you, the young riders of today, who will be the horsemen and horsewomen of tomorrow. I offer you these ideas in this my last book with the hope that, after I am long gone, when you are in positions of authority, something I say here will lead you to bring about changes for a happier, more rational world for all riders and their mounts.

A Judge Speaks

I N spite of my denunciation of judges in general, I'm not really out to exterminate the breed. Without judges, what would our happy horse-show organizers do with their long weekends? Besides, there are good judges. I feel signally honored to be able to present here the views of one of the best equitation judges in America, Carson Whitson, of Talladega, Alabama.

Carson Whitson is that rarity among horsemen—an expert rider who is widely read, a scholarly reader who rides. His scholarship is devastating, deflating, humiliating. Neither in conversation nor in letters have I ever succeeded in mentioning a book, an idea, a theory, or a fact about horsemastership which he didn't know more about than I did. I doubt that there is an important work on horsemanship published in English within the past two hundred years that he has not read or at least skimmed through. He is steeped in the lore of the horse.

Carson Whitson's practical experience matches his scholarship. A member of the last Officer Candidate School horse class to graduate from the Cavalry School at Fort Riley, he is an A.H.S.A. judge, a past-president of the Alabama Hunters and Jumpers Association, a breeder of Thoroughbreds, a former Honorary Huntsman—and above all a teacher and judge of

Carson Whitson on Hassim Bey, an Arabian Stallion. Photograph by Carl Raswan

horsemanship. The hunter trials and combined training event he sponsors annually at his farm near Talladega have become a Mecca for Southerners who appreciate fine horsemanship. Excepting only classical high school riding—a European monopoly —there is hardly a field of horsemanship in which Whitson does not qualify.

This rare blend of practice and theory, distilled by reflective insight, is evident in the following observations on judging written especially for this book.

Judging Horsemanship

By CARSON WHITSON

HORSEMANSHIP is a many-sided subject. Nobody ever knows it all. On most of its various topics—conformation, riding, schooling, stable management, care of the horse's health, and so on—many excellent books have been written. The one subject it seems difficult to get any concise, clear-cut information about is one with which most of us who show horses are vitally concerned—judging in the show ring, specifically the judging of performance horses and the riders' horsemanship. Judging is such a personal thing it is difficult to lay down hard-and-fast rules.

Yet it is obvious that in order to perform his job efficiently a judge must have some rules to go by, a set of standards. He must have a thorough theoretical background as well as a great deal of practical experience. Years ago I read an article written by an old army horseman in *The Cavalry Journal* that laid down three basic rules in judging horsemanship. Here they are:

1. Know the requirements of the class you are judging.
2. Know the type of horse, or the type of riding.
3. Have a quick and accurate way of recording your observations.

Let's examine these three fundamental requisites in detail.

Knowing the requirements of the class is not difficult. These are usually printed in the program and generally are copied from the rules of the A.H.S.A. Sometimes there may be ground rules that the show committee has seen fit to include for some special reason or to meet local conditions. But a thorough familiarity with the A.H.S.A. rules governing the class you are judging is absolutely essential.

Knowing the type of horse you are judging requires a great amount of knowledge. Regardless of the type or breed, you can define a good horse as one that has many good points, few indifferent points and no bad points. The horse with the most good points which apply to the particular kind of work required automatically becomes the right type. So with horses it is chiefly a matter of conformation and temperament, whether stock horse, hunter, jumper or Saddle Horse.

Judging each rider's horsemanship, however, is a bit more complicated. Here it is chiefly a matter of balance. Depending on the kind of work the horse is called on to do, a rider's balance will vary with the center of gravity of the horse. For example, the rider of a racking Saddlebred will have a different balance from the rider of a hunter going at a hand gallop. A great French cavalry officer summed up in one terse sentence all that can be said of riding and schooling horses: "The rider's body should become a second *balancier*." The horse's head and neck are his balancer, and when the rider's body acts as a second balancer he has, in effect, become part of the horse. Theoretically, there is then nothing left for the rider to learn, and there is nothing more for the horse to learn. Carrying the rider as a part of himself, he naturally assumes any attitude or gait without interference.

A quick and accurate way of recording one's observations is something most judges work out for themselves. Human nature being what it is, each of us thinks that his own system is as good as, if not better than, anyone else's. It is doubtful if any standard of judging equitation or horsemanship classes will ever be universally accepted; nor, I think, would it be altogether wise, as it might kill individual initiative, reducing the judge to the status of a clerk. Knowing of no published card for judging horsemanship or equitation classes, however, and having seen only one in a book that irritated rather than inspired me, I dreamed up one of my own. After having used it for years now, I find it most convenient and helpful. [1] It has gotten me out of more than one tight spot when an angry parent demanded to know why I had tied his child so low, or not at all. (And don't think many parents don't want to know!) By merely referring to my card I could easily pinpoint the rider's faults.

Interpretation of Symbols on Judging Chart. Courtesy C. Whitson
Rider No.

1   *Head bent forward, eyes looking down.*
2   *Shoulders slumped, loin broken out, buttocks tucked under.*
3   *Elbows behind hips, hands too low, back of hand vertical with wrist broken in. Reins too long.*
4   *Stiff elbows, hands too high. Reins short.*
5   *Rider overbalanced to front.*
6   *Rider overbalanced to rear, hanging on reins, hands too high.*
7   *Rider unbalanced to right.*
8   *Rider unbalanced to left.*
9   *Faulty base of support: toes turned out too much, weight on back of thighs, daylight under knees, back of calves gripping horse, stirrups not across broadest part of boot sole and at a right angle to long axis of foot.*
10   *Toes turned in, weak leg position below knees, back thigh faulty, ankle broken out.*
11   *Stirrups too short.*
12   *Stirrups too long.*
13   *Legs pulled back with heels up, stirrup leathers behind vertical.*
14   *Feet on the dashboard, leathers ahead of vertical.*
15   *Lower legs loose, swinging like pendulums.*
16   *Many faults: head bent forward, eyes on ground, shoulders and back slumped, buttocks tucked under, hands too high and hanging on horse's mouth, loose ineffective legs with toes pointed down. Rider completely out of balance at all gaits.*

[1] Copies of this judging card may be obtained from Carson Whitson, Talladega, Alabama.

CLASS NO. _____

The figure represents the correct seat mounted. Any deviation or fault may be shown by three symbols: A line ━ , An arc ❱ , or An angle ❯

FAULTS are given a value of 1 to 2 above the pelvic bones and 2 to 4 below depending on degree of fault.

The gait at which the fault occurs is indicated by a dot behind the number.　　● Walk　　∶ Trot　　⫶ Gallop

A fault reoccurring at more than one gait is indicated by the dotted number in line with symbol indicating the fault. Use of inexpensive red ballpoint pen is suggested for contrast.

OVERALL PERFORMANCE Faults are scored
　　1 - Excellent;　2 - Very Good;　3 - Good;　4 - Fairly Good;
　　5 - Poor;　6 - Very Poor.

COMMON FAULTS Listed Below —
Head down, eyes down or wandering.
Slumped, loin broken out, buttocks under.
Elbows in rear of hips, not flexed, no straight line from elbow to bit viewed from horizontal or vertical.
Loss of balance to front or rear or side.
Faulty base of support, thighs, knees, calf or leg, tread of stirrup.
Ankles broken out, feet turned in or out, leathers not vertical, short or long.

1st					
2nd					
3rd					
4th					
5th					
6th					
7th					
8th					
JUDGE _____					

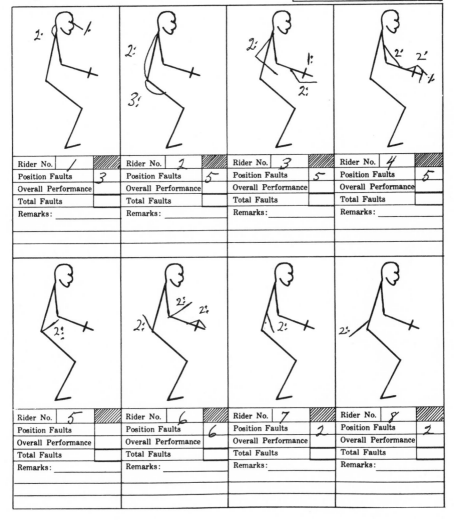

Rider No.	1		Rider No.	2		Rider No.	3		Rider No.	4	
Position Faults	3		Position Faults	5		Position Faults	5		Position Faults	5	
Overall Performance			Overall Performance			Overall Performance			Overall Performance		
Total Faults			Total Faults			Total Faults			Total Faults		
Remarks:			Remarks:			Remarks:			Remarks:		

Rider No.	5		Rider No.	6		Rider No.	7		Rider No.	8	
Position Faults			Position Faults	6		Position Faults	2		Position Faults	2	
Overall Performance			Overall Performance			Overall Performance			Overall Performance		
Total Faults			Total Faults			Total Faults			Total Faults		
Remarks:			Remarks:			Remarks:			Remarks:		

Rider No.	9		Rider No.	10		Rider No.	11		Rider No.	12	
Position Faults	13		Position Faults	14		Position Faults	2		Position Faults	4	
Overall Performance			Overall Performance			Overall Performance			Overall Performance		
Total Faults			Total Faults			Total Faults			Total Faults		
Remarks:			Remarks:			Remarks:			Remarks:		

Rider No.	13		Rider No.	14		Rider No.	15		Rider No.	16	
Position Faults	7		Position Faults			Position Faults			Position Faults	78	
Overall Performance			Overall Performance			Overall Performance			Overall Performance		
Total Faults			Total Faults			Total Faults			Total Faults		
Remarks:			Remarks:			Remarks:			Remarks:		

REMARKS: _____

Whenever possible, I like to have a clerk who understands my system mark my card as I dictate. There are two main reasons for this. First, I never have to take my eyes off the horse and rider I'm scoring. Second, indirectly I am teaching the clerk, usually a young person, who will be one of the judges of tomorrow.

It is self-evident that no judge could make a detailed analysis of each rider's faults in a large class and with limited time. Nor is this necessary. In any class where all the contestants are in the ring at one time, contrast and comparison are the criteria. Here is how I go about it:

First, with all riders at the walk, I make a list of those riders who fill my eye and leave a good impression. (And here I might add that one of the greatest helps to a judge of equitation classes the management of a show can give is providing armbands for *both* arms as well as a large number on each rider's back.) When I find myself beginning to repeat riders, I move the class to a different gait, the trot.

Now I begin a second column, similar to the first. Riders that looked very good at the walk may show faults at the trot, while others may show considerable improvement. Again, when I find myself repeating the numbers of certain riders, I know it is time to call for the next gait, the canter.

At the canter (or gallop) I make a third column. When I begin repeating numbers, I pull the class back down to the walk and change to the other hand.

Again I work the class at the three gaits, checking each rider already marked and adding to the list others I think I might have overlooked. By that time I have, I believe, accurately spotted the best riders in the class.

My next step in the elimination process is to begin a fourth column. Taking the first rider listed in column No. 1, I look to see if his number recurs in the next two columns. If it does, I list him in column No. 4. I repeat this with all other riders I have marked. In a large class I usually wind up with about a dozen riders listed in column No. 4. Here, I know, is where the ribbons will be tied. With the field thus narrowed down, the rest of the class can be excused from the ring. I call out those who are left for more work, if time permits.

The A.H.S.A. rule book lists movements a judge may require riders in an equitation class to perform.

After I have worked each of the remaining riders left in the ring, sometimes two or more of the riders appear to be equal in ability. When confronted with a situation like this, I do not hesitate to seek help from better judges than I am—the horses themselves. I ask the riders to swap mounts. By seeing which one gets the smoothest performance out of a horse he may never even have seen before, I am left in no doubt about where the ribbons should go. Equestrian tact is best learned from riding a number of horses. No two respond in exactly the same manner. How a rider applies the aids, how he meets the resistance of his horse, and how he reacts in a difficult situation are of great importance in judging horsemanship. Although two riders may have equal skill, the superior horseman has greater emotional control. Loss of temper sometimes makes the difference between a mere rider and a real horseman.

Several years ago, for example, I judged a show in a part of the country that takes its riding seriously and has turned out a number of excellent riders. One particular class was for older riders, advanced Pony Clubbers; some of them were good enough to have won in national rallies. I decided to make it a bit rough. Now the rule book says that a judge may call a class to ride without stirrups; it does not specify any particular gait. I called for a sitting trot and then a posting trot without stirrups, the riders to execute several changes of pace at the trot. Believe me, that made tying the ribbons much easier.

Later I asked a friend's daughter who had been in the class whether the young people thought I'd been too rough on them. She replied, "They loved it."

I frankly admit that a posting trot without stirrups is a gymnastic exercise that would be tiring if kept up for long, but it certainly will make a rider hollow out his loin and incline forward from the hips—or hang on to the reins.

I have found that the chart I originally intended for judging in the ring is equally useful when I'm conducting a riding clinic or in checking the progress of a pupil. It can be used for any type of equitation but is especially helpful in classes that require solo performances, such as stock horse classes and equitation over fences.

Judging Horsemanship. The five photographs, with diagrams and comments, show how Carson Whitson judges a horsemanship class and how he marks his card. At any moment he can check back on a rider's performance and at the conclusion of the class he has a clear record minus any memory-jogging or guesswork.

Mr. Whitson's comments merely indicate the sort of thoughts that run through his mind when he is watching a rider. These remarks, of course, do not appear on the card. Only the figures and symbols marking each diagram go down on the card. However, should the judge wish to jot down any special remarks, space has been provided for that.

The photographs were taken when Tonka was three years old and Linda was eleven.

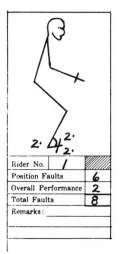

Rider No.	1	
Position Faults	6	
Overall Performance	2	
Total Faults	8	
Remarks:		

No. 1. Mount moving at free walk on loose reins. Rider in balance; elbows properly flexed; feet too far home in stirrups, ankle joint not broken in, heels not down far enough probably because irons are too far home, thus reducing ankle joint flexibility. Ankle joint not broken in sufficiently probably due to rider's foot being near outside rather than inside of stirrup.

315

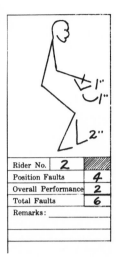

Rider No.	**2**
Position Faults	**4**
Overall Performance	**2**
Total Faults	**6**
Remarks:	

No. 2. Mount flexed properly from ears to tail on arc of turn. Rider's left hand slightly low because rein is too long; rein action exaggerated. If reins were properly adjusted, rider could have made turn without displacing hands by changing from yielding to fixed hand. Foot correctly positioned in iron, but leg is a bit too far forward with stirrup leather ahead of vertical.

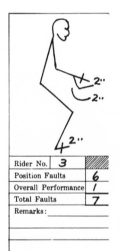

Rider No.	**3**
Position Faults	**6**
Overall Performance	**1**
Total Faults	**7**
Remarks:	

No. 3. Rider's body position good but reins are uneven, left rein hanging loose. Left hand is too low, would have to move behind rider's knee to make contact with mouth. Left leg in good working position but foot is too far home in stirrup. Mount's attention is distracted; he is not framed by the aids. Rider should adjust reins evenly and leg horse up to the bit. Is rider unaccustomed to carrying a crop?

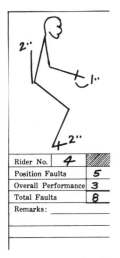

Rider No.	4	
Position Faults	5	
Overall Performance	3	
Total Faults	8	
Remarks:		

No. 4. Rider is posting by rising from foot, body moving up and down; rider is behind her mount. Should post by pivoting over knee with spine stretched. Left rein is too long. Foot slightly too far home in stirrup.

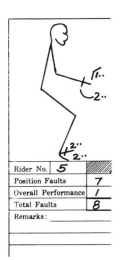

Rider No.	5	
Position Faults	7	
Overall Performance	1	
Total Faults	8	
Remarks:		

No. 5. Mount's attention is distracted; he's playing schoolboy-looking-out-the-window. Rider's heels insufficiently down, feet too far home in stirrups. Her wrists look stiff. Is she concentrating too hard on holding hands in proper position? If she had light contact, with all arm joints relaxed, stiffness in wrists would disappear. Mental as well as physical relaxation is needed for good hands.

317

The choice of symbols or markings to use on the chart is an individual matter; anyone can dream up his own code system. In the chart illustrated I have made no attempt to score a class but have merely indicated the symbols I use to pinpoint faults.

In pointing out these faults there is a great temptation to become involved in explaining just why they are faults. However, if one understands the reasons why, then the how, what and when usually become evident.

Seán on his new filly, Tabu. "Here we go again!"

Index